PE.

MW01223856

Killing Me Softly

Dr Philip Nitschke was the first doctor in the world to legally administer voluntary euthanasia. He is now director of the death with dignity organisation, Exit International. Born and raised in rural South Australia, Philip studied physics at Adelaide and Flinders universities, gaining a PhD in laser physics. Rejecting a career in the sciences, he travelled to the Northern Territory in 1972 to work with land rights activist Vincent Lingiari and the Gurindji at Wave Hill, and later became a Parks and Wildlife ranger. After a serious accident, Philip turned to a career in medicine, graduating from Sydney University in 1988. He returned to the Northern Territory in 1989 to practise medicine, later becoming involved in the debate that surrounded the passage of the Rights of the Terminally Ill Act in 1995. Philip lives in Darwin.

Dr Fiona Stewart is a public health sociologist who has worked as an academic, newspaper opinion writer and consultant. She became involved with the voluntary euthanasia move-ment after meeting Philip Nitschke at the Brisbane Festival of Ideas in 2001. Since this time Fiona has assumed responsi-bility for Exit International's strategic direction and research agenda. She has postgraduate qualifications in public policy and law, including a PhD from La Trobe University. Her first book, *Internet Communication and Qualitative Research*, was published in 2000. Born in Melbourne, Fiona now lives in Darwin.

*This book is inspired by and dedicated to the spirit
and determination of Mordechai Vanunu*

killing
me
softly

Dr Philip Nitschke
& Dr Fiona Stewart

PENGUIN BOOKS

PENGUIN BOOKS

Published by the Penguin Group
Penguin Group (Australia)
250 Camberwell Road, Camberwell, Victoria 3124, Australia
(a division of Pearson Australia Group Pty Ltd)
Penguin Group (USA) Inc.
375 Hudson Street, New York, New York 10014, USA
Penguin Group (Canada)
10 Alcorn Avenue, Toronto, Ontario, Canada M4V 3B2
(a division of Pearson Penguin Canada Inc.)
Penguin Books Ltd
80 Strand, London WC2R 0RL, England
Penguin Ireland
25 St Stephen's Green, Dublin 2, Ireland
(a division of Penguin Books Ltd)
Penguin Books India Pvt Ltd
11 Community Centre, Panchsheel Park, New Delhi – 110 017, India
Penguin Group (NZ)
Cnr Airborne and Rosedale Roads, Albany, Auckland, New Zealand
(a division of Pearson New Zealand Ltd)
Penguin Books (South Africa) (Pty) Ltd
24 Sturdee Avenue, Rosebank, Johannesburg 2196, South Africa

Penguin Books Ltd, Registered Offices: 80 Strand, London, WC2R 0RL, England

First published by Penguin Group (Australia), a division of Pearson Australia Group Pty Ltd, 2005

10 9 8 7 6 5 4 3 2 1

Cover design by Lynn Twelftree © Penguin Group (Australia)
Text design by Karen Trump © Penguin Group (Australia)
Typeset in Sabon by Post Pre-press Group, Brisbane, Queensland
Printed and bound in Australia by McPherson's Printing Group, Maryborough, Victoria

National Library of Australia
Cataloguing-in-Publication data:

Nitschke, Philip Haig, 1947– .
Killing me softly: voluntary euthanasia and the road to the peaceful pill.

Includes index.
ISBN 0 14 300303 8.

1. Euthanasia – Australia. 2. Euthanasia – Law and legislation – Australia. 3. Right to die – Australia. I. Stewart, Fiona Joy, 1966– . II. Title.

179.70994

www.penguin.com.au

Acknowledgements

The publication of *Killing Me Softly* has only been made possible through the goodwill and support of many people, including our agent Lynne Spender, the staff at the Australian Bureau of Statistics, the Australian Institute of Health and Welfare and various Parliament House libraries. Professor Colleen Cartwright of the University of Queensland gave generously of her expertise as did Dr Wendy Gunthorpe, who is the nicest quantitative researcher one is ever likely to meet. Janine Hosking and Steve Hopes have worked closely with us, allowing us unfettered access to the rich material in Janine's documentary film *Mademoiselle and the Doctor*.

Kerri Dennis, our coordinator at Exit International, kept the office running when we were knee-deep in research and writing, and we are very grateful to her. Thank you to Penguin Australia's publishing director Bob Sessions for wearing his convictions on his sleeve, and putting these sometimes controversial thoughts into the public domain. Thanks also to our editor, Saskia Adams, who is not only clever and insightful, but who has made the process of pulling the book together a sheer joy.

Within Exit International, we would like to thank the following people for their professional and personal support: Judy Wedderburn, Cesare Pradella, Derek Humphry, Dorothy Simons, John Edge, Lyell and Marianne Crane, Amanda

McClure and Mary Fahy. We would also like to thank Gwen Nitschke and Pam and Gordon Stewart. In addition there are many other Exit members and patients whose voices resonate throughout this book: ordinary Australians who have made this project worthwhile. It is *for them* that we have persevered in bringing this to life and it is *because of them* that we maintain hope for the future; hope that politicians will not only find the guts to act on this issue but respect people's right to create their own choices should the politicians fail to do so.

Fiona Stewart's acknowledgements: Words can't express Philip's contribution to this book. He is an inspirational co-author and I thank him truly.

Philip Nitschke's acknowledgements: Fiona took a jumbled mountain of half-finished papers and ideas and turned them into this book. It wouldn't have happened without her and I feel immensely lucky, grateful and proud of what she has achieved.

Contents

Foreword

There is arguably no more controversial public figure in Australia today than Dr Philip Nitschke. Often referred to as 'Doctor Death' by his detractors, he is both frequently condemned as a dangerous villain and acclaimed as a compassionate hero.

Anyone who has been the subject of significant media coverage will tell you how inaccurate its reporting can be. Understandably, Dr Nitschke wrote this book to correct the misconceptions about him and to tell his story in his own words. And what a story it is. *Killing Me Softly* is not so much an autobiography as it is an interesting account of where the voluntary euthanasia (VE) movement in Australia has come from and, more importantly, where it is going.

Philip originally became involved with the VE cause in 1995 when I as Chief Minister first mooted introducing right-to-die legislation in the Northern Territory parliament for those who were terminally ill. At the time, Philip also passionately believed that, with appropriate safeguards, dying individuals should have the right to take their own lives, and that this right should be prescribed in law. In this book, a decade on, he tells us why he has changed his mind about pursuing legislative reform.

Following the Australian Medical Association's hostile response to the Territory's VE legislation – 'the worst example

of the profession's insufferable paternalism', as Philip puts it –
he describes the dramatic events that followed the passage of
that groundbreaking legislation, including the stories of the four
people who used the NT law to find relief in death. Readers
will feel a lump in their throat as they discover why several of
Philip's not-so-fortunate patients – such as Max Bell and Esther
Wild – died horrifically, despite meeting all the requirements of
the NT legislation.

Philip Nitschke is one of those rare individuals who dedi-
cates himself so completely to his cause that what most would
consider 'normal' life aspirations – for example, wealth and
security – come far down on his list of priorities. As he puts it,
'Doing the bare minimum for the VE cause is not an option.'
Being a man who views treading on toes as a legitimate tac-
tic in achieving one's objectives, it is no wonder that during the
course of his work he has disconcerted so many, including sec-
tions of the VE movement itself. Most politicians hate him; his
peers have tried to have him deregistered; Right to Life groups
despise him; and to the Catholic Church he must represent the
very devil. Yet to thousands of Australians, particularly the sick
and the elderly, Dr Philip Nitschke is a hero – a lone individual
who understands completely their fear of suffering in dying and
is prepared to risk prosecution in his campaign to help them.

In this book Philip paints a pessimistic picture of the possibility of an Australian parliament in the near future adopting VE
laws, despite overwhelming community support. His frustration
at the intransigence of our elected representatives, together with
being besieged by so many Australians wanting a means to end
their lives calmly and with dignity, has driven Philip to initiate

research to develop a 'Peaceful Pill'. Able to be made from readily available substances that cannot be banned, the availability of such a pill will challenge contemporary views on suicide and improve the quality of remaining life for the hopelessly ill. More than that, it will – intentionally – sideline the role of politicians in the future of the debate completely.

This book contains information about why doctors do not want the common practice of slow euthanasia examined too closely; what is wrong with palliative care; the heart-rending decisions regarding euthanasing very ill babies; and a discussion about giving prisoners sentenced to life the option of suicide. It is sure to absorb and challenge every reader. This is not a 'how to die' manual, but a must-read for anyone who believes they and their loved ones should have control over when and how they will die.

Marshall Perron

Introduction

Coming to Grips with Death

This book is about the Australia I know. Not the modern, prosperous civil society we might think we live in, but the country in which many ordinary people face impossible circumstances every day. In this nation our end-of-life choices are so limited that pain and suffering are commonplace for many who deserve better.

It need not be like this. We need not shun death, hoping that it will just go away. We need not force misery upon our sick and our elderly in their last hours, days, weeks and years. New strategies to deal with this issue are vital and they are needed now. They are needed because voluntary euthanasia (VE) legislation has been defeated at every turn in the nation's parliaments. They are needed because the long arm of the Church already reaches too far into the lives of non-believers. Finally, they are needed because we have members of a medical profession whose practices towards patients reaching the end of their lives are often duplicitous and demeaning to those they are supposed to be assisting.

My decision to go public with these thoughts on our right

1

to die when and how we choose stems from my frustration at the disparity between political and medical double-speak and the needs of ordinary people. Barely a day passes when I am not called upon to talk to people from all over the country about their end-of-life options. While I am aware of the significance of my position – as a doctor trying to tell it straight – I also feel obligation and a sense of expectation. Not sometimes, but every day when I read the heartfelt requests from Australians who write: 'Dear Dr Nitschke, please help me die', or 'please help my mother', or please help a father, wife, husband, sister, brother . . . on and on it goes.

These letters detail the truly tragic situations some Australians find themselves in. And it is not just the sick who are seeking help, but also elderly people who think their time has come and that the decision to die should be theirs and theirs alone. Old age often brings increased frailty, sickness and, for some, a world-weariness. For these people too, all choice at the end of life is denied. In addition, many adult children of ageing parents and partners with sick spouses are asking the same questions. What are our options? What can we do when we don't have a law? How can we help our suffering parents without risking prison and jeopardising our own families?

These men and women plead with me to provide them with the information they need about how to die. They want to know. They have a *right* to know. I answer their questions as honestly as I can, running the gauntlet of the law in the process.

As I have dealt with the increasing numbers of people who implore me for information about their end-of-life choices, so my views have changed about where a civil society should be headed on this issue. Should we be pursuing legal reform? Should we just give up? Or should we be thinking outside the legal square for our own solutions? Until recently I would have argued that a law on voluntary euthanasia would provide all the answers. Like everyone else in the pro-choice movement, I used to think that a law would enshrine *and* protect people's rights. More recently my views have changed. In this book I explain why.

Rather than focusing upon the possibility of legislative change, in *Killing Me Softly* I take a different and more controversial approach by exploring the role of DIY (do-it-yourself) technologies. I investigate how new and readily obtainable methods can provide people with real end-of-life choices. At a public level, these technologies will be a watershed for those seeking control over when and how they die. At a very personal level, these technologies will allow me to stop saying sorry: 'I'm sorry I can't tell you how many of these tablets you need to take to ensure you die tonight'; 'I'm sorry I can't tell you what the law will do to you if you hold your wife's hand as she dies'; 'I'm sorry I can't organise slow euthanasia for you'; 'I'm sorry we can't safely talk about this on the phone'.

After eight years of apologising for not answering people's questions swiftly enough or adequately enough, I can apologise no more. This book is to help me stop saying sorry. In sharing my thoughts here, I am hoping to encourage all Australians to think more openly and creatively about end-of-life choices and what they may mean for them personally, as well as for their families and friends, both now and in the future.

Finally, *Killing Me Softly* is about my journey. For many

years I have had offers from writers wanting to tell my life story. Many an enterprising journalist has found me a figure of curiosity. Yet, like many Australians, I am cautious of the media. And despite their best efforts to prise my world apart, my personal life is just that – personal. I am fairly shy, and talking about myself is not something I do easily. However, this book will allow me to tell my story in my own words – and only as much as I want of it, without any fear of misrepresentation.

Killing Me Softly need not be read in any particular order. It includes factual accounts of the law relating to voluntary euthanasia and my own anecdotes and experiences as well as my new and sometimes radical understandings about the issue. And there are many other people's voices within these pages, too – those of ordinary Australians who have written letters to the newspapers, as well as the voices of politicians, some of whom undertake their job with great integrity. Then there are the voices of my patients, workshop and clinic participants and others, some well known, who have been interviewed in the course of our research.

I ask the reader to come with me on this journey and be open to the ideas I present. While I do not have all the answers to the VE issue, I have one deep-seated belief – that things have to change. This book is a starting point.

A point of clarification

Killing Me Softly is the product of my work within the area of voluntary euthanasia over the best part of the last decade. It is not, however, a 'how-to-die' manual. The following chapters contain no hints, tips or descriptions about how to ensure you or your loved ones obtain a peaceful death. My organisation Exit International's inventions such as the Peaceful Pill and the CoGenie – devices that continue to receive extensive media coverage – are discussed only at a theoretical level. Why have I not included such information, given I am a proponent of people's right to know? The answer to this question is legal. This book would not have been published if I had done so. I do, however, expect to publish such information – which is so widely sought, both here and internationally – in the near future; be it about how to make a Peaceful Pill, or how to buy Nembutal in Mexico. For further information, or to join Exit International, please see the form on page 355 or email info@exitinternational.net.

Postscript

At the 2004 Sydney Film Festival, the documentary film *Mademoiselle and the Doctor* had its world premiere. Produced and directed by the Academy Award–nominated Sydney filmmaker Janine Hosking, this film is about my work with Exit International. The film and *Killing Me Softly* complement each other, both discussing, describing and ultimately advocating a person's right to exercise choice in how they live and die. Further information about the film can be obtained from Janine by emailing janinehosking@bigpond.com.

Chapter 1

Will the Real Philip Nitschke Please Stand Up?

I am often asked about my life story and whether I came to support voluntary euthanasia through personal experience, and my answer is no. I came to it as a reaction. In part as a reaction to the arrogance of the Australian Medical Association, and in part because I believe that end-of-life decisions are a key element in any human rights platform. And, just as the feminists of previous decades lobbied long and hard for reproductive rights for women, I thought it only a matter of time until how we die would become as passionately argued.

In recent years, numerous versions of my story have been told by a third person, usually a journalist. And the right-to-life lobby have, of course, also told their version, eagerly dwelling on the mistakes of my youth. When I read about myself in the media, I often feel someone else is being described. I know I am not alone in having this reaction. Anyone in the public eye is open to scrutiny and has to acknowledge that they have little control over what is said about them and how. Having a thick skin is essential for those who speak out.

Over the years, however, it has both amused and shocked

me that I have been frequently portrayed as a zealot, as someone obsessed with their cause. I believe it is easy to label as
zealous anyone attempting to push the envelope. I can think of
others who share this label with me. While I do not like this tag,
I am certainly committed to voluntary euthanasia and I see
the provision of real end-of-life choices as the last bastion of a
human rights agenda. But it is not the only issue of importance
to me.

My commitment to social justice is deep, a seed that was
planted early in my life. Growing up in the 1960s I wanted to
make a difference on a variety of issues and believed that I could.
Now I am focused primarily on the right-to-die cause. And my
commitment is not waning. Rather, the unfulfilled needs of the
patients I see every week, and the encouragement I receive from
strangers as I walk down the street – any street – strengthens
my resolve and keeps my feet on the ground.

Over the years I have also been portrayed as a loner. Of
course, I don't dislike my own company, and choosing to live
on the outskirts of Darwin means that I can't see my neighbours, and we like it that way. But a loner? Not particularly.
Although I have never married, female partners have been
central to my life. The time I like best is that spent in romantic,
domestic harmony: going out to dinner, riding our old Cossack
motorbike with sidecar, spending time at the pub. Nothing
extraordinary.

My great love of the desert has frequently been mentioned
in profiles about me, and it's true that when I'm home in the
Territory – and that is not often enough – I try to go bush.
However, it is not something I need to do alone. While camp

fires, beer and the breathtaking beauty of the desert remain the staples of my life, having someone there to share it makes things complete.

I am also regularly depicted as a man who cares about little other than my work: someone who works too hard and too long. As much as I dislike this description, I can understand its origin. Back in 1997 when I founded the Voluntary Euthanasia Research Foundation (VERF, now known as Exit International), I knew I was creating a huge amount of work for myself. That is the nature of starting something new.

These days, however, I am surrounded by a small, dedicated staff, and an ever-growing team of volunteers. Nevertheless, the buck still stops with me. In the absence of other doctors formally supporting Exit's work, I still bear the burden of organising workshops, visiting patients, speaking at conferences and fronting the media. I am often on the road, and yes, I do live out of a suitcase a lot. But doing the bare minimum for the VE cause is not an option. Nor is it what the hundreds of Australians who call and email me expect.

Yet, like most working people, I am always trying to create a better work–life balance. And, like some, I am making progress towards that goal.

Early days

I was born in 1947 in the small South Australian country town of Ardrossan to schoolteacher parents, Gwen and Harold. I am the youngest of three children. My older brother and sister, Dennis and Gailene, both live in Adelaide, as does my mother.

My father died in Perth in 1984. He had remarried after my parents divorced in 1977.

My father was a product of his time and great-grandson of F. W. Nitschke, one of the Lutherans who migrated from Germany in the nineteenth century with Captain Hahn in the *Zebra* to take up land at Hahndorf. Dad was a stubborn and difficult man. Sadly, we were never close. But when there was an emergency, and there were a number, he always came up with the goods. I recall the time he saved my life when, as a ten-year-old, I sucked a collar stud into my throat. While I gestured frantically, unable to speak and deafened by the sound of blood pumping faster and faster in my ears, others in the room ignored me with the dismissive comment, 'What's wrong with the boy?' Not my father. He looked at me for a moment, then upended the kitchen table on his way over to me and grabbed and upended me in turn, dislodging the stud with a blow to my back.

My mother is a remarkable woman. With no secondary education at all, she married young and learnt teaching on the job as my father's assistant in too many small country schools to mention. When she divorced my father forty years later she had to make the best of her situation, learning a whole new set of survival skills. Now eighty-three, she reminds me whenever I visit that the most useful thing about having a doctor for a son is the chance it offers to obtain lethal drugs when the time comes. My mother has quite a sense of humour.

While I was growing up, we were constantly on the move. Every few years my father was given a new teaching post, and the family would pack up and travel to another country town.

I would be dumped in a new school, often mid-term, and would once again have to make new friends. In secondary school, I went to five schools in five years. Perhaps this is why I do not mind an intermittent suitcase lifestyle today. Moving around is very familiar to me.

At school, I discovered early on that mathematics and the sciences were my forte. In Year 10, to continue my education I had to go to Adelaide and a private Lutheran boarding school was selected. My mother wanted me to go on to university and I liked this idea, but I found the private-school culture stifling, and after a year I begged my parents to let me return to the state system. This they did and I attended Henley High School in Adelaide for my final school year. I began boarding with a married couple in the suburb of Fulham Gardens. Unfortunately, this situation worked out badly also. There wasn't really a name for it then, but what happened to me I imagine would today be called sexual harassment, delivered under the guise of helping me with my studies. In any event, I found it frightening. I sensed a risk and I did not want to be a victim. I did not know how to raise the situation with anyone. I told no one, including my parents. I felt trapped, and I wanted to escape.

I needed someone to hear my cry for help. The method by which I eventually achieved this was to kill the couple's pet dog. My father was a keen hunter and by the time I had reached my teenage years I had been on plenty of hunting expeditions with him, owned my own rifle, and had shot my fair share of rabbits. I did not have my rifle with me in Adelaide, but I did have my hunting knife, and I cut the dog's throat. At the time I could see little difference between a dog and a rabbit.

While I knew what I had done was wrong, the outcry that followed was unexpected. For example, I never thought my misdemeanour would make the Adelaide *Advertiser*, but it did. And at the time I was also surprised that I was marched off to a doctor to make sure I was a normal (even if slightly eccentric) teenager. Indeed, it was this willingness on the part of my father that I see a doctor that allowed me to avoid going through any juvenile court proceedings.

I have never tried to hide the incident, but I did not imagine how this youthful, desperate mistake would one day be used by my political opponents. The right-to-life lobby now bring it up frequently as apparent evidence of my bloodthirsty nature. However, nothing could be further from the truth.

In retrospect, I can see that talking about what was happening to me would have been a much better way to deal with the situation. But I was too afraid to discuss it with anyone. I saw it as a problem I had to solve, rightly or wrongly, by myself. I am now, of course, sorry about what happened, but I did manage to escape from that awful situation.

The following year, at age seventeen, I started a science degree at Adelaide University and managed to attract controversy again, this time when I staged a citizen's arrest. One night, while my Morris Minor was parked outside the St Clare Youth Centre in Woodville, my portable radio was stolen from my car. I was furious and wanted it back. At police headquarters in Angus Street the desk officer was understanding but put it bluntly: 'Look, hundreds of radios are stolen every night. We'll take the details, but your chances of recovery are very slim.' Not to be deterred, I again saw this as another problem that I would have to solve on my own. I wanted my radio back and there was no one else offering to help.

My plan was to leave an imitation radio on the dashboard of my father's Holden, which was driven to the same spot by my friend James with my girlfriend Jenny in tow. I was concealed in the boot while those two went inside to have fun at the youth centre. Freezing and armed, I waited for the crime to be repeated. And it was. This time, however, instead of making off with another radio, the would-be thief got the barrel of my Browning .22 automatic rifle pointed at him as I marched him to a nearby house to await the arrival of the police.

The incident was reported the next day on the front page of the Adelaide *Advertiser* and I ended up giving my first television interview. While some of the public thought my actions heroic, the police were understandably not impressed that I had taken the law into my own hands. Thus, in less than a year, two incidents had occurred in my life that had me both publicly vilified and acclaimed. I learnt that solving one's own problems could be risky.

My generation – Vietnam, land rights and my growing social conscience

My undergraduate years at Adelaide University from 1964 to 1968 were spent living away from home, getting involved in university politics and studying science. I soon chose to major in physics, the subject I was best at. I did not study very hard, however, as I always passed easily. It was during these years that I met my first medical student and was once lucky enough to be smuggled into the dissection room of the medical school. I was envious; why hadn't anyone at Henley High suggested I study medicine? Back then, there seemed to be only two higher-learning options mooted: arts or science. Frustrated, I attempted to change courses from undergraduate science to medicine but, to my disappointment, my application was rejected.

During my time at university the Vietnam war was raging and conscription came in. Since I was just about the right age, like everyone else I had to think fast to work out how to avoid the South-East Asian jungle. A sad acquaintance from my boarding-school days, Errol Novak, became the first conscript killed. He, who I knew to have missed out on everything else in life, was the recipient of a state funeral, and I watched sombrely as the gun carriage slowly drew his coffin down King William Street. Meanwhile we all waited anxiously to see if in the ballot our draft number would be chosen, and in those early years many of my acquaintances were called up.

Some of my friends courageously became conscientious objectors, but I took a soft, safe option and joined the University Air Regiment. All the while, my politics moved further and further to the Left. Indeed, my opposition to the war prevented me from accepting a tempting offer from Boeing in Seattle to work with them in the area of acoustic physics and noise abatement. While the job and the lifestyle were enticing, the fact that I could be called upon for military service in the US army quickly ended any dreams of life as a professional physicist in America. Boeing could not guarantee that I would not be enlisted for Vietnam, and I could not take the risk.

In my final undergraduate year, I believed I had found my

niche. A project I devised saw me trying to create Australia's first hologram. I was intrigued by the concept of a three-dimensional image hovering in space, an image that could be captured in time and frozen as an exposure on a glass plate. Working with the world's weakest laser (it was all I had access to) and using the world's slowest photographic plates presented immense technical problems. Exposure times of three hours with required mechanical stabilities of millionths of a centimetre just about had me beaten. My last chance of making it work was to use the seismic vault in the basement of the physics school, exposing the photographic plate late on a Sunday night when there was not much traffic and hence no vibration.

My initial tests were encouraging, but the year was ending and time running out. On the last Sunday night that was available, I found the door to the vault locked, even though I had been given permission to use it. I was damned if my experiment was going to be thwarted! The door was off its hinges with one kick, and three hours later, the holographic plate was being processed. The next day I was the star of the department, with everyone visiting the lab to view the ghostly reconstructed image. At the same time I was summoned to the office of the head of the physics school. While Professor Carver was understanding about my actions with the door, he was adamant that formal disciplining would follow, and I paid $5 towards the wilful damage I had caused to university property.

A few weeks later I received first-class honours and moved on to Flinders University to start my PhD in laser physics. Atop the intellectual scientific pyramid, it was physics that had been used to create earth-shattering nuclear weapons. While I abhorred their purpose, I admired the science behind them. I found physics exciting, revered by many, and I was thrilled to be a part of the study of it. I was also seduced by the dream physics might realise – that of obtaining clean, unlimited energy from sea water. My PhD was to be a small part of that vision. Four years later I had the PhD, but the dream seemed no closer.

My thesis was entitled 'Laser Diagnostics of Normal Ionising Shockwaves'. On one level this topic was innocent enough, but as my project came to an end I discovered that the university was accepting general research funding from American companies that were involved in the production of arms – what we might now call weapons of mass destruction. Instead of asking the senior faculty to look into it, I took the path of criticising the university publicly for their promotion of what in my youthful eyes was a war-hungry agenda. In doing so, my voice ended up on the ABC's 'AM' radio program. I spoke of how angry I was about my research being funded indirectly by the US military; funding that hadn't been declared. Professor Brennan, the head of the physics school, was understandably not impressed with my going public on the issue. I was called into his office to explain my actions and it was made clear to me that, in his opinion, it had not been a good physics career move.

As my PhD drew to a close I looked briefly into the idea of postdoctoral studies. A transition into academia would have been difficult, but not impossible. However, my heart wasn't in it. I had spent too many years as a student activist, spouting dissent against the establishment. I wasn't ready to join it.

From little things . . .

At that same moment my imagination was fired by other issues. In 1971 I attended a talk by an Aboriginal man from the Northern Territory called Captain Major (Lupna Giari) who was on one of his early university circuit speaking tours. From the Gurindji tribe of the Wave Hill area, Lupna was one of a group who was trying to garner support – political and financial – for the tribe's land rights claim at Wave Hill station. The station was in the Victoria River area of the Northern Territory, about 400 kilometres south-west of Katherine, and part of the sprawling Vestey cattle empire.

The Gurindji's land claim eventually became the first successful one by an Aboriginal tribe in Australia, although it was not until Gough Whitlam became prime minister in 1972 that a section of the station was actually handed back. Even then it was only after the Gurindji had spent more than a decade on strike, refusing to do the mustering and station work required by the pastoral industry. Vincent Lingiari had led the Gurindji people back to a place on the station called Wattie Creek and there they camped and waited. That historic time is encapsulated in the well-known song by Paul Kelly and Kev Carmody, 'From Little Things, Big Things Grow'.

When I first heard the story of the Gurindji, they were still waiting, still on strike, and I wanted to join the struggle. Their cause struck a chord with me. White Australia's treatment of Aboriginal people had been – and still is – horrendous. I have never forgotten Frank Hardy's words on the subject in his 1968 book *The Unlucky Australians*:

To this day the Aborigine is treated as less than a man, his situation is appalling. His destiny and very identity is decided by his white superiors. He can live only on terms dictated by the people who despise him. He is paid less, educated less, segregated, rendered landless, discriminated against, insulted, dispossessed, deprived of dignity, his women molested. This is a crime committed by you or in your name.

How do you plead?[1]

My original plan was to go to Wave Hill to be a community gardener for the Gurindji. I knew little of gardening, nor did I have much interest in it, but I was open to any occupation in order to be able to stay there. My girlfriend Jenny came with me. As luck would have it, not long after we arrived the person employed to manage the books and write the necessary letters to Canberra left the community. As the only other literate man there (and the only white man), I was asked to step into the role. I stayed in this position from 1973–4. Jenny and I found the conditions the toughest we had ever experienced. We lived in rough sheds of scrap galvanised iron that were unbearably hot in the Dry and awash in the Wet. We had no refrigeration, no power and an unreliable HF radio communication. The community, some 200 strong at times, battled immense privation and disease to make a single point: they wanted their land back.

At Wattie Creek – or Daguragu as it is now called – I wrote and answered official correspondence on Vincent's behalf. I signed the cheques when horses were purchased or cattle were sold and more or less acted as the administrative manager of the community. Jenny befriended the women, was given a skin name and 'adopted' by a family. While I never learnt the Gurindji language, I immersed myself in their culture and activities. It was a tough, exciting and dangerous time as we waited for Canberra to give the land back to its original owners.

After only a few months with the community I became publicly identified with the Gurindji cause. I was vocal in the letters page of the local newspaper (*The Katherine Informer*), and critical of the thinly disguised racism that prevailed in the town. People were afraid of what was happening at our camp. What would it mean for the pastoral industry nationwide if Vesteys caved in and the Gurindji got their land back? In this tinderbox environment, I often found myself targeted in bars by people looking for fights, and sometimes they couldn't be avoided.

I'd been at Wave Hill only a few months when my father came to visit. He had always been interested in Indigenous crafts, and was therefore curious about my life with the Gurindji. One night as dusk settled over the camp, a Toyota laden with beer cartons rolled in, driven by the local Wave Hill policeman who was accompanied by Len Hayes, the brother of the Wave Hill station manager, and a 'yella fella' contract musterer called Sabu Singh. Trouble was in the air.

Gurindji elder Pincher Numiari took me aside, warning me to get out of the camp for the night. I left, but my father chose to stay. As I watched from a distance in the dark, I saw these men push and shove my father and threaten him with a beating. Their message was clear: 'Your son's a troublemaker – both of you should get out of the Territory now.'

It was therefore with some amazement that I recently noticed in Katherine a new, larger-than-life statue of the now famous Territory stockman, Sabu Singh. Commissioned by the Northern Territory Cattlemen's Association, it is positioned at one of the main intersections on the Stuart Highway. I was not impressed. For an industry built on honest Aboriginal labour, I thought this man a poor choice in recognition. It seemed to me another example of the white man's version of history again overriding that of the Aborigine.

My interlude at Wave Hill came to a sudden and unexpected end in 1974 when Jenny left me for a dangerous (but apparently highly desirable) American on a motorbike. James Powell had drifted into Katherine on one of the weekends we were in town on station business. A Vietnam vet from America's mid-west, he had a macho charisma that I seemingly lacked. Jenny climbed on his bike, they left for Mt Isa, and I fell in a heap. Throughout my time at Wave Hill, I had seen myself as a bit of a hero; someone facing immense difficulties with calm stoicism. However, that image disintegrated as James's Honda 450 headed off down the Stuart Highway. It must have been obvious I was in a bad way, for the community decided I needed time-out. Vincent called me to his camp and tactfully suggested I take a break and fix myself up. I took his advice and shifted to Melbourne for a while, driving cabs and conducting on trams, drifting for over a year in a new city with new friends and relationships, before the lure of the Territory had me packing my bags and driving north again.

Back Outback

When I returned to Alice Springs two years later, I answered a job advertisement in the *Centralian Advocate* for a ranger with the Northern Territory Parks and Wildlife Service. I was offered the position and kept it for the next six years, basing myself in Central Australia. Of life-changing significance during this time was the birth of my only child, Philip, in 1977. While not altogether planned, Philip's arrival gave my life a new dimension. My relationship with his mother Paddy was difficult and destined never to last, but our common bond in our son keeps us in touch to this day.

Based in Alice Springs and working at Simpsons Gap, 15 kilometres west of the town, I loved rangering. The MacDonnell Ranges are a stunning part of Australia and tourists who visited often commented that I had the best job in the world. For some time I agreed with them. I worked closely with Bob Darken, then senior park ranger. Bob, ex–wool classer, ex–Territory policeman and ex–pastoralist, was a rough, idiosyncratic but delightful man who ran the park as his own private fiefdom, standing up to anyone who complained. In the years we worked together, I admired him greatly – but never more than the time he stood up for me when a poison-pen letter arrived in the Alice Springs Parks office, urging my immediate dismissal.

The author, Mike Reed, a ranger at Katherine low-level camping ground (the place where I had often stayed on monthly trips in from Wattie Creek), clearly disliked me. At the time I wondered why I was being harassed, and put it down to the racism that prevailed in Katherine and the hostility commonly shown to whites working on land-rights issues. Although years had passed since my work with the Gurindji, Reed had taken it upon himself to point out that the Parks Service had hired a real 'troublemaker' whose sole goal was to further black interests in national parks. Reed went on to claim that I was a communist, sponsored by Left interests alien to our country, and I had lied about my background and tertiary qualifications.

Bob Darken was shown the letter in Alice Springs. He drove back to the park and ordered me to pack my bags, saying that if 'anything in that letter is true, I want you off my park'. By the time I got into Alice Springs to view the letter, it was with the Parks and Wildlife lawyers. It had suddenly become privileged correspondence and I didn't see it for another twenty years when, one day, it arrived anonymously and unexpectedly on my fax machine in Darwin.

The injustice of not being able to defend myself against claims in a letter I had not seen soon had Bob back on my side and that is where he stayed. However, in the ensuing months and years I found myself being passed over repeatedly when promotion was due. Meanwhile Mike Reed made a meteoric rise through the ranks and became the Northern Territory Parks and Wildlife director. He was being groomed by the white conservative pastoral lobby for a political career during which he would come to represent the worst elements of redneck Territory culture. Our paths were to cross again a decade later when I became an intern at Royal Darwin Hospital and found Mike Reed was the Territory's Minister for Health. (Although I must say I got some satisfaction in 1997 when, as deputy chief minister, Reed – who always pushed an anti-gay agenda – was caught out buying pornographic videos [*Highway Hunks* and *Hot Firemen*] from a Sydney sex shop, only to claim they were for the purposes of 'research'.)

I would eventually resign from Parks and Wildlife, but it wouldn't be because of Mike Reed. During my time as a ranger I joined the Army Reserves. Two trips a year on double-pay, the opportunity to learn new skills and a break from rangering all took my fancy. At the end of one of these two-week periods, I was at the Larrakeyah barracks in Darwin, preparing to celebrate the successful completion of an advanced four-wheel-drive training course that we had just taken in Arnhem Land. I was sitting on a huge esky on the back of a stationary truck. Suddenly the truck started up, turning unexpectedly, and off I came. Landing badly, my heel broke away from my foot. I remember saying to the admitting doctor as I arrived at the old Darwin Hospital, 'Doc, I think I've broken my ankle.' He replied gravely, 'You'll wish you had.'

Three operations later, I still walk with a limp and occasionally endure pretty strong pain. At the time all my plans had to be reassessed. While the $100 000 I was eventually awarded for 'pain and suffering' and 'loss of future income' seemed like a lot of money then, I would still rather have kept my foot intact. Not only was I on crutches for six months, I couldn't continue rangering. I had to find something else to do.

One door closes, and another opens . . .

A career in medicine had never ceased to be of interest to me and it seemed that at that point it was worth giving it one last try. All my previous attempts to enter medical school had failed. Either it was too difficult to change courses or the universities were not interested in my application. As I recovered from my accident, I sent off applications to all the Australian medical schools and was surprised to be accepted by Sydney, Melbourne and Adelaide. It seemed my physics PhD was finally coming in handy.

Having never lived in Sydney, I liked the idea of experiencing a new city. And while I found the rote learning of medicine boring and relatively easy, the actual subject material was wonderful. Like many doctors, I am fascinated with the inter-relationships and complexities of the human body and its experience within its environment, and I was particularly taken with the study of the history and philosophy of medicine. My first few years at Sydney University were therefore inspirational. By the fourth year of study, however, I was more jaded than excited by the life of a medical student. As a mature-age student – I was thirty-five when I commenced first year – my friendships with other medical students were frequently strained. I felt that their often privileged backgrounds gave them poor insight into the complex social issues that lie at the interface between medicine and politics. The idea of taking a year's break from the course had begun to appeal to me. And it was at that time that the compensation payment for my accident finally came through.

To everyone's amazement, I spent most of my payout on a 32-foot sailing boat, a cutter-rigged sloop known as *Squizz*. With my partner at the time, Marlise, I set off to sail around Australia for a year. But while we were taking time-out in

Hobart, moored in Constitution Dock, a radiophone call came in. It was Sydney Uni ringing to tell me if I did not return immediately I would lose my coveted place in the course. With this ultimatum, I bit the bullet and sailed back to Sydney, finding a mooring in Botany Bay. But I found that final year of medicine insufferable. I could not finish it soon enough.

Back to the north

Once my medical degree was behind me, I took to the road and headed north again. The further towards the Territory I travelled, the more I felt I was ridding myself of those frustrating Sydney years. I recall listening to the car radio as Graeme Connors' song 'North' confirmed that the Territory was the place to be. An internship at Royal Darwin Hospital was waiting, and I started there in 1989.

I soon discovered my working life at the hospital would be far from peaceful. Not long after arriving, my background in physics saw me appointed as the hospital's radiation protection officer. It was then things started to go wrong. In an incident triggered by the arrival in Darwin Harbour of the nuclear submarine *USS Houston*, I felt obliged to speak out once more. On 24 March 1993, I arrived at work in the emergency department to see a notice directing all medical staff to attend a training session on dealing with nuclear accidents and emergencies. The session had to be carried out that day, as – the note went on to explain – there would be a nuclear-powered submarine in Darwin Harbour the following day.

I was supposed to be the hospital's radiation protection

officer, but the notice came as a shock to me, and it was a ludicrous suggestion that staff could be trained in this complex area of medicine in just twenty-four hours. Angered by the incident, I made a public statement as spokesperson for the Medical Association for the Prevention of War, a statement that ran that evening on ABC radio's 'PM' program.

All hell broke loose. I was dragged into the office of the hospital's general manager and given twenty-four hours to explain why I shouldn't be disciplined for a breach of the Public Service Act. The Department of Health issued a media release denying that my statements about the lack of safety protocols at the hospital were accurate. But other doctors rallied in support of my actions, and after a flurry of public statements the Department of Health issued a public apology to me and I thought the incident was behind me. How wrong I was.

Two months later I was asked to give evidence to a Senate committee in Darwin seeking Territorians' views on disaster preparedness. I presented a submission under parliamentary privilege, and spoke freely about the deficiencies I'd seen at Royal Darwin Hospital. Within twenty-four hours of my giving evidence, my old adversary, and now Territory Health Minister, Mike Reed issued a press release that ended with the ominous statement: 'If Dr Nitschke doesn't like the situation, I have no doubt the Royal Darwin Hospital will be able to scrape by without him.' A few days later this was followed by a letter from the hospital telling me that my services as a doctor would no longer be required when my contract finished.

I was stunned; medical staff contracts were *always* renewed – after all, they can never get enough doctors to work in the

Territory. Everyone viewed this act as punishment for my actions over the *Houston*. Junior medical staff threatened strike action and the Department of Health rapidly set up an enquiry to avoid industrial action.

Months went by. The first enquiry was boycotted by staff as a department whitewash. The AMA became involved and recruited Dr Peter Arnold from its Federal Executive for an 'independent' inquiry, which produced a report that was immediately restricted because of fear of litigation by senior medical officers who claimed they were defamed. During this most stressful period it was support from my partner at the time, Tristan, a trainee paediatrician, that got me through, although it took a toll on her career, and eventually on our relationship.

Justice – of sorts – eventually came when I convinced the Senate in Canberra that there was a good case that my loss of employment had been directly linked with my evidence given under privilege. The issue was then referred to the Senate Privileges Committee. After two hearings, one in Canberra and one in Darwin, with the Territory's Department of Health represented by QCs and with me defending myself and even attempting my own cross-examination, the 55th Report of the Senate Committee of Privileges was tabled in Federal Parliament in June 1995.

While the report did find that I had been discriminated against, it could not establish that this had been because of the privileged evidence I gave. It did, however, urge that a remedy should follow from 'those who have punished Dr Nitschke for what should have been his right as a citizen'.

As a result, the hospital offered me my job back. But with

Mike Reed still at the helm of the Department of Health, I could see a repeat of the Parks and Wildlife situation: years of remaining on the ladder's bottom rung. And by this time, I had no desire to return. The bureaucracy of the hospital and my ideas clearly did not mix. Instead, I decided to start my own after-hours general practice: Austdoc Mobile.

With my newly purchased Barina car, I took to the streets of Darwin, providing medical home visits to the city's drug-using and sex-worker populations. Since the Territory did not yet have a methadone program, the plight of narcotic-dependent people tapped into my concern for social justice. To this day I am pleased I undertook that work. It gave me a huge sense of satisfaction and taught me much about human nature and social and economic discrimination. And again, it took me to that troubled interface between medicine and politics.

It was during my work with Austdoc Mobile in 1995 that I first heard the Northern Territory Chief Minister Marshall Perron speak out on ABC radio about his proposed Rights of the Terminally Ill Bill. I instantly thought what a good, brave idea it was, but did not know at the time that my life was about to change forever.

Chapter 2

Lessons from Darwin

When Territorians first learnt of Marshall Perron's proposal to legalise voluntary euthanasia, everyone I talked to gave the same response: Perron is on the right track. He was a clever politician, but looking back I believe that he was not fully aware of the global significance of his proposal. Time ensured that he soon became so. Marshall had long believed that a person suffering and near death should be able to ask for assistance to end their life peacefully. But it was not until he read a speech by Monash University Professor Helga Kuhse that he really saw that there was no '*rational* argument against VE for a competent terminally ill adult'.[1]

Initially, I took little interest in the issue. After all, the bill was simply commonsense to me. If I was terminally ill, I would want to be able to choose to die. I would not want others telling me I had to wait until my suffering worsened before I got any help to end it. Why would anyone else want to?

Yet within days of Perron's announcement, the medical profession declared its opposition to his bill with a statement by the head of the NT branch of the Australian Medical Association

(AMA) and right-to-life advocate, Dr Chris Wake. Wake said that 'killing patients is not a proportional or proper response to terminally ill situations'.[2] He went on to say that 'AMA members will have nothing to do with the drug protocols and the like necessary to enact the legislation'.[3] The message from the medical profession was that they would wreak havoc on the legislation, no matter what the people or the politicians wanted.

Why the vitriol, I wondered. What was it that the AMA was so afraid of? And what about the patients? What did those who were seriously ill and dying want? Did the AMA ever ask them? Once again, my indignation was ignited. I felt the AMA was out of line. They had no right or role in dictating end-of-life choices to the Australian community. So while I had certainly never voted for Marshall Perron's Country Liberal Party – indeed I had stood as a Greens candidate in the 1995 federal election – I felt his proposal had merit. And I was annoyed that the AMA would deny Territorians this type of legislative approach to a dormant social issue.

Throughout my life, and even during my medical career, I had hardly heard the word euthanasia mentioned. In medical school in the mid-1980s the issue never raised its head. But, probably like most people in society, I had a clear view of what I would want my end-of-life choices to be. The idea of the medical profession coming along and attempting to use its power to impose its view on the issue I found breathtakingly arrogant. Even though I had only been a doctor for a few years, this was the worst example I had seen of the profession's insufferable paternalism. I resolved to set myself apart from the AMA and show that they did not speak for all Territory doctors.

The way I demonstrated this to Dr Wake and the AMA was to garner the signatures of twenty-two other Territory doctors who were prepared to state publicly that they supported the proposed legislation. On 8 May 1995 we ran the following half-page advertisement in the *NT News*, under the name Doctors for Change.

> **Doctors for Change**
>
> A public claim has been made that the medical practitioners of the Northern Territory are opposed to the introduction of the Private Member's Bill on the Rights of the Terminally Ill.
>
> *This is not the case*
>
> The undersigned doctors are registered practitioners within the Northern Territory and are of the opinion that with the provision of safeguards, voluntary euthanasia should be available to all those terminally ill patients who make such a request.
>
> There is a need for legislation to govern this practice and we support in principle the proposed Bill.
>
> Signed: Twenty-two doctors
>
> Doctors for Change

This advertisement led to my being interviewed, and my views about the legislation were reported in the local media. Consequently, my voice was used by the national media as the counter to statements made by the AMA. Although we were strange bedfellows, Marshall Perron and I became the spokespersons of this new movement.

The first place in the world

On 25 May 1995, after much nail-biting, the Northern Territory became the first place in the world to pass legislation that allowed a sick person to ask a doctor to help them die. The bill was passed by just one vote. A thirteen-month period was set aside for the development of regulations to control the new law, and enactment was set for 1 July 1996. The deciding vote was cast by the Aboriginal Member for Arnhem, Wes Lanhupuy, who said:

> Mr Speaker, I can assure you that, in the 11 years that I have been in this Parliament, this is the most difficult bill that I have ever had to examine and ponder on. I have had sleep-less nights over it for a whole range of reasons . . . Based on such considerations, I believe a person should have the right to be able to determine what they want if they are of sane mind.
>
> It is my intention to support the bill.[4]

Wes's support for the bill surprised me. Throughout the campaign run by Dr Wake, allegations had been made that the legislation was 'racist' and 'culturally insensitive'. It was also said that Aboriginal people viewed the bill as a new version of the 'poison waterhole', by which White Australia would again promote genocide. Even though Wake's own survey of 300 Territorians (of whom seventeen were Aboriginal) was unable to confirm this view among the Indigenous community, the dam-age was done.[5] Support from the Left faded. By the time the vote was to be taken, no one was prepared to predict the result.

I really did not expect the bill to be passed, so when it was, I was stunned. I had sat in the public gallery of the parliament for most of the night. After hearing a number of speakers – enough of whom were against the bill – I thought that all was lost and I left. I had already postponed patients that I was due to see as part of my nightly mobile medical practice, so I returned to work.

The news of Lanhupuy's deciding vote came through on the radio as I was in between patients. While I digested the news, it was another thirteen months before the magnitude of the legislative achievement fully dawned on me. It was not until I saw the world's media, replete with satellite dishes, set up in front of Darwin's Parliament House on 1 July 1996 that I would feel excitement, exhilaration and a responsibility for what had come to pass.

The right stuff

In watching the enactment of VE bills elsewhere in the world since 1996, I have come to realise that certain ingredients are required for the successful passage of a law on VE. In the mid-1990s in the Northern Territory, we had all that was needed. For example, we had a charismatic politician who was prepared to stand by his beliefs. More than this, though, Marshall Perron was something of a legend in the Territory. His long involvement with Darwin gave him unique insight into the local psyche, something he was able to put to good use as he carved out his successful political career.

Perron is also a straight talker. He doesn't mince words and can be a powerful force in any debate. He has that admirable talent of taking the people with him. A politician from the conservative side of politics, his leadership on VE reinforces the fact that the issue of one's right to die with dignity transcends political divisions and ideological differences. Over the years strong support for VE has come from the likes of Petro Georgiou and Amanda Vanstone in the Liberal Party, Bob Brown in the Greens and Jenny Macklin, Carmen Lawrence and Simon Crean in the ALP.

A second factor in the initial success of the ROTI bill in the Northern Territory parliament is that it has no upper house. This makes the passage of legislation more efficient. The government of the day is all the more powerful when the checks and balances of the house of review of the traditional Westminster system are absent. This was the case in 1995 in the Territory and it worked in voluntary euthanasia's favour.

A third factor that helped get the ROTI bill through is that the Northern Territory is the least religious place in Australia. According to *Social Trends 1994*, 18 per cent of the Territory's population consider themselves to have no religion. This compares to 10 per cent in New South Wales and a national average of 12 per cent. Territorians are also the most likely people to leave the religion question in the census unanswered.[6]

Finally, the Territory has a mindset that is different from everywhere else in Australia. In this part of the world, car registration plates contain words like 'Frontier', 'Barra Country' and 'Outback' – words that conjure up Territory fact and myth. And this is the point. Territorians can be rough, rugged and cynical as hell about the gentrified south. In some ways, the Territory welcomed a VE law precisely because no one else had one. No other state or territory was tough enough to find a legislative way to deal with this political hot potato.

The *Rights of the Terminally Ill Act 1995* – what was it all about?

The ROTI Act was a cautious, carefully-written piece of legislation. While it might have been radical in that it allowed for the world's first case of medically-assisted voluntary euthanasia, the Act was relatively conservative in that it only catered for those who were terminally ill. The Act also had many stipulations and even more safeguards.

To qualify to use the Act, a person had to be over eighteen years of age and, in the treating doctor's opinion, 'suffering from an illness that will, in the normal course and without the application of extraordinary measures, result in the death of the patient'. This is to say that the person had to be terminally ill and 'experiencing pain, suffering and/or distress to an extent unacceptable' to that person. To prove that this was the case the patient had to consult three medical professionals in addition to their own doctor. A mandatory 48-hour cooling-off period applied once all consultations and paperwork were completed.

In regard to the consultations, one of these had to be performed by a psychiatrist in order to certify that the person was not 'suffering from a treatable clinical depression in respect of the illness'. The second needed to be carried out by a 'medical practitioner who holds prescribed qualifications, or has prescribed experience, in the treatment of the terminal illness from which the patient is suffering'. A further stipulation involved palliative care. The Act stated that there could be no 'palliative care options reasonably available to the patient to alleviate the patient's pain and suffering to levels acceptable to the patient'. This safeguard ensured that no one would request VE because they could not access palliative care. Rather, the two had to go hand in hand. Finally, the person did not need to be a long-term resident of the Territory to access the Act. A late amendment to the Act gave the coroner the role of watchdog over the implementation and monitoring of the legislation.

The following is a copy of the paperwork that was required to be completed by the patient and their doctors.

Request for Assistance to End my Life in a Humane and Dignified Manner Form

I, _____, have been advised by my medical practitioner that I am suffering from an illness which will ultimately result in my death and this has been confirmed by a second medical practitioner.

I have been fully informed of the nature of my illness and its likely course and the medical treatment, including palliative care, counselling and psychiatric support and extraordinary measures that may keep me alive, that is available to me and I am satisfied that there is no medical treatment reasonably available that is acceptable to me in my circumstances.

I request my medical practitioner to assist me to terminate my life in a humane and dignified manner.

I understand that I have the right to rescind this request at any time.

This form was then signed and dated in front of the patient's own doctor who then completed their section that stated:

> DECLARATION OF WITNESSES
> I declare that –
> (a) the person signing this request is personally known to me;
> (b) he/she is a patient under my care;
> (c) he/she signed the request in my presence and in the presence of the second witness to this request;
> (d) I am satisfied that he/she is of sound mind and that his/her decision to end his/her life has been made freely, voluntarily and after due consideration.
> Signed: Patient's Medical Practitioner

The signature of another medical practitioner was also required. This final section read:

> I declare that –
> (a) the person signing this request is known to me;
> (b) I have discussed his/her case with him/her and his/her medical practitioner;
> (c) he/she signed the request in my presence and in the presence of his/her medical practitioner;
> (d) I am satisfied that he/she is of sound mind and that his/her decision to end his/her life has been made freely, voluntarily and after due consideration;
> (e) I am satisfied that the conditions of section 7 of the Act have been or will be complied with.
> Signed: Second Medical Practitioner

In terms of the specific action that would cause death, the ROTI Act stated that a medical practitioner could prepare, administer and give a lethal substance to a patient. This same person had either to provide 'the assistance and/or is and remains present while the assistance is given and until the death of the patient'. This meant that while I did not have to administer the lethal drug – I invented the Deliverance Machine before the enactment of the ROTI Act to make patient self-administration possible – I did have to be present at the death.

After the death of the patient, the same medical practitioner had to sign the death certificate and then report it to the Coroner. This was done by forwarding the death certificate and the patient's medical records as they related to the terminal illness and death of the patient. This was to be done as soon as possible after a death.

In summary, the ROTI Act confirmed the right of a terminally ill person to request assistance from a medically qualified person to voluntarily terminate their life in a humane manner. Furthermore, it provided procedural protection against the possibility of abuse of the rights recognised.

In the thirteen months that followed the ROTI bill's passing, but before its enactment, the first of several dying patients began arriving in Darwin, believing the law to be already in place, and sought me out as a doctor who they thought could help them die. When Marta Alfonso, who was suffering from bowel cancer, arrived from Spain and found to her disgust that she would have to wait another eight months for the law to be operational, she contacted 60 Minutes and told her story. A few weeks later she checked into a motel, took the lethal drugs she had obtained and died. As I waited out those thirteen months, I received a rapid education in patient rights, medical options, end-of-life decisions and palliative care.

On 1 July 1996 the *Rights of the Terminally Ill Act 1995* became law. Yet the ink on the Act would never be allowed to dry. What we did not know at the time was that even before it was enacted, conservative federal Liberal backbencher Kevin Andrews was talking to Prime Minister John Howard about the possibility of introducing a private member's bill in Federal Parliament to overturn ROTI.[7]

Attacks on the legislation intensified significantly in the eight months after 1 July. White ants came from far and wide to eat away at the ROTI Act. These attacks were largely underwritten by the Catholic Church, with Kevin Andrews as the master of ceremonies. But all gnawed away at the legislation at a steady pace.

White ants in Darwin

Primarily, the attacks came from within the Territory government's own ranks and these started on the very eve of the vote. After many years in parliament and after having made his mark with the issue, Marshall Perron chose the night of 25 May 1995 to resign as Chief Minister. In retrospect this was unfortunate, as it allowed staunch Catholic and anti-euthanasia politician Shane Stone to take over.[8] And, as fate would have it, Stone – a close friend of John Howard – was charged with the ROTI bill's full implementation.

One of the highly effective ways by which the new Act was undermined was through the Territory's Department of Health joining forces with anti-euthanasia activist Chris Wake. Together, Wake (operating on behalf of the AMA) and the department were extremely successful in ensuring that Territory doctors shunned the ROTI Act. This was primarily achieved by the department mailing all doctors a letter that detailed an obscure legal risk, suggesting that doctors could face retrospective prosecution if the Act was ever deemed unconstitutional. Even though the ROTI law was never found to be so, the damage done was as significant as it was lasting. It would take another three months for doctors to see through the propaganda of Wake and others such as the Catholic Bishop of Darwin, Ted Collins.

With the media by our side

Not long after the ROTI Act became law, I was contacted by Max Bell, a taxi driver from Broken Hill. Max, sixty-seven, had stomach cancer and surgery had left him with constant nausea, vomiting and an inability to eat anything solid. He had put his house on the market, had his pet dog put down and drove north in his taxi to Darwin to make use of the new Act. As the most prominent Territorian doctor in support of the legislation, the onus was on me to help Max qualify to use it. While this might sound easy – and I thought it would be – at the time it was to prove infuriatingly impossible.

On Max's arrival in Darwin, it was clear that he had paid a high price for his six-day drive. Desperately ill, I had him admitted to Royal Darwin Hospital, and there he languished for the next three weeks. In that period, I tried desperately to get the specialist medical signatures the Act required if Max was to be eligible to use the law. I needed to find a surgeon, a palliative care specialist and a psychiatrist. To my amazement, I could not find one doctor who was prepared to come and see Max and provide their name to the necessary paperwork. Such doctors didn't have to support voluntary euthanasia, I told them; they simply had to confirm (a) that Max was dying, (b) that he had had his palliative care options explained, and (c) that he was not mad. But such was the fear within the medical community, fuelled by reports that doctors who cooperated with the legislation could be retrospectively punished, that none would come forward. I rang every specialist in the Northern Territory. No one wanted to become the second public face of the VE cause and risk their own medical career and practice. Chris Wake and the AMA's scare campaign was successful. Marshall Perron came to the hospital to see Max, but no doctor would. We had the world's first law, but it wasn't working.

At the end of three terrible weeks, Max signed himself out of hospital. It was clear he wanted to take matters into his own hands back home. I managed to stop the sale of his house as he set off to drive himself back to Broken Hill. He was disgusted and angry at what he saw as the cowardice of the Territory's doctors. He was furious with me too for not warning him that this could happen. His accusation, 'You didn't do your homework, boy' was made, and then he was gone.[9]

A week later I joined Max in Broken Hill, where I found him camped in his empty house. I and a few of his friends bought him a bed and bits of crockery and I stayed with him for the remaining three weeks of his life. As his health failed, he was finally moved to a palliative care bed at the Broken Hill Base Hospital. There, heavily sedated with morphine, Max died over a period of three days. He died precisely in the way he most dreaded – slowly, and with the process completely out of his control.

Yet Max's ordeal was not completely in vain. When the mood is right, the media can work powerfully in one's favour. On this occasion it was the work of *Four Corners* journalist Murray McLaughlin that provided the pivotal moment; a moment that was to help make the ROTI law succeed in practice. Earlier that year, Murray had introduced himself to me, asking if I knew of anyone intending to use the new Act. When Max made contact it seemed a good idea to put the two in touch. This meeting resulted in an ABC-TV crew meeting Max in Katherine and filming the last leg of his road trip to Darwin. Despite being so sick, Max was pleased to be involved in something that might help his cause.[10]

Max and Murray got on well, and the filming continued during Max's stay in Darwin. The end result was an episode of *Four Corners* titled 'The Road to Nowhere'. This program was to prove a powerful piece of media, raising many questions about why a terminally ill man like Max was unable to use the law.[11] While Max never received the euthanasia he desired, the images of his terrible suffering in the *Four Corners* program were responsible for inspiring the first Territory doctor to break ranks and sign the requisite paperwork for another person's request to die several months later. My faith in the power of the media was sealed. Today, Max's cab lives on as my car and, like his memory, travels with me around Australia.

The story of Bob Dent

The doctor who was brave enough to sign the paperwork for another patient's request to die was surgeon Jon Wardill and it was for the death of Darwin man Bob Dent that he acted. On 22 September 1996, Dent became the first person to successfully make use of the ROTI legislation and I became the first doctor in the world to legally administer voluntary euthanasia. Jon Wardill was integral to making this happen, as was Sydney psychiatrist John Ellard, who flew to Darwin to see Bob. The drought had broken.

Bob Dent, who was suffering from prostate cancer, died using the Deliverance Machine. The machine is a laptop computer connected to a syringe driver. When the reservoir of the syringe is filled with a lethal drug such as Nembutal, and an intravenous line connected to the patient, the person can self-administer the drug. The Deliverance Machine restored the balance, placing the patient's family centre-frame and leaving me, the medical practitioner, to retire to the corner.

Bob and his wife Judy had invited me to have a meal with them in the hours before Bob planned to die. As I sat down to that Sunday lunch, my mouth was so dry I couldn't swallow. I sipped on a glass of stout to moisten my mouth. But it was only a sip. I had no appetite, certainly no thirst, and I was worried that the alcohol – even that small amount – might affect my judgement.

At the end of a most difficult hour for us all, Bob retreated to the verandah and lay down on the lounge. I nervously prepared the equipment and brought it over to him. To my surprise, the needle of the cannula went into his vein on the first attempt. Insertion can often be difficult and I had worried that there could be trouble. Next, I connected the line to the machine. Once set up, I was able to move away and Judy took my place.

One last time, I asked Bob if he was sure of his decision. He answered by reaching for the laptop computer. There was nothing more to be said. Bob pressed the 'Yes' button to each of the laptop's three questions as soon as they appeared on the screen: 'Are you aware that if you go ahead to the last screen and press the "Yes" button, you will be given a lethal dose of medications and die?'; 'Are you certain you understand that if you proceed and press the "Yes" button on the next screen that you will die?'; and 'In 15 seconds you will be given a lethal injection . . . press "Yes" to proceed.' (If the wrong button was pressed or a button was pressed outside of a specified time limit, the program would stop and the process would need to begin again.) As I watched, I realised I was drenched in sweat. While waiting the fifteen seconds for the machine to start, I was aware that Bob's death would be a world first. While I didn't feel particularly good about it, I was certainly glad Bob was getting the peaceful death he so desired.

Bob gave one last sigh and, as Judy was holding him, fell into a deep sleep. Five minutes later, while still in her arms, he died. Judy and I sat quietly for what must have been a good half hour. Slowly, she gestured for me to come over. I certified Bob's death and left them.

The story did not hit the media until the following Wednesday, and then all hell broke loose. Calls came in from journalists on every continent, all wanting interviews for radio, TV and newspapers. Every year now, we call 22 September Bob Dent Day. Every second year, Exit International bestows the Bob Dent Award, one that recognises outstanding contributions to the right-to-die movement. The first recipient of this award was Greens Senator Bob Brown. In 2003, the Queensland activist John Edge received it.

From September 1996 to March 1997 three more people made use of the Northern Territory's ROTI law. All of these people were my patients. They included Janet Mills (from Naracoorte in South Australia), Bill (from Darwin) and Valerie (from Sydney). Another woman, Esther Wild, qualified to use the law (see chapter 6), but Kevin Andrews' bill overturned the legislation before she was able to utilise it.

The personal toll on me during this period was enormous. I never set out to administer? – practice? – oversee? (I'm not sure of the right words to describe my role) voluntary euthanasia. But, as the first doctor in the world to use VE legislation, I felt an immense weight of expectation and responsibility upon me. It proved to be a disturbing task and a lonely place to be. The difficulty of being so intimately involved with these people's deaths was stressful enough; then there were the political attacks on the Act that increased in severity as the law started to operate more effectively. During this time, my relationship with my partner Tristan began to falter. Obsessed with the cause and with little time for anyone or anything else, I was hell to live with. Who could blame her for being unhappy? While part of me still thinks that I did not have any choice about how to live through those months, my behaviour during that time remains a major regret.

Soon after the ROTI bill was passed, media reports began outlining the opposition that the legislation would be facing federally. Not only was there to be a high-court challenge, but the possibility of a private member's bill being introduced by Kevin Andrews was also being reported.

The Kevin Andrews bill

The Liberal backbencher MP Kevin Andrews first presented his private member's bill to the Australian parliament on 9 September 1996. To this day I maintain that the passage of this bill could have been prevented. But the cards were stacked against us, and at the bottom of the pack was the issue of our Constitution. Canberra is able to override Northern Territory, ACT and Norfolk Island legislation through use of Section 122 of this document. This section grants the Commonwealth the power to make laws for the government of any territory of Australia. This power rides roughshod over proper regional democratic processes.

The months between the ROTI Act's passing and the introduction of the Andrews bill were intense. The legislation was attacked from all angles. Take the machinations of the Lyons Forum (the secretive organisation of the far Right of the Liberal Party) and the 'Euthanasia No' campaign as an example. This campaign was made up of a wide-reaching network of people, many from within the Lyons Forum and Catholic Church–based propagandists. With ringleaders including former Young Labor president Tony Burke – now a member of the shadow cabinet – and Sydney businessman Jim Dominguez, the 'No' campaign was well-funded and effective.[12] In the words of journalist Michael Gordon, the campaign was a 'story of a network [where] all the principals [were] Catholics – its influential connections, its single-mindedness and the tactics it employed'.[13]

Involved in the 'No' campaign also were some rather prominent players in the Australian media, not least among them *The Australian's* then editor-in-chief, Paul Kelly. A powerful ally of the 'No' crusade, Kelly openly used his position at the newspaper to promote 'No', ensuring his personal opposition to voluntary euthanasia was extremely effective.

Another source that helped undermine the ROTI legislation (albeit unwittingly) came from within the state-based voluntary euthanasia societies. To my dismay, as I travelled from state to state during 1996, trying to encourage the VE societies to mount a coordinated, national campaign to save the ROTI Act, I knew something was not right. The responses I received were patchy, and although I managed to get representatives from Queensland, South Australia and the ACT together for a strategy meeting in Canberra, there was little willingness to pool resources and mount a national campaign.

The Voluntary Euthanasia Society of Victoria argued that they were unwilling to put money into a project that would not directly benefit that State. Later I met with the president, Dr Rodney Syme, and the then executive officer, Kay Koetsier, whereupon they expanded on this view. Syme explained that while the society was prepared to pay for survey work that could benefit Victoria, there would be no involvement in a national campaign to lobby federal politicians. Koetsier went so far as to claim that the passage of the Andrews bill could even bode well for Victoria. When I asked Koetsier to elaborate on this extraordinary claim, she said that if the Senate voted in favour of the Andrews bill, there would be a national outcry. Then the then premier of Victoria, Jeff Kennett, would take it upon himself to 'do the right thing' for the people of that State, and pass right-to-die legislation. History tells us otherwise.

In retrospect, it is little wonder that the 'Euthanasia No' campaign was so powerful. Not only did the Commonwealth have the Constitution on its side, but the media, the Church and a large network of influential and wealthy people pulled out all the stops to defeat the ground-breaking Act.

The parliamentary word

In an unprecedented occurrence, the Kevin Andrews bill was debated in the Senate for the best part of four days. The speeches heard in both houses of parliament were some of the most emotional ever made by Australian politicians. While some MPs spoke about the rights of the individual, others' views were fuelled by the dogma of the Catholic Church. Some talked critically of state/territory versus Commonwealth powers.

Within both major parties, opinion was split. The words of ALP frontbencher Anthony Albanese were eloquent and passionate. He said: 'This debate is hard – real hard. It is hard because it is about death.' He went on:

Most people are uncomfortable talking about dying . . .
[Yet] this debate, as hard as it may be, is important. The
outcome of this debate will reflect on our maturity both as
a parliament and as a nation for it will determine the manner in which we seek to control each other's lives.

I oppose this [Andrews] bill because I support human
dignity. I oppose this bill because I support freedom of
choice. I oppose this bill because I support civil liberties.
I oppose this bill because my Christian upbringing taught
me that compassion is important. I oppose this bill because
modern medical practice should be open and accountable,
not covert and dishonest . . .

I oppose this bill because I oppose the moral posturing
of the Lyons Forum. I oppose the hypocrisy of those who
say, 'This debate is so important' and then vote to debate it
upstairs in sideshow alley.

Most importantly, I oppose this bill for one critical
reason, and that is this. We have all accepted that this parliamentary debate should be a matter for our conscience.

How arrogant to then suggest that the ability to exercise conscience should be taken from a seriously ill patient
who wants to die. There is nothing moral about our exercising a free conscience vote as members of parliament
and then voting to deny to others the right to exercise their
conscience.

What possible right do Kevin Andrews, Leo McLeay,
Lindsay Tanner or Anthony Albanese have to have exercised Bob Dent's conscience for him? It was his decision
and he had a right to do that.[14]

In contrast, Kim Beazley kept his comments in parliament to a minimum, although he did offer some elaboration on his support for the Kevin Andrews bill during a doorstep interview at Canberra University:

> I think it's a sad thing. I'm not a supporter of euthanasia, as you know. I'm a believer in palliative care and in properly funding it. And I do think there are an awful lot of pressures on old people and if we go down this road, we'll end up with something very close to the Dutch experience, and I think that would be bad.[15]

History has of course proven Beazley embarrassingly wrong in his summation of the Dutch VE laws (see the 'slippery slope' discussion on page 134) and he is clearly ill-informed in thinking palliative care always provides the answer to end-of-life suffering. Nevertheless, Beazley's opposition to our right to die with dignity remains.

Of those who focused on territory rights, it was the Territory's own Senator Bob Collins who led the way. Although a hostile opponent of the ROTI law, Collins was angry at the vilification of both the Territory and its politicians by federal parliamentarians. He was especially critical of Kevin Andrews and Senator Eric Abetz from Tasmania. He was angry at Andrews for his audacity to think that 'Territorians have no rights, only obligations'. Collins was also scathing of Abetz when the Tasmanian had tried to argue that 'the Northern Territory parliament exists only by the grace and favour of the Commonwealth parliament. What the Commonwealth parliament gives, it can also take away'. 'This', said Collins, 'from a senator from a state with about twice the population of the Northern Territory's, and five times its representation in the House of Representatives and six times its representation here in the Senate'.

Other politicians focused more on their own moment in history. Citing the eighteenth-century libertarian Edmund Burke in some detail, Barry Jones followed Burke's lead, stating that he as 'your representative' 'owes you, not his industry only, but his judgement; and he betrays instead of serving you if he sacrifices it to your opinion'.[16] Jones's mistake – and that of other politicians who drew on Burke – was to believe that it was appropriate for politicians to dismiss the 'opinion' of their electorates in favour of their own prejudices. Sure, the political paternalism of Burke might have suited the uneducated, illiterate electorate of Bristol more than 200 years ago. But it is nothing short of arrogant to suggest that politicians should do our thinking for us today. If Burke must be treated as the patron saint of politicians, then those who quote him should reacquaint themselves with another well-known Burke quote used by the Whistleblowers' Society: 'All that is necessary for the triumph of evil is that good men do nothing'.

That sinking feeling

This period of personal and political turmoil drew to a close on 26 March 1997 when the Kevin Andrews bill, formally known as the Euthanasia Laws Bill, passed its final stages in the Senate of the Federal Parliament. Letters to the editor in the *Sydney Morning Herald* the next day summed up many of our feelings about the event:

I have heard that early this morning, in the Senate, the lights went out.[17]

As did this one:

I don't understand why these evangelists of their own belief systems have the right to take away another individual's right to end his or her own suffering.

This is the worst kind of politicking, far worse than acting out at Question Time, making errors with expenses or jetting around on fact-finding missions. I don't care what 'God' a politician chooses to follow, but when his belief affects others I consider he has overstepped his already poor standing in the community.

My heart goes out to those who are suffering and those wanting to help them within the law.[18]

Two days later, the Governor-General Sir William Deane ratified the bill and the Northern Territory ROTI Act ceased to exist. I was devastated. The way I felt is perhaps best encapsulated in a photo taken by a Fairfax press photographer that shows me standing on the steps of Parliament House, surrounded by the journalists of the press gallery, with burning copies of the ROTI Act and the Northern Territory's Constitution at my feet. Prior to the successful passage of the Andrews bill, the writing had been on the wall. I knew the ROTI Act was lost, and I suspected that if I was going to make a scene, this was the day to do it. The burning was to me a symbolic act, as I felt the wishes of most Territorians lay in ashes at the feet of our federal politicians.

The phoenix that rose to become Exit International

As the fog lifted in the weeks following the success of the Andrews bill, it became clear that while the ROTI Act was no more, the need for people to have access, if not to voluntary euthanasia, then to information about end-of-life options remained. Sick people still wanted to die. And so my focus changed. Political lobbying was over. The previous twelve months had been as intense as they had been public and they had taken their toll. Yet I found that my work was just beginning. I established the Voluntary Euthanasia Research Foundation (VERF) for people wanting to find out more and began a workshop and clinic program that has since spread to all Australian capital cities and more recently to New Zealand.

One of the other challenges I took on in 1998 was to run against Kevin Andrews in the federal election. Putting my money where my mouth was, I moved to Melbourne to stand in Andrews' own electorate of Menzies, in Melbourne's eastern suburbs. During the campaign I worked closely with the Voluntary Euthanasia Society of Victoria. In contrast to the poor effort they had made defending the ROTI legislation in Federal Parliament, they put their total support behind my challenge, and it gave me some insight as to what might have been possible when we were trying to preserve the ROTI Act. If only. Over $120000 in donations came in, an amount that still stands as one of the highest records for campaign funds ever raised by an independent candidate. On election day we secured nearly 10 per cent of the primary vote. While I'm not sure how worried Kevin Andrews was on that day, we were pleased that the safe Liberal seat of Menzies was forced to count preferences for the first time. This seemed suitable payback for the misery that Andrews' bill had caused.

> May I wish Mr Kevin Andrews a long and excruciatingly painful life.
>
> – Letter to the Editor, *Sydney Morning Herald*[19]

With the 1998 election out of the way, my attention turned to the world stage and I flew to Zurich to attend the Conference of the World Federation of Right-to-Die Organisations. There I spoke at length on the concept (first put forward by Huib Drion) of the Drion Pill. Building on the conceptual work of Drion, I presented my early thoughts on what the development of a 'Peaceful Pill' project might involve. (See chapter 11 for a full discussion of the future of the Peaceful Pill.) Given the unlikelihood of another VE law being passed in Australia, I was already aware that new strategies were needed.

VERF, the foundation I established, has since been renamed Exit International, and since 1997 more than 3000 people have attended Exit's programs. Now a lot of my year is taken up travelling around Australia and New Zealand, with regular trips to the US and Europe. More importantly, perhaps, all my spare time is now devoted to the pursuit of technologies that offer real choices for people sick of waiting for another law to be enacted. I call these the CoGenie and the Peaceful Pill projects, and Exit members have welcomed the chance to be involved in their development. Interestingly, these devices continue to attract a significant amount of media both in

Australia and overseas. A technological answer for those who are ill and suffering seems to have captured the public's imagination.

While this level of interest is pleasing, there is a downside. The constant media exposure I experience has led to the accusation that I am media hungry or just simply macabre. The upside is the growing number of people joining Exit so they can discover some real end-of-life options. And while I am committed to conducting Exit's workshops and clinics around the country, I have to admit I am also worn out by it all, and from being away from home so often and those I love. I am now fifty-seven and have friends who are retiring. For me, however, it seems my commitment to assisting the ill and the elderly means I am busier than ever. Dying with dignity is a growth industry. So when I am not on the road, I am usually in Darwin, busy in the laboratory working on the Peaceful Pill, testing old drugs and looking for ways to modify new drugs so that they may provide people with a peaceful, timely death. I'm also now spending time creating an experimental toxic plant nursery. But, like environmentalists and other human-rights activists, I am hopeful that I will – eventually – achieve my own redundancy. What better goal to aim for?

The road ahead

For Territorians, and many others, the ROTI legislation is gone but not forgotten. Every day in Darwin I get pats on the back and encouragement to 'keep at it', from ordinary people. But only when the Territory achieves statehood will we have any chance of restoring the law. However, with a Catholic as Chief Minster, even this seems doubtful. In 2004, Clare Martin made it clear that VE is not on her government's 'agenda'.[20] In response, Marshall Perron – whose seat of Fannie Bay Martin inherited – has accused her of having neither the 'experience nor maturity when it comes to dealing with VE at a legislative level'.[21] And he's right.

The death with dignity road in Australia has been long and hard and seems to be never-ending. But I would not have swapped my place with anyone. I have recovered, at a personal level, from the stress following the failed legislation and the anguish of that difficult time. And I remain inspired by the possibilities of new technology and excited by the challenge of the Peaceful Pill. I hope to see in my lifetime a society in which any rational adult can peacefully and reliably end their life at the time of their choosing. It's what I continue to work towards.

Chapter 3

The State of Voluntary Euthanasia Laws around the Globe

In recent years, brave politicians in the state parliaments of New South Wales, South Australia and Western Australia have introduced voluntary euthanasia (VE) bills and each state has seen them defeated. The resounding trouncing of all bills and the ROTI Act conveys a powerful message to us all. Legislation enshrining one's right to die with dignity at a national or state level appears less likely to succeed now than ever before. While other countries move increasingly closer to addressing the issue, Australia is left idling, and our sick and dying continue to endure horrible deaths. These people have little ability to influence the medical decisions being made about them, and this should anger anyone with a social conscience.

In this chapter I examine Australia's position within a larger, global context and look at the progress of VE legislation internationally. How does our now invalid ROTI Act compare to laws since passed in other parts of the world? What options have other countries adopted that we haven't? Does it matter that Australia has been left behind legislatively, or should we be focusing on other approaches for a way forward on end-of-life choices?

Death with dignity in Oregon

America has a spotted history of law reform on voluntary euthanasia and physician-assisted dying. At the current time, Oregon
is the only state in the US where physician-assisted dying is legal.
VE remains illegal everywhere else.

Oregon first passed the Death With Dignity (DWD) Act
in 1994 after a Citizen Initiated Referendum, although it was
not finally implemented until 27 October 1997. (In the inter-
vening period, the Act was subject to legal challenge that
prevented it being used; this is why the Northern Territory
was the first place in the world to experience VE legislation.)
The Death With Dignity Act allows people who are terminally
and/or hopelessly ill to ask their doctors for lethal medication.
Patients must make two verbal requests and one written
request that is fully witnessed. Two doctors must agree on
the patient's 'diagnosis, prognosis and the patient's capability'.
The patient must administer the lethal medication themselves. The
Oregon law explicitly prohibits euthanasia, which is defined
as involving someone other than the patient administering the
medication.

The DWD legislation is reported on annually by Oregon's
Department of Human Services. Their sixth review was released
in 2004, revealing that forty-two people used the DWD law in
2003. The law is reported as having had no effect on the overall death rate in that State. 'Loss of autonomy', 'a diminished
ability to participate in activities that make life enjoyable', and
'loss of dignity' were the three most frequently cited end-of-life
concerns by those who used the law.[1]

It is ironic that the Oregon Act passed into law in the same year that the ROTI Act was overturned. Globally speaking, it seems we finished the year on par.

End of Life Choices (formerly known as the Hemlock Society)

End of Life Choices is America's most prominent and active voluntary euthanasia and physician-assisted dying organisation, founded by Derek Humphry in 1980. With over 30 000 members, the group provides a 'Caring Friends' network: free in-home or telephone counselling with trained volunteers and healthcare professionals. Caring Friends has been the flagship service of the organisation, and evidence of their practical commitment to end-of-life choices. However, the group has recently taken a conservative turn, dissociating itself from its original practical orientation in favour of a focus on legislative reform. The organisation today is far removed from Humphry's founding vision some quarter of a century ago.

The consequences of this ideological transference include End of Life Choices actively distancing itself from Dr Jack Kevorkian in the years leading up to his sentencing in 1999, despite all the while referring to him patients in need.[2] More recently, its decision in 2004 to withdraw a substantial annual grant for Exit's research and development program is another example of their desire not to be seen pursuing 'DIY' end-of-life options.

The Netherlands' approach

Over the past twenty years, the Netherlands has gradually decriminalised voluntary euthanasia and it is now legal. The gradual nature of VE's introduction in that country is said to have been behind its success. VE now falls under the *Termination of Life on Request and Assisted Suicide (Review Procedures) Act 2002*. Broadly speaking, the law makes it possible for doctors to administer VE in a range of circumstances. In several important ways, the Dutch law is much more liberal than our ROTI Act was.

While assisting someone to die is still a crime under the Dutch penal code, the 2002 Act makes VE legally permissible. In short, the Act stipulates that a request for VE must be voluntary and 'well considered'. The patient must be aged over sixteen years and there must be 'no other reasonable solution' for the situation they are in. If the person is between twelve and sixteen years and has a 'reasonable understanding of his interests', the doctor cannot ignore a request for VE, as long as a parent or guardian agrees with the termination-of-life decision. Also, the patient must consult at least one other independent physician.

Since 1990 the Remmelink Reports (investigating both reported and unreported VE deaths) have documented the impact of the changes to the law where VE is concerned. The most recent of these was published in May 2003. To date, the reports have revealed the proportion of deaths in the Netherlands as a result of voluntary euthanasia to be constant.[3] In the third of these reports, it was suggested that this type of monitoring is helpful in creating a well-informed debate and contributes to ongoing social acceptance of VE.[4] Transparency has its benefits.

The Belgium follow-on

In September 2002, Belgium became the second country in the world to pass VE legislation, much to the disgust of their influential Catholic clergy. Belgium's law is similar to that of the Netherlands, though there are several key differences.

Belgium is unique in that it provides all patients with access to free painkilling medication. This is to ensure that no patient requests VE as a result of their poverty, or because their pain cannot be treated. Also, if a person is not in the terminal stages of their illness, a third medical opinion needs to be sought. Lastly, patients must be over eighteen years of age. As the Belgian Socialist Senator Philippe Mahoux has said, a dying person in pain is 'the only judge of their quality of life and the dignity of their last moments'.[5]

The sleeping Swiss lion

Assisted suicide has been legal in Switzerland since the 1940s. Indeed, assisted suicide in that country need not be performed by a medical doctor. While historically the Swiss Academy of Medical Sciences has held that assisted suicide is 'not a part of a physician's activity', according to Swiss MP Dick Marty in 2003 the academy 'performed a U-turn and told doctors they could help the terminally ill die but only under strict conditions'.[6]

Ludwig Minelli of the organisation Dignitas is the most high-profile non-physician assisting with suicide in Switzerland. Minelli is a human-rights lawyer. American *60 Minutes* recently reported that his service has become very popular. Dignitas is said to be struggling to meet demand and to have temporarily closed their books.[7]

Yet the situation in Switzerland does not mean that all assisted suicide is legal. Rather, assisted suicide falls under Article 115 of the Swiss penal code. As such it is 'a crime if and only if the motive is selfish'. What is important in Switzerland is motive, not intent.

When an assisted suicide is declared, a police inquiry is undertaken, as is standard for all 'unnatural' deaths. If a selfish motive cannot be proved, there is no crime. By all reports these deaths are open-and-shut cases.[8] Interestingly, Swiss law also states that the 'permissibility of altruistic assisted suicide cannot be overridden by a duty to save life'.[9] This safeguards those assisting in the suicide, as long as the motivation is altruistic.

The Kiwi experience

Like Australia, New Zealand has recently seen the VE issue appear on the front pages of its newspapers and discussed in its national parliament. Unlike Australia, I suspect our neighbours are rapidly developing the social and political preconditions that might make a VE law possible.

To start with, there have been several high-profile cases where allegations of euthanasia have been made.[10] And then there is the case of Lesley Martin. In May 1999, Martin – a trained intensive-care nurse – helped her mother, Joy, to die. Joy was suffering from bowel cancer. Lesley explains that before her mother fell hopelessly ill, she promised her that she would not let her suffer. Lesley says that this was the promise of a dutiful and loving daughter.

Without legislation that 'acknowledges the existence of euthanasia and governs its existence', writes Lesley:

> All you have is hope and, maybe, a promise.
>
> The hope that your passing will be quick and peaceful.
> Failing that?
>
> The hope that the care available will maintain your quality of life *as you would wish it* until your last breath.
> Failing that?
>
> The hope that you will be under the care of a realistic and compassionate doctor who will help, albeit covertly.
> And finally, failing that?
>
> A promise from someone who loves you.[11]

When Lesley published her book *To Die Like a Dog* in 2002, she knew that she might be charged with her mother's death. And she was. In the book, Martin admits openly to having increased Joy's dose of morphine.[12] She also admits to smothering her with a pillow. In March 2004, Lesley was found guilty of the attempted murder of her mother. She was acquitted on the other charge of attempted murder by smothering, and was sentenced to fifteen months in jail. (She was released in December 2004 after serving half of this sentence.) Lesley's imprisonment was a travesty of justice – her only deed was to help end her mother's suffering. As a dutiful daughter, she kept a promise to her closest of kin.

One has to question what sort of society we live in when we punish a compassionate person like Lesley. She wrote:

Why am I telling my story? Because it didn't have to be that way.

Joy didn't have to face her death with fear and uncertainty and I shouldn't have had to take her in my arms as a last resort; desperate and broken by the battle. No one should ever be driven to that when it is known that doctors do help.

I know from my years of nursing that doctors are performing euthanasia when the need arises.[13]

If Joy had had the option of openly discussing her fears and wishes for a merciful release with a compassionate doctor, it all could have been so different. Up close, her daughter is an attractive forty-year-old, middle-class woman. Her activism on the VE issue since her mother's death has been vigorous and effective, leading to her establishing her own death-with-dignity organisation in the process. Through her book and her trial, Lesley became a household name in her country. She was the bright, new face of VE – not only in New Zealand but internationally. The world's media followed her case closely.

While I thought that the aftermath of the Lesley Martin story might pave the way for successful VE legislation in New Zealand, the recent turn of public opinion against her has made me think otherwise. Since her imprisonment, Lesley has been demonised in the media – an experience I know only too well. Her cardinal 'sin' was to initially reject the option of home detention. In doing so, the accusation was levelled that she cared more for the right-to-die cause than for her ten-year-old son Seanie or her husband Warren. When she did finally apply

for home detention, the parole board was reported as stating
not only that they saw Lesley's rehabilitation as an 'unrealisitic'
prospect, but that she was an 'undue risk to the community'.
Perhaps most unfairly they concluded that Martin could only
reapply for home detention if she accepted without condition
'the impropiety of breaking the law'.[14] Lesley of course maintains
that because she is not sorry for helping Joy to die (and would
do the same again), she cannot acknowledge that what she did
was wrong. For Lesley home detention was never granted.

Despite Lesley's experience, and in spite of the defeat of
Peter Brown's private member's bill for legalising VE in New
Zealand in July 2003, a parliamentary VE committee is still
alive and well in that country. With 2005 being an election year
for the Kiwis, it will be interesting to see what emerges. Will
it result in a future VE law? I would like to think so, but the
pessimist gets the better of me once again.

Quo vadis?

With VE back in the public's mind in New Zealand, the
differences between that country and Australia could not be
more obvious. Back home, neither the Liberal nor the Labor
party has shown interest in VE for a very long time. While
the Greens might be active on the issue, they cannot do much
alone.

Ian Cohen was elected as the first Green member of the New
South Wales state parliament in 1995, and was re-elected in
2003. The following is a summary of Ian's views on VE:

I support end-of-life choices. This stems from my belief in the individual's right to choose and that another's religious convictions should not impinge on the decisions of those who do not share particular beliefs.

DIY technologies are a necessary stop-gap because of the illegality of VE. This situation would be remedied with legal VE and proper medical care. That said, the CoGenie and the Peaceful Pill give people choice and security. As such, they are humane options.

It is vital that people can feel in some way empowered in the process of dying, not helpless victims of others' methods. I personally demand the right to die by a method of my choosing. It is a basic human right of modern technological society.

The Australian Democrats – once strong supporters of VE – now seem half-hearted in their commitment to a legislative turn-about. In South Australia, Democrat leader Sandra Kanck has worked hard to present VE bills to their parliament, but in early 2004 it was also the Democrats who rejected an important opportunity to introduce a Citizen Initiated Referendum (CIR) to that State's democratic process. It was a CIR that earned Oregon its legislation in the mid-1990s, and a CIR could be an important mechanism that would ensure the passage of a VE law. Federally, the Democrats' Victorian Senator Lyn Allison introduced a private member's bill to overturn the Kevin Andrews bill of 1997. But that was in early 2004, and there has been an election since. As with any proposed legislation, if an election is called the bill must start its arduous legislative road all over again.

Public polling on VE continues to show that four out of five Australians support end-of-life choices. I have never before known such a well-supported issue. Yet our politicians – those who are supposed to represent us – remain recalcitrant to the end. So while many Australian right-to-die groups believe that the future still lies in agitating for a VE law, I have to now say I do not agree.

First, political trends suggest that an Australian VE law is years away from being enacted. Yet I have patients who do not have the luxury of time. These people are sick *now*. They face painful and drawn-out deaths *now*. Second, history has taught us that what the parliament gives, the parliament can take away. There can be no legislative certainty. Take the Netherlands, for example. In her opening speech to the Dutch parliament in September 2003, Queen Beatrix of the Netherlands proclaimed that euthanasia and abortion legislation were to be 're-evaluated'. And that was announced in a country where VE is no longer a sensitive social issue.

And what about Oregon? The Death With Dignity legislation has been under attack ever since George W. Bush was elected. His former Attorney General, John Ashcroft, declared it his life's work to challenge the DWD law by decree.[15] His successor Alberto Gonzales will no doubt follow his lead.

It is this universal lack of certainty – even once laws are passed – that makes new strategies for end-of-life choices so vital. This is one reason why Exit International has changed its objective to primarily examine practical strategies. In focusing on the practical, Exit offers private clinics, introduction and practical workshops and our new Peanut project whereby members come together to create their own Peaceful Pills. This project utilises existing suicide laws. If a person makes a Peaceful Pill themselves, they break no law: suicide in Australia is legal. However, if a group of elderly or sick members teach each other how to make a pill, would they be breaking a law that prohibits advising, counselling or assisting with a suicide? No one is sure.

Exit clinics and workshops are always in demand, with enquiries increasing constantly. The Peanut project is an excellent example of mass civil disobedience on the part of the participants. It is a small sign of things to come, especially when the generation who invented this type of political strategy – the baby boomers – find themselves facing death head-on.

Exit's aim is to be there, continuing to highlight the issues for a way forward.

Chapter 4

An Unholy Trinity – Medicine, Law and the Church

Euthanasia should be permitted, not because everyone should accept that it is a right, nor because to fail to do so violates a defensible conception of the sanctity of life, but simply because to deny a person control of what, on any analysis, must be one of the most important decisions of life, is a form of tyranny, which like all acts of tyranny is an ultimate denial of respect.

– John Harris, Sir David Alliance Professor of Bioethics, Manchester School of Law[1]

When thinking about death and how we understand the dying process, a number of key influences emerge. These include the professional 'discourses' of medicine, the law and, of course, organised religion, particularly Catholicism and fundamentalism. Individually and with each other, these discourses shape our world and, with that, our understandings, decisions and experiences of death and dying. To understand these influences and to make better sense of people's attitudes towards dying, we need to examine each discourse and how they collectively influence the VE debate.

Medicine

Dying as a medical event

In this twenty-first century, dying is closely controlled and monitored by the medical profession. According to the French theorist Michel Foucault, medical knowledge sits atop the hierarchical pyramid of knowledges, ways of knowing.[2] But just as childbirth has not always been the domain of doctors, decisions about dying have not always involved doctors and specialists. Indeed, it is only fairly recently that medicine has acquired its gatekeeping role with regard to dying. It previously spent many years queuing behind religion to get the toehold that it now has.

La Trobe University sociologist Professor Alan Kellehear, who has written widely on society's changing perceptions of death and dying, argues that in the sixteenth century the dying person was a controlling figure around the death bed. With the rise of the discipline of medicine in the nineteenth and twentieth centuries, however, power began to shift much more to doctors. Now, in this century, the experience of death and decision-making about dying is more likely to be shared by patient and doctor.[3] This means that the dying person – and, to varying extents, the person's family – have more to do with doctors than was previously the case.

In Australia today, dying generally takes place in an institution, an intensive care unit, a hospice, a palliative care service or a nursing home. This is an important point, because this set of circumstances brings together doctors, other health professionals and sick people, allowing the former unprecedented involvement in determining how a person dies.[4] Therefore in practice, as in the scholarly literature, dying is medicalised, even if patients have marginally more control than they might have had one hundred years ago.

Medical privilege

Challenging the stranglehold of the medical profession on the dying process is an important first step towards empowering patients. The attitudes of the profession and its doctors tend to be paternalistic and all-knowing. Although I am quick – especially as a doctor – to acknowledge that medicine often has a truly wonderful power to liberate individuals from the devastation of disease and pain, at its worst, medicine can act as though it has all the answers, and doctors can pretend they can 'walk on water'.[5]

Take the education of medical students as an example. On one level, students are taught anatomy and physiology. But their education doesn't end there. They are also taught to privilege their own expert knowledge over all others, including that of their patients. In this respect, medicine enjoys considerable professional and social privilege. And it is medicine's perception of its own importance that explains its track record in overriding patient wishes and its insistence that it alone knows what is 'in the patient's best interests'. Indeed, with the advent of new medical technologies, this arrogance has allowed the profession to reach previously unknown heights of authority.

The way of the future

Every year I am called upon to speak to a medical student society at a university somewhere in Australia. I undertake these engagements with enthusiasm. Young medical students inspire me. They are keen listeners, engaging with the theory and practice of choice in dying, unlike many of their older peers. Indeed, I recently received a letter from a student thanking me for speaking to their society. Contained in this letter was a lament at the lack of training that is currently offered by medical schools in regard to end-of-life decisions, in terms of both palliative care options and voluntary euthanasia.

The future of end-of-life choices lies with these students. Failing to educate them about these issues is not a good start.

How the medical profession views death

Traditionally, medicine has regarded the death of a patient as an affront to its expertise. Indeed, medicine's main response to death has been to prolong it.[6] Death is somehow considered evidence that you have failed in your role as a doctor. This sentiment was tellingly expressed by the then newly elected MP Dr Brendan Nelson in 1996 when addressing the Australian parliament. During an adjournment of the debates concerning the Kevin Andrews bill, Nelson stated: 'I have cared for many people who have died – I hope that is not a reflection on my medical skills.'[7] It would seem this fear of patients' deaths on the part of doctors is indeed widespread.

The enduring belief is that 'good medicine' continues to primarily be about curing the sick. Successful medicine is yet to reconcile itself to the fact that a good death can be part of the professional toolkit. Medicine's privileging of life over death, regardless of quality, is, in part, why decisions that reject technology – for example, decisions that turn life support machines off – continue to be so controversial. They show how far the profession still has to go before being able to accept a patient's wish to die. Indeed, it seems that it will be a long time before all doctors will be able to grant their patients permission to die at the time and place of their choosing.[8]

What sort of doctor am I?

While I support what is known as the participatory model of dying – where doctor and patient both have a say in the decision-making – I do not believe this model operates in our society to a great extent. While some claim that doctors and patients can already speak freely in this country about end-of-life decisions (within legal limits, of course), the steady increase in the number of people who are approaching Exit for advice and information tends to suggest otherwise. New members frequently tell me that the main reason they sought information from Exit is because they felt unable to talk about death with their own doctor. The space is not there.

In a recent interview for *New Scientist* magazine,[9] I was asked what set me apart from the American doctor Jack Kevorkian, currently serving a ten to twenty-five year sentence for the second-degree murder of a motor neurone disease sufferer. It wasn't hard to pinpoint a difference. Despite my huge admiration for Kevorkian, in my view he practised medicine within a biomedical framework. He was much more centre-stage than I have been or would wish to be in similar situations.

I believe if medicine must be involved in the dying process, then the new public health ethos (which stems from the 1986 Ottawa Charter for Health Promotion of the World Health Organization) provides a good guide on how to go about it. In a nutshell, this charter places the patient centre-stage in all decision-making.[10] The individual's ability to undertake decisions that affect them is respected in a way that puts it at odds with the traditional, biomedical approach. Thus doctors are said to have been forced to 'concede their professional autonomy'. They have had to enter 'into a partnership with patients in end-of-life decision-making',[11] and patients and their families now fully expect that their views are heard and respected.

While this new approach is laudable, many doctors continue to disregard the voice of their patients. This is one reason why the demand for Exit services is increasing. Studies show that doctors routinely 'ignore patient wishes for end-of-life treatment despite being obliged to abide by legally binding living wills'.[12] Other doctors are happy to concede *some* power to their patients, but only as far as the law permits. They continue to be wary about crossing the fuzzy lines. I have chosen not to be and openly utilise the many grey areas that the law presents. While I try not to break the law, the lack of legal definition on some points (for example, assisted suicide) means that I am constantly – however inadvertently – testing the boundaries. Is providing a person with factual information about terminal sedation – slow euthanasia – breaking the law? No one can accurately say. Is answering questions about lethal quantities and types of drugs breaking the law? Again, who knows? What I do know is that in my willingness to answer end-of-life questions honestly, I am behaving differently from many doctors. My approach is to help people gain access to the information and knowledge that will assist them to make their own informed choices.[13] Am I assisting people to suicide? Perhaps. Is this the right thing to do? You decide.

From voluntary euthanasia to physician-assisted dying

In this era of the new public health ethos and shared decision-making, it is important to note the shift in the way some doctors are involved in a person's dying, a shift from voluntary euthanasia to physician-assisted dying (PAD). PAD is a fancy term that describes the move by doctors away from active and towards passive involvement in a patient's death. Let me explain.

With voluntary euthanasia, the doctor would normally be responsible for administering a lethal injection to a patient. With PAD the doctor takes a step back from being significantly involved and, for example, may simply provide the patient with a prescription for lethal drugs. These drugs are then taken by the patient themselves. The Oregon Death with Dignity legislation permits PAD while banning VE.[14] Do you see the difference?

Having the doctor step back and thereby grant the patient more control was the rationale behind my inventing the 'death machine', the Deliverance Machine. This device allowed patients to self-administer lethal drugs. (See chapter 9 for a more detailed description.) I invented the Deliverance Machine after the Rights of the Terminally Ill Act was passed because I did not want to be the one holding the syringe that would lead to the death of another person. Like many other doctors, I do not believe this is our role. However, unlike some other doctors, it is not because of any selective adherence to the Hippocratic oath. My commitment to PAD stems from the belief that in many circumstances the doctor has no role at all. Dying need not be a medical experience.

Interestingly, at a meeting of the NuTech[15] group in Seattle in January 2004, my approach to patient empowerment was confused with cowardice by a Canadian delegate. Such accusations miss the point. I believe a person's decision to die should be theirs alone. As public health researcher Beverley McNamara has argued, a seriously ill person's quality of life is 'influenced largely by their ability to participate in decisions that are made about them'.[16] Nowhere is this more relevant than in the final moments of life. The moment of death is not the time for the doctor to be the focus of attention. Rather, they might simply be one of a network of people who are present, nothing more.

The ROTI legislation of the Northern Territory required that a doctor be present at the patient's death. This is why I was with the four people who used the Act. So while the legislation clearly prioritised the role of the medical professional in its requirement for three doctors to sign the patient's paperwork, the Deliverance Machine helped de-medicalise Bob, Janet, Bill and Valerie's decisions to die. The machine ensured that the personal space of the dying person, so commonly colonised by the medical profession, was returned to family and friends. For Bob Dent, it was his wife Judy who was at his bedside, holding him when he died. For Janet Mills, it was her husband Dave. For Valerie, the last person to use the ROTI Act, it was her five adult children. In technical terms, this means that my role during the life of the ROTI Act was not to provide VE at all. Rather, because of the machine, it was PAD – physician-assisted dying.

The Hippocratic oath

A further reason why palliative care professionals and doctors have such trouble with requests for hastened deaths is that it may contravene their understanding of the Hippocratic oath, to which they are bound. For those to whom the Hippocratic oath is sacred, a request for hastened death is an unconscionable question, one that challenges the very fundamentals of the medical profession.

The accusation that the Hippocratic oath has been broken is persistently levelled at doctors who assist patients to die with dignity. Indeed, when we wrote to former RSL president Bruce Ruxton, inviting him to participate in this book, Bruce took Fiona to task for apparently breaking her Hippocratic oath. While Fiona is a sociologist and not subject to such an oath, there is still confusion over whether euthanasia was ever actually disallowed in the original version. According to Professor Howard Markel of the Centre for the History of Medicine at the University of Michigan, there is plenty of historical evidence that 'many ancient Greeks and Romans who [when] confronted with a terminal illness preferred a quick, painless death by means of poison'.[17] So not only was there an absence of laws prohibiting suicide, it was 'not uncommon' for physicians to recommend suicide to terminally ill patients.

While the oath has certainly changed over the years – the modern oath allows women to practise medicine and it allows surgery (both of which were prohibited in the original version) – any ban on euthanasia seems less clear cut. This is perhaps why pledges prohibiting euthanasia have been found to be contained in only 14 per cent of the many versions of the Hippocratic oath that are currently used in medical schools in the US and Canada.[18] As Derek Humphry and Anne Wickett have argued, the Hippocratic oath is 'more a tradition' that has been used to guide 'physicians over the centuries than a literal promise to do or not do something'.[19] When I graduated from the University of Sydney in the late 1980s, we were not even offered the opportunity to take the oath.

Voluntary euthanasia and the medical profession

It is commonly said that medicine has 'responded mostly to the problem of death by postponing it'. With this in mind, it is not surprising that studies reveal doctors and nurses to be far less supportive of VE than the general public.[20]

For example, in 1999, Betty Kitchener and Anthony Jorm of the University of Canberra pooled data from several Australian surveys and found that while around 78 per cent (and sometimes more) of the Australian public support VE, only 57 per cent of doctors were supportive.[21] Reasons put forward for this hesitance included fear of legal recourse; objection at the perceived breaking of the Hippocratic oath; religious beliefs; and inadequate training around end-of-life decisions.[22]

Studies have also revealed strong differences between doctors' attitudes to passive and active euthanasia. This is despite many philosophers arguing that there is no substantial difference between the two, and certainly no difference that would stand up in any rational argument. The intended outcome of death is the same.[23] Despite this, the medical profession largely supports passive euthanasia (via the doctrine of double effect – see chapter 6), yet they are hostile to active euthanasia. But there are some glimmers of hope – a number of medical professionals openly support patient end-of-life choices, but they are few and far between. In Australia, the Doctors Reform Society has been a lone voice in support of VE.

In the years before and after the ROTI Act, Robert Marr was often heard as the spokesperson for the Doctors Reform Society. He has been a Sydney doctor for twenty-nine years. The following is an outline of his views on VE:

> I support the right of terminally ill people to choose how much suffering they are willing to endure at the end of their life; I support the right of dying people to choose voluntary euthanasia after being offered the best palliative care available.
>
> I have come to hold these beliefs after more than twenty years as a doctor, having seen many dying patients suffer unnecessarily, even though they had good palliative care. For example, my own father suffered greatly in the last months of his life when he died from the paralysing illness motor neurone disease.
>
> I have also observed how compassionate doctors *do* help dying patients shorten their lives in a secret, covert manner. It is time these matters be brought out in the open. It is essential that voluntary euthanasia is legalised, otherwise it will only be available to a limited number of dying patients who can find a cooperative doctor.

Some professionals in other disciplines also object to the anti-VE rhetoric of the mainstream medical profession. Indeed, one recent call for the legalising of VE in the United Kingdom was made by Lesley and Len Doyal in the prestigious *British Medical Journal*.[24] The Doyals are both professors, Lesley of public health and Len of medical ethics. The AMA, on the other hand, has been particularly active in its criticism of VE legislation and those who promote it, going so far as to mount several campaigns to secure my medical deregistration, for example. With such persistent hostility, it seems unlikely that mainstream medicine will become a friendly or supportive voice on the right-to-die issue any time soon.

My ongoing battle with deregistration

When law and medicine combine, the force against the individual and the doctor who dares to challenge the status quo can be very powerful. This is something I have discovered through personal experience.

Most doctors do not expect to find themselves being disciplined by a medical board or council unless they do something terribly wrong. Deregistration is a shame reserved for the foolish and the unethical. Clearly, I don't consider myself deserving of either label, yet the AMA – my own professional association – has lodged complaints about me to the medical boards of various Australian states on four occasions. These complaints have been made in Victoria, South Australia, Western Australia and Queensland. I may well be the most harassed doctor in the country.

The first attack on my professionalism came in 1998 from

the then president of the Victorian AMA, Dr Gerald Segal. Segal objected to my intention to commence introduction workshops in that State. Subsequent complaints against me have followed a familiar vein. I have been accused of breaching medical professionalism by allegedly 'advising', 'counselling' or 'assisting' patients on ways and means to end their lives.

In Victoria, I tried using the Freedom of Information Act to obtain the documents on which these allegations were based. After a battle with the Attorney-General, Rob Hulls, I was granted access to news clippings and Media Monitor transcripts only; things I could have obtained myself elsewhere. The dozens of remaining file notes, letters, faxes and legal advice were said to be 'privileged'. So much for government transparency.

More recently, the New Zealand Medical Council has made enquiries about my workshop activities in that country and the matter is now with my solicitors. Again, the concern is that I am promoting suicide by advising, counselling or assisting people who come to Exit workshops.

How have such groups formed their opinion of me when they have never attended one of my workshops? Through media reports, of course. The outcome of all these cases (with New Zealand pending) has been that the medical boards have handballed the complaints to the local police, claiming that they – the police – are the appropriate authority to investigate since the allegations against me are of a criminal nature.

However, in all of these cases the police have not taken the matter further, and at the time of going to press I remain a registered doctor in all states and territories of Australia.

The law

Law and medicine – an unholy alliance?

Like medicine, the law is a powerful force in the regulation of death. It is the law that creates the very framework that determines how dying is experienced. And, as legal theorists and others note, the law is often a means of reinforcing control over an individual, rather than a way of freeing them to make their own decisions.[25] Far from protecting a person's end-of-life right to self-determination, I see the law as prescribing a fairly rigid set of rules in the form of hoops through which patients and their families must jump. This can leave the dying person's wishes compromised, and detract from their ability to decide how or when to die. These constraints can have potentially tragic consequences, especially if the dying person asks their loved ones to help them die, which in turn exposes family and friends to significant legal risk – maybe even a prison sentence.

Anita Idol and John Kaye of the University of Adelaide have written about the impact of the law upon people's end-of-life choices by looking at parliamentary debates on VE in South Australia in 1995. They argue that the law grants decision-making power not to the person who wants to die, but to the medical profession. This means the patient is dependent upon the opinion of the expert(s); they are at the mercy of the doctor's professional opinion. This interpretation shows the law maintaining an 'illusion of freedom' while the individual's rights and choices are undermined.[26]

It's worth thinking about. In the Northern Territory, a person could only access the ROTI legislation under a strict set of guidelines. The patient had to be suffering from an illness that would result in death, and the patient had to be of sound mind, etc. These criteria, as Idol and Kaye have pointed out, make objects of people – objects to be ordered, checked, regulated and controlled. Yet many doctors think this is the way things should be, and such arrogance knows no bounds. In an article by Dr David Kissane of the Centre for Palliative Care at the University of Melbourne (to which I also have my name), this attitude is made clear.[27] Published in *The Lancet* in 1998, Kissane argued that during the life of the ROTI Act, medical practitioners occupied a 'gate-keeping function in which the vulnerable [were] protected through the wise application of the law'. In noting what he saw as the limitations of the gate-keeping role of doctors, Kissane was implicitly, and even explicitly, calling for more control.[28] Patients, he argued, need protection and guidance. On reflection, I wonder what became of the patient's voice for Kissane. It seems the patient had no voice – or at least none that was worthy of consideration.

Dying people need *real* choices. If a VE law is created, it must be done in a way that empowers, rather than diminishes, the dying person.

Bill's story

Bill X[29] was the third person to use the Northern Territory's ROTI legislation. Diagnosed with terminal stomach cancer, he had undergone a long period of hospitalisation, surgery and palliative care. Bill knew that ahead of him lay further deterioration. He did not want to wait around to die, saying he had 'had enough'.

Bill contacted me in early 1997. He had been a Darwin

resident for many years, living in suburban Nightcliff. Like all patients who sought to use the ROTI Act, much paperwork had to be completed before he could do so. For Bill, as for the others, this meant that I had to find the signatures of a medical specialist, a psychiatrist and a palliative care doctor. While I had no trouble getting two of these on Bill's behalf – Bill's own surgeon unreservedly signed off one of the forms, and his palliative care doctor the other – finding a psychiatrist was a little harder.

After much ringing around, it was Darwin psychiatrist Len Marinovich who finally said he would have a consultation with Bill to see if he was depressed or otherwise psychiatrically ill. If all went well, the required documentation would then be complete. The only problem was that Marinovich would not come to the hospital to see Bill. Rather, this dying man had to attend the psychiatrist's consulting rooms in the Darwin suburb of Tiwi.

For most people, such an attendance would not be a problem, but Bill was distressed at the prospect – he was, after all, very sick, and he was scared stiff that Marinovich might find him depressed and not sign the paperwork. So Bill kept putting the visit off, hoping he might 'cheer up'. Finally, he had to face seeing Marinovich and we made the visit together on the day he was hoping to die. Bill wanted to die at home, so the plan was to visit the psychiatrist en route to Bill's apartment. An ambulance was arranged, one that would take Bill from the hospital to the psychiatrist's, and then on to his home. He was too weak to walk and needed a wheelchair and considerable assistance.

Upon his arrival at Marinovich's rooms, the receptionist

insisted that a 'first visit form' be completed. It was at least five pages long. The process was gruelling. Bill could hardly sit up in the wheelchair, let alone answer questions. I protested to the receptionist, pointing out that completing the form was surely not necessary, given that the visit was not only Bill's first but would be his last, as he would die in two hours' time. However, she stood her ground. The protocol would prevail.

What would also prevail was the up-front consulting fee. I protested again; surely payment could be made later? But no, $200 was needed at once or nothing was going to happen. Bill searched his bag; he only had $40. So while he sat in the wheelchair, in his hospital gown and with his small overnight bag on his lap, I made a dash to the car to collect my cheque book. I still have the stub for that $200 cheque, undoubtedly the most important payment of Bill's life.

The assessment by Marinovich, when it finally began, took far less time than the arduous completion of the preliminary paperwork, and thankfully he signed the form that would allow Bill to die. Once back in the ambulance, we travelled to Bill's modest flat and carried him up the stairs to a home that had been empty for the past three months. The St John's people remade his bed, made him comfortable and said a sad goodbye. We were left alone, and early that same afternoon Bill died, eased into the afterlife to the soundtrack of the British TV series *The Choir*. A month later, two of Bill's friends hired a small plane and sprinkled his ashes over Darwin Harbour just as he had requested.

Bill was a quiet, solitary man, but he was not the pathological loner that Melbourne palliative care professor David Kissane had tried to assert in his *Lancet* article. To claim Bill wanted to die because he was lonely is an insult and shows no respect for the man. Rather, Bill wanted to die because he had terminal cancer. He had symptoms that could not be treated; symptoms that made his life a misery. And he had had enough of the battle.

The ROTI legislation eventually worked for Bill, but no one should have been subjected to that form of psychiatric assessment when so desperately ill.

Some MPs stand proud and tall

I do not believe that parliament should be debating the Euthanasia Laws Bill, regardless of what chamber it might be in. Questions such as euthanasia and other moral issues are the responsibility of the individual.

It is arrogant in the extreme that we, as members of parliament, should put our morality on others. Because we have a particular religious belief or feel strongly on a moral issue, what right have we to insist that others concur with our view?

– Colin Hollis, ALP Member for Throsby[30]

The South Australian Voluntary Euthanasia Society and the politics of the Australian VE movement

While I may be critical of the role of the law in death and dying, there are plenty who support a legalistic approach to the issue. For example, most VE societies have an explicit focus upon law reform, at the expense of finding practical solutions. The South Australian Voluntary Euthanasia Society (SAVES), one of several state-based right-to-die organisations in Australia, is an example. Its primary aim is to engineer 'a change to the law in South Australia so that in appropriate circumstances, and with defined safeguards, death may be brought about as an option of last resort in medical practice'.[31] Along with the Victorian VE Society (VESV), the legal focus of SAVES distinguishes it from Exit and places it at the conservative end of the spectrum of the global VE movement. And this is an important point of difference. While Exit is concerned with both political *and* practical strategies, organisations such as SAVES maintain a faith in the legislative process.

In an early cut of the *Mademoiselle and the Doctor* documentary, SAVES spokeswoman Mary Gallnor was asked if she could see a collaborative approach being possible for Exit and her society in the future. She explained her reluctance in the following metaphorical way:

> It's so important I think that we do remain separate . . . you know, if you put blue ink with white ink you get a paler blue, whereas you want the deep blue and you want the pure white. And it's not useful to change the whole mix. You know you've got to stay pure and sure of what you are trying to achieve.

The President of the VE Society of Victoria, Dr Rodney Syme, goes one step further, suggesting that some of Exit's activities make it particularly difficult for him at the state level. 'In Victoria', he writes:

we constantly find in our conversations with politicians that many are concerned by your activities. Since VESV aims to change the law, whereas you seem determined to challenge the law, VESV needs to be seen to be clearly separate from Exit . . . This explains why, at times, we may seem not to support you, even though fundamentally we support the same goal – dying with choice and dignity.[32]

So while the Victorian and South Australian societies differ from Exit in their shared commitment to law reform, it is SAVES that has been the more successful lobbyist in state parliament. In the last decade, several right-to-die bills have been introduced there. The most recent of these was resoundingly defeated in June 2004, thirteen votes to eight, in the Legislative Council. While much of the legislative activity in that State is due to the hard work of South Australian Democrat leader Sandra Kanck, even she has called the 2004 defeat of the Dying with Dignity bill 'bitterly disappointing'.[33]

The introduction of a VE bill in any state could be a good thing, but what is really important is that such bills progress to the point of legislation. To date this has only occurred in the Northern Territory – albeit briefly – where unique conditions prevailed. In the Victorian parliament, no bills have ever even been presented. When discussing the failure of any SA bills passing into legislation, Sandra Kanck has replied that it is a slow process, 'like water dripping on sandstone'. Although I admire her efforts, in my mind the presentation of repeated bills only exhausts the proponents of legislation while maintaining an illusion of progress.

The right to die – is voluntary euthanasia the last frontier in prison reform?

The idea of making VE permissible for prisoners and those sentenced to death by the state is not new. The Egyptians, for example, allowed execution by suicide, as did the Stoics. After all, that is how the Greek philosopher Socrates came to die – by being forced to drink the cup of hemlock. More recently, however, the idea of euthanasia for prisoners has re-emerged from an unlikely source . . . or was it?

During the parliamentary debate prior to the passing of the Kevin Andrews bill in 1996, this idea was proffered by the Liberal member for the seat of Bowman in Queensland, Andrea West. Arguing in support of the Andrews bill, West suggested that it would be 'more appropriate to offer the same circumstance [voluntary euthanasia] to life-sentenced criminals and to those who committed heinous crimes against humanity. They truly deserve to die'.[34] This is surely an interesting point. While it is unlikely that all prisoners would see themselves as 'deserving' to die, there are certainly some who have shared their wish to die quite publicly. Others have simply gone ahead with dying by their own hand, contributing to the awful statistic that suicide by hanging is the most common cause of death for prisoners in Australia.[35]

One prisoner who wants to die and who has sought my advice on VE is convicted murderer Jonathan Horrocks. Horrocks opened fire in the Eagle Bar of La Trobe University in Melbourne in August 1999, killing the manager and wounding several others. He is currently serving a life sentence in Barwon Prison near Geelong. To date, Horrocks has written several letters to me, each seeking my support for his campaign to be allowed VE. His reason is that he would rather be dead than face a lifetime in prison. With the spectre of prisoners hanging themselves so vivid, at a philosophical level I can see no difference between Horrocks' request for VE and that of any person on the outside. The right to a peaceful death should be one of the defining factors of a civil society.

While Horrocks is not the only prisoner whose execution would attract public support, he is the most high-profile who is seeking it voluntarily.[36] He wrote to me:

> I am sure the public would welcome the end of many notorious criminals, not to mention the saving in tax dollars . . . it will cost the taxpayer approximately $90 000 a year to keep me until I die and I for one would rather see that money go to hospitals . . .
>
> If it seems a bit too drastic to push for this, perhaps a call for the option of death to be offered to life sentence prisoners would be a better support angle.[37]

In my mind, Horrocks has a point, but not from the argument of the burden he places on the public purse. If unending incarceration is understood – and it can be – as a form of state-sanctioned torture for which the state has not been charged, ethical questions need to be asked. Torture is clearly what Horrocks believes his imprisonment to be. At the very least, his request deserves to be taken seriously. He wrote:

My current incarceration is constantly frustrating and offers no worthwhile meaning for living as the system is grossly corrupt and no better correctional/rehabilitation ideal will ever be introduced . . . I feel the only recourse for my crime is to end my life. Hence, my life is meaningless and has no purpose so I repeat that I am firmly committed to ending it.

My reply was:

To force a person to endure chronic suffering, without the option of access to a peaceful death, is inhumane and could be seen as torture.

Exit believes that those who suffer chronically from whatever cause, so that they see a peaceful death as a preferred option, should be given access to the means to obtain this.

Short of linking Jonathan Horrocks with MP Andrea West, there is little that I can do to assist other than continue to tell prisoners like Horrocks that I empathise with their plight. While the manufacturing process of both the Peaceful Pill and the CoGenie might be straightforward, these methods are of little use to a prisoner like Horrocks, with no access to the necessary equipment or ingredients for manufacture. Similarly, the information he could obtain on the Internet is also of little use, not having access to the means necessary to make any device. A bedsheet fashioned into a noose may well prevail, to the shame of us all.

Why the law is not the answer

While some people believe that the regulation of dying by legislation is necessary, I particularly object to law and medicine's mutual delegation of decision-making and gate-keeping to each other – and at the expense of the dying person. In this respect, I maintain that the law not only operates to constrain our right-to-die choices, but, in collusion with the medical profession, strips the dying person of any power.

For all these reasons, I increasingly believe that a VE law will not give people more choice over when and how they die. In my view, such a law would have enough constraints to leave me wondering if it was at all worthwhile. My change of heart on this important issue is a work in progress. For years in interviews with the media, the issue of law reform has been raised, and I have been asked, 'Do you support this or that bill?', 'Why is a law on VE so important?' and 'Why do you often say that politicians are gutless?' and for years I have responded by answering 'Yes, absolutely', or 'Of course we need a law'. It is only now that I am beginning to think more creatively about end-of-life choices and what can and can't be achieved in our times.

Curiously, as I change my position on the usefulness of a VE law, other activists like Derek Humphry (the author of the seminal book *Final Exit*) have chosen to back the legislative process as the best way to attain end-of-life options. In an interview in an early cut of *Mademoiselle and the Doctor*, Humphry wears his support for the law as a badge of honour:

> Now I much admire the people who are going for legislation only . . . I've always fought for legislation and if you

look to my writings, to my books, I've always ended up by saying: 'Wouldn't it be better if we all had intelligent, democratic legislation?'[38]

While I move beyond supporting legislative change and towards developing practical end-of-life strategies, Derek seems, in this interview at least, to be relinquishing his previous strong commitment to the same in favour of law reform. For now, Derek and I must agree to disagree. What we are more likely to agree upon, however, is the persistent and insidious power of the Church.

The role of religion

The word of God

The stranglehold of the Church on the right-to-die issue (and on other contentious issues such as abortion, embryonic stem cell research and gene therapy) has its roots deep in the theological past. Their claims to truth on how we should die have been many years in the making. Even today the Catholic Church and other fundamentalist denominations such as the Assemblies of God wield significant power, and it is the challenge of the right-to-die movement to contest this power at every turn. So what is the Church's problem with an individual's right to determine the time and place of their death?

In Judeo-Christian philosophy, the body tends to be seen as the property of God. Indeed, this point was made clearly to me at the 2003 Life Week debate at Sydney University. We are, as my opponent Catholic Bishop Anthony said on the day, the 'image of God'.[39] Our bodies *are* God. Following this line of thought, the body is not the property of the individual concerned. If your body is not yours to own, then how can it be yours to dispose of? But this may not be the only reason for the Church's hostility to end-of-life choices. The President of the VE Society of Victoria, Rodney Syme, believes the Church's objection to VE might also lie in the scriptures:

> The scriptural reason for this opposition . . . is presumably based on the Commandment Thou shalt not kill, a very simple, non-discursive, unqualified directive . . .[40]

In noting the Church's formal opposition to our right to die, it is important to acknowledge that there are dissenting voices within the wider Christian Church. The views of retired American Episcopalian Bishop John Shelby Spong are one example. For many years I have been an admirer of this bishop for his sharp insight and wit, and for his willingness to engage with the VE issue within a Christian framework, so I was excited when I met him in San Diego in early 2003. When he told me of his long-standing admiration for my work, I realised the VE issue need not always treat Christianity as its arch enemy. Shelby Spong also reminds me that while I may talk about the Church as an amorphous whole, there are glimmers of light for change.

An exception to the rule?

Until his retirement in 2002, John Shelby Spong was the Bishop of the Episcopal Diocese of Newark for twenty-four years. The following is an excerpt from an interview with him that was published by the Death With Dignity organisation in Vermont, USA, in 2003. Spong gave a similar speech when we shared the stage at the annual conference of the Hemlock Society in San Diego in January of the same year. On how he came to support VE, Spong says:

> As a priest and bishop for more than forty years I have been privileged to live with people on their journeys through life and into death. I learned much in that process. I value, indeed treasure, life. I see it as a gift of God. I have no desire to hasten its end prematurely. At the same time I see no value in extending life beyond the limits of meaningful relationships. To me life is honoured when it can be laid down in an appropriate manner at the appropriate time. I defend the right of every individual to determine what that manner and time are for him or her. I see no conflict between this and my religious convictions.

On his own church's view of his standpoint, Spong says:

> The subjects of physician-assisted suicide and active euthanasia are regularly debated in the Episcopal Church. There is majority support for passive euthanasia, but only minority support for active euthanasia. I fail to see the distinction given the development of medical science. I think we are simply not yet comfortable stating the obvious. The Episcopal Church mirrors the debate in our nation. As that debate moves forward, I believe my church will move with it.

On how he guides his parishioners on the subject of hastening death, Spong says:

> Hastening death is not the way I would describe my point of view. Seeing death as natural, not something evil, sinful, or even to be avoided is what I support. I seek to embrace death as a friend and not to be so committed to avoiding it that I cling to existence when it has ceased to be life. A breathing cadaver is not a witness to the goodness of life.

On the topic of fundamentalist Christians, Spong says:

> Fundamentalist Christians fight many losing battles. Women should keep quiet in church! Creation science is a proper alternative to evolution! Homosexuality is inherently evil! I see no reason to engage these points of view. Knowledge will challenge yesterday's ignorance and yesterday's prejudice quite adequately. I prefer to move with the people who are able to move and to love the others while ignoring their arguments.[41]

> It has always been my view that a fundamental human right is for one to be able to end one's life with dignity. Prolonged life is inherently inhumane.
>
> — Greg Barnes, lawyer and columnist with *The Mercury* in Hobart

I support people being able to choose how their life ends, as long as they are in a position to make a considered, well-informed choice in a calm manner.

It seems obvious to me that the person whose life it is has the most at stake. So why should anyone else be able to tell her or him when and how to die? John Stuart Mill said that the state should interfere with individual liberty only to prevent harm to others. There may be some exceptions to that principle, for example, where people are likely to be careless with their own interests, and not wear seatbelts or motorcycle helmets. But voluntary euthanasia and physician-assisted suicide are not like that. If people are terminally ill, or have an incurable condition they find unbearable, they are not harming themselves by avoiding continued life.

I am against pointless suffering. I think most people are. Unfortunately, some are in the grip of a religious ideology that assumes suffering has a point. That's fine for them, they can live their life on that basis. But they shouldn't force others to do so.

– Peter Singer, Ira W DeCamp Professor of Bioethics at the University Center for Human Values, Princeton University

With God in our thoughts

So what is the impact of religion upon the theory and practice of end-of-life choices? In one random study of 514 adults in the United States, the belief that life belongs to God was found to be directly linked to levels of opposition to the legalisation of VE.[42] Where study samples have included medical professionals, it has been reported that the more religious a doctor or nurse, the less likely they are to support VE.[43] The trend is well-established. Interestingly, it appears that educational background, theoretical knowledge of euthanasia and clinical experience do not make a difference to how medical staff feel about the VE issue.[44] Rather, it is religious belief that remains the most significant determinant of support levels for VE among both health professionals and the wider community.[45] It seems the religious battle lines are drawn, and there is very little common space between us.

The Pope's recent call for politicians to ensure their political work is informed by their religious beliefs is a worrying sign of how Church and state may not be as separate as we think.[46] In Australia, it seems to have fallen to Federal Health Minister and good Catholic Tony Abbott to take the running on several moral issues, including abortion and stem cell research. The Pope's bidding? You bet. For this reason, we need to watch carefully for the involvement of the Church in the behind-the-scenes influencing of politicians, politicians who are supposedly representing their electorate. Yet the act of bringing religion into the parliament is a sin of which more than one Australian MP is guilty, especially if the speeches at the time of Kevin Andrews' challenge to the ROTI Act are anything to go by.

Take Queensland MP Danna Vale as an example. In her speech in support of the Andrews bill, Vale took guidance from Catholic Bishop Christopher Toohey when forming her views on why the Northern Territory had got it so wrong. The bill, said Vale,

> is not about a person being able to have the choice of when they wish to die. It is about the legally sanctioned administration of death . . . It is about the ultimate violation

of the fundamental paradigm upon which our society is structured. It is about the corrosion of our own humanity. We are really on dangerous ground here.[47]

But it is not just the Catholics like Kevin Andrews or Tony Abbott that need to be watched where religion and politics are concerned. This 'marriage in heaven' can occur on all sides of the political spectrum. For example, while there are those in the Labor party such as Kevin Rudd who are relatively open about their staunch Christianity, there are others like Peter Garrett who have been much more secretive about the role of God in their politics and in their anti-VE standpoints.

For me, the right of politicians to choose a faith and live by its dicta is fine in their private life. But politicians are not elected to be foot soldiers of this or that religious leader – at least not in Australia. When politicians implicitly or explicitly bring their religion to work, the least they should do is make full disclosure of this to their colleagues and certainly to their electorate, preferably prior to their election. Once we have this level of disclosure we – their constituents – might begin to see why some politicians vote in particular ways in parliament.

Kevin Andrews' quest to overturn the ROTI legislation did not stem from his dislike of Northern Territorians. Rather, it derived from his Catholicism. Andrews should have had the integrity to admit his role of errand boy for the Pope. History might then have told a different story. If the Andrews bill had been presented to the parliament as an initiative if not of the Catholic Church, then at least of a staunch Catholic fulfilling his duty, it very well might have been voted down.

Peter Garrett on voluntary euthanasia

When the former Midnight Oil frontman announced he would run as an ALP candidate for the seat of Kingsford Smith in the 2004 federal election, Peter Garrett was depicted in the media as a radical greenie who would bring a new generation of politicians into the Labor fold. What most people didn't know then and don't know still is that Garrett is a committed Christian. Indeed, there has been little scrutiny of Garrett's conservative views on issues such as abortion, stem cell research and euthanasia. Instead, the media has settled for describing Garrett's religion as 'very personal to him and [something] he doesn't like talking about'.[48]

For this book, we asked Labor's new member of parliament a number of questions about his views on voluntary euthanasia and Exit's activities. His responses proved unique, with perhaps the exception of former RSL president Bruce Ruxton, who shares Garrett's strident opposition to end-of-life choices:

> **EXIT:** Are you a supporter of people having end-of-life choices that may include voluntary euthanasia or doctor-assisted dying? How have you formed this opinion?
>
> **GARRETT:** I am not in favour of voluntary euthanasia nor of doctor-assisted dying other than when doctors, with the informed consent of the patient or patient's legal guardian, cease attempts to keep the patient alive when terminally ill.
>
> **EXIT:** Do you think Australia needs a law on end-of-life choices? Why?
>
> **GARRETT:** No, not until there is a more thorough and comprehensive public debate and a clear and consistent consensus

amongst a majority which produces policy choices for parties to advance.

EXIT: What is your general opinion of the new DIY technologies that Exit International is developing, e.g. the carbon monoxide generator (CoGenie) and Peaceful Pill?

GARRETT: I am not in favour of technologies of this kind and do not believe attempting to bypass legislation is the appropriate way for advocates to introduce these technologies.

While I have no objection to Garrett's Christianity, this man's hesitance to speak about his religious adherence, given his own assertion that a person's 'faith or belief framework . . . influences all your activities', concerns me greatly.[49]

The rise of the Assemblies of God and the Family First Party

Like its American parent organisation, the Australian Family First Party has recently emerged as a growing force in Australian politics. The group first fielded a candidate in the South Australian state election of 2002. I stood in that election for a seat in the Legislative Council and found myself targeted by full-page ads in the Adelaide *Advertiser* asking the electorate 'Are you dying to vote for Dr Nitschke?' I didn't win a seat but Pastor Andrew Evans did. Family First's Senate candidate in Victoria, Steve Fielding, won a seat in the 2004 federal election.

Vocal in their opposition to VE or, as they put it, 'anything that hurts families', this party is changing the face of Australian politics. Through a pre-election deal with the Howard Government, Family First is working hard to incorporate 'family impact statements' into a wide range of policy areas on the part of the

government. In the 2004 federal election, Family First preferences helped the Howard Government win key marginal seats.
From Family First's perspective, Chairman Peter Harris was able
to seek – and presumably obtain – the support of Liberal candi-
dates in 'opposing human cloning, stem cell research, euthanasia
and abortion'.[50] Describing the Prime Minister as 'very recep-
tive' towards the idea of family impact statements, Harris said
that Howard has 'indicated very strongly that he would support
that position and support that impact statement for submissions
to Cabinet'.[51]

While the Australian public will have to wait until July
2005 to determine the actual impact of Family First upon the
Australian political landscape, the horizon does not look good
as far as VE is concerned. With its extreme Right religious connections, and given that the party was, in part, founded on an
opposition to my own candidacy in the 2002 South Australian
election, the rise and expected power of Family First appears an
anomaly in a country that is increasingly secular.[52]

The future of the right-to-die movement

In my mind, better end-of-life choices in the future lie very
clearly in the opportunities presented by new technology. And
that's just as well, since legal windows are closing far faster than
they are opening. I don't just refer to the overturning of the
Northern Territory legislation, but the failure of VE bills since
presented in all states. The likelihood of a VE law being enacted
in Australia in the next decade at least, I believe, is extremely
remote.

And what about the medical arena? Is there hope of support for patient choice from this quarter? Available evidence suggests not. Indeed, the Australian Medical Association continues as one of the most conservative of voices in the right-to-die debate, while refusing to acknowledge that doctors covertly practise a form of slow euthanasia all the time. It is this type of impasse that leaves patients looking for solutions elsewhere.

And then there is the Church. If the success of Kevin Andrews' private member's bill proved anything, it was that Christians make for a highly effective and well-funded lobby group. Catholics, together with other Christian fundamentalists such as the Assemblies of God, have proven they can influence and determine public policy when so-called 'matters of conscience' are at stake. The behind-the-scenes lobbying that led to the Andrews bill's success demonstrates that the Church is a force to be reckoned with. Its blatant disregard for the rights of non-Catholics and non-Christians reinforces an intolerance for any standpoint that does not reflect its own ideology.

In the face of these types of constraints, people who want their end-of-life choices to be theirs alone have nowhere to go. It is ironic that this should be the state of play at precisely the time when the so-called 'Me' generation is starting to demand choice in retirement and soon, I predict, choice in dying. Perhaps one's right to die with dignity will become the baby boomers' swan song.

> There is only one thing wrong with dying and that is doing it when you don't want to . . . There is nothing wrong with doing it when you want to.
>
> – Professor John Harris[53]

Makes me feel all warm and fuzzy. I don't have to worry about what's best for me. A very few altruistic-minded wise persons in Canberra tell me what's best. I feel good. I don't need God. I have them.

– Letter to the Editor, *Sydney Morning Herald*[54]

A generational perspective

As our demographic profile continues to change, and as the baby boomer generation starts to enter its twilight years, the demand for answers to end-of-life questions will only increase. The 'Me' generation will insist on being heard. It is a generation that knows much about the effectiveness of mass civil disobedience. I am sure of this, for this is my generation. I was at the Vietnam moratoriums. I was there watching the Aboriginal people sit down on their land. I learnt much then and I look to and apply these same tactics in my work today. These are the tactics that inspired twenty-one people to sit with Nancy Crick when she died – safety in numbers. And these are the tactics that inspire Exit's Peanut project, where people join together to make their own Peaceful Pills.

Just as the boomers marched in the streets for gay and women's rights and for an end to the Vietnam war, I have no doubt they will be back. This time they will be rallying together and lobbying for their right to die with dignity when and how they want. With many of them having witnessed their own parents' unhappiness in nursing homes, most will have no intention of following suit. Who can blame them? The boomer generation will demand information, they will demand options, and woe betide any doctor, politician, pastor or priest who stands in their collective way.

Nancy's Friends

One tangible method by which Exit hopes to meet the needs of the baby boomer generation is through the creation of a new network known as Nancy's Friends. Launched at our 2003 national conference, this network aims to relieve patients' dependence upon the medical profession for reliable information and advice about death. The result? A groundswell of people who feel more empowered and in control of their choices in dying.

Nancy Crick died at her Gold Coast home on 22 May 2002 with a large number of friends and family present. (See chapter 9 for a full discussion about Nancy Crick.) Nancy's death challenged the laws of the State of Queensland. Indeed, the presence of so many people at her death threw the government into turmoil, and it took a full two years for the Queensland Director of Public Prosecutions to decide that charges would not be laid against those twenty-one people.

Based loosely on the Caring Friends program of the End of Life Choices organisation in America, Nancy's Friends provides free home counselling and advice to people who are contemplating end-of-life decisions. Nancy's Friends is staffed by dedicated volunteers. The group seeks to ensure that people are well informed about end-of-life options and that no one dies alone. Nancy's Friends also aims to see that an individual's desires and end-of-life choices are respected insofar as possible. Like Caring Friends, Nancy's Friends abides by the law. The means by which a death is hastened remains the responsibility of the person wishing to die.

Nancy's Friends will soon operate in all states and territories of Australia and New Zealand. Further information is available at www.exitinternational.net.

The answer is technology

As a way forward, I believe the most important area of Exit's current work is our research and development program. Focused upon a range of smart but simple technologies, this program offers some real and practical end-of-life choices for the future. Using the political strategy of mass civil disobedience, Exit's R and D is about creating accessible and tangible options for all of our members who seek them. These choices circumvent the constraints imposed by the medical profession, the law and, most certainly, the Church. Once these methods can be manufactured simply, cheaply and without expert knowledge or equipment, choice in dying will become a reality. The medical profession and others who seek to censure and gate-keep the end-of-life decisions of ordinary Australians will then, finally, be sidelined.

Chapter 5

Palliative Care – Between the Truth and the Lies

A generation ago, the term 'palliative care' was unheard of. Today, the palliative care movement is a respectable and thoroughly mainstream branch of modern medicine that presents an argument with which we all agree. Everyone from the Prime Minister down approves. The Church approves. The law approves. And, in most cases, patients and their families approve.

Put simply, we all support the shift in medicine away from the predominant focus on 'cure at all costs' towards the treatment and management of symptoms for those who have a life-threatening illness. We all acknowledge that there are things that can be done to make death easeful. Ironically, perhaps, this new form of medicine is at loggerheads with those who believe that choice in dying should be available to people who are terminally ill. In this chapter I explain why.

Defining palliative care

In 1990, the World Health Organization (WHO) defined palliative care as 'the active, total care of patients whose disease is not responsive to curative treatment'. WHO characterised palliative care as a form of treatment that:

- neither hastens nor postpones death
- provides relief from pain and other distressing symptoms
- integrates the psychological and spiritual aspects of patient care, and
- offers a support system to help the family cope during the patient's illness and in their own bereavement.[1]

In theory, palliative care represents a radical departure from traditional medicine in that its focus is not curative. Distinct from other branches of medicine that concentrate on diagnosis, treatment and cure, palliative care professionals aim to treat dying as a social experience rather than just a physical condition. And unlike traditional medicine, palliative care aims to put the patient in the centre of the picture. In this respect the patient is supposed to be an active stakeholder. I will now examine whether the discipline has been able to deliver in practice on these laudable aims.

Some history about the palliative care and hospice movement

It is commonly held that the hospice or palliative care movement had its origins in London in 1967 at St Christopher's Hospice, though the term actually harks back to medieval times, when a hospice meant a wayside place of rest and refuge for pilgrims.[2] English nurse Cicely Saunders is now widely recognised as the founder of the movement. A religious woman (she was once a Billy Graham counsellor), history has recorded Saunders as extending end-of-life care from the purely physical towards something that she called 'total care'. For her, total care also included the emotional, social and, importantly, spiritual dimensions.

With its roots firmly within Christian theology, it was not long before hospice care came to be known as palliative care or palliative medicine. It was Dr Balfour Mount, a surgeon at the Royal Victoria Hospital in Montreal, who played an important role in the name change. Mount is thought to have coined the new term in order for it to better fit modern, secular society, to give it more gravitas and to create respect for it among the medical profession. He was aware that words like 'palliation' and 'medicine' would ensure the discipline sounded more acceptable to the conservative medical establishment and would, it was hoped, provide palliative care practitioners with a new legitimacy.

The Johnny-come-latelies of the medical profession

Despite its name change, palliative care's quest for acceptance by the mainstream medical profession has been only partly successful. Terminally ill patients who attend Exit clinics are often in the last stages of their life, and they frequently report their symptom control is far from perfect. Furthermore, their medical management is usually being provided by the specialist they had during earlier stages of the disease, when cure was the goal.

When I tell them they may get better pain control from a palliative care specialist and suggest they seek a referral from their doctor, too often they come back to me with a story of failure: 'I mentioned your idea of a palliative care referral to my oncologist and he said, "Don't worry about that, they'll only offer you more morphine, and I'm already doing that. It'd just be a waste of time".'

Clearly many doctors still see palliative care practitioners as lightweight, Johnny-come-lately dabblers: not real doctors, and not doctors who actually ever cured anyone. At this point, I occasionally choose to intervene and it's not hard to get results. I ring the treating specialist and simply say, 'Your patient has come to see Exit; it seems they're having difficulty getting a palliative care referral from you.'

There is usually a few seconds of silence, followed by a mad scramble to get the referral arranged. No doctor can afford to have it claimed that it was their failure to provide adequate palliative care that drove a patient to Exit.

Palliative care in Australia

There are currently 111 hospice care units in public hospitals in Australia, with palliative care beds available in both urban and rural areas.[3] While these services are called upon at a steady rate, demand is also said to be increasing. With our ageing population, it seems safe to say that palliative care is set to become a growth industry. Given the ongoing demand for these services, it is not surprising that medical schools now include palliative care in their undergraduate curriculum. This shows how far the discipline has come and its increasing acceptability to the medical establishment.

When I was in my final year of medical school at Sydney University in 1988, we were told that we were the first year to receive lectures on palliative care. These lectures were delivered by Narelle Lickiss, who is now Professor of Palliative Care in the same school. As a doctor who has been an advocate of palliative care since the beginning, it is not surprising that Lickiss is opposed to VE. She made a hostile submission to the NT government inquiry looking into the ROTI legislation before it was passed into law, and she did the same at the Senate hearings in support of the Kevin Andrews private member's bill.

When it comes to those involved in palliative care medicine, opposition to VE is the norm, not the exception. That patient choice is supposed to be a centrepiece of palliative care seems to count for little where requests for hastened death are concerned. Roger Hunt, a palliative care expert from Adelaide, calls this the 'rhetoric-reality gap'.[4]

So what exactly constitutes this new form of end-of-life medical treatment, and why is it so often at odds with patients' wishes?

The Watts family's view

I am strongly in favour of a more accessible legal regime to allow doctor-assisted dying. My grandfather went through a terribly tragic seven years in a vegetative state with advanced Alzheimer's disease before he died. This put incredible strains on my grandmother and the wider family, and was directly a product of medical intervention at a nursing home. This outcome was contrary to his expressly stated wishes early in life.

– Tim Watts, newspaper opinion writer and founder and director of the
Generation Next Think Tank – OzProspect.org

Without question I am a supporter of end-of-life choices. Our
society is remiss in not providing for this. The key issue is
choice – while we have the capacity to make it. Strangely, we have
a situation where society promotes individuality and autonomy
while denying us these rights at the very end. My father was absolutely unafraid of death – and was unafraid all his life. Yet there
was no mechanism for allowing him (or us to help him) make the
transition he anticipated with such equanimity. The system – as it
stands – failed an intelligent, profound and courageous man.

Despite the rhetoric, there is no real palliative care for certain conditions. My father died miserably and in pain after seven
excruciating years bedridden in a nursing home. To what end? He
was not 'made comfortable' – there was no comfort to be had.

– Jackie Watts, Tim's baby boomer mum

An alternative treatment

At its core, palliative care is said to be a wholistic form of medical treatment. While traditional Western medicine is focused
upon the physicality of a person – that is, their sick body –
palliative care claims much more. The wholistic focus of the
discipline means that the patient's illness is seen as just one
aspect of their existence. In addition to the sick body, the mind
and the soul are also acknowledged as being in need of
psychological and spiritual help. The palliative care professional

therefore takes a three-pronged approach to the body, mind and soul.

And palliative care doesn't end with the patient. The patient's family – their feelings and attitudes, along with their ability to look after the relative in a hospice or at home – are all part of the equation too. In this respect, it is not hard to see why palliative care has become such an important part of end-of-life medicine. Its willingness to think beyond the patient's body has provided welcome relief for many who, in the more traditional setting, have felt themselves sidelined from decision-making and from retaining any control as their disease became the main signifier of their existence. The words of Austrian writer Jean Amery starkly illustrate this experience:

> Fettered, drilled through with tubes, fitted on both wrists with painful devices for my artificial nourishment. Delivered and surrendered to a couple of nurses who came and went, washed me, cleaned my bed, put thermometers in my mouth and did everything quite matter-of-factly, as if I were already a thing, *une chose . . .*[5]

The multidisciplinary approach

Palliative care is different from traditional medicine again in that it adopts an interdisciplinary approach. Instead of decision-making being the sole domain of medical doctors and specialists, other health workers such as social workers, counsellors, pastoral care workers and volunteers all have a say. This method is designed to uphold the importance of the patient as a whole. That is, the individual, rather than the symptoms, is being treated. However, while there is noble intent at work here and while the aims might look good on paper, there still remain too many examples of where the patient's wishes have been lost, drowned in the plethora of advice proffered.

In social scientist Beverley McNamara's field research of two palliative care units in the early 1990s, one Australian palliative care nurse was quoted as saying:

> We burble on about control – you know, palliative care is all about handing control of this person's life back to the patient and back to the family; we don't own the patient and we don't control them. [But] woe betide the patient who doesn't do what we want them to do. And they sense this, they will say: 'Well, where is this control?'
>
> This family that would just give their eye teeth for the morphine to be put up, they will say: 'Well, who is really listening to us?' So I think we are really paying a lot of lip service to this issue of control. I think it's mythology, the way the program is going now.[6]

The patient-centred approach

Within this multidisciplinary context, palliative care claims an emphasis, in theory at least, upon collaboration with the patient. Decisions are said to be made in consultation with them. It's joint agreement all the way.

This commitment to the patient's wishes should be the defining feature of palliative care. This change has come partly from the new public health ethos and partly because the medical profession has had little choice but to change. As Keith Reed, the campaign manager for the Voluntary Euthanasia Society in the United Kingdom, has noted:

> Individuals are no longer willing to be told what to do. Empowering the patient is the new driving force in regular medicine. People's attitudes have led that. They are trying to ensure they have fundamental rights.[7]

These days, people expect to be heard and good medical practice demands this be so. And not just heard, but consulted too, and their views respected. This is why a patient's request for a hastened death must be considered with the utmost seriousness, and why end-of-life choices need to be seen as part of what Canadian sociologist Russell Ogden calls the continuum of palliative care. Given that such care was founded on the principles of 'emotional, spiritual and informational needs' of the patient, Ogden argues that euthanasia must be a consideration; certainly at a theoretical/conceptual level, and in law at a practical one.[8]

In the Northern Territory when the ROTI legislation was still valid, a request for VE always occurred within the context of palliative care. All the patients who used the legislation had had this care, provided by doctors like the courageous Brian and Lyn Reid who were prepared to consult with interstate experts and deliver the best palliative help. All patients had received advice on how to best deal with their symptoms; some had taken the advice, some had not.

Nancy Cato's story, by her daughter Bronley Norman

My parents, Eldred Norman and writer Nancy Cato, never had much respect for convention. They believed in the rights of the individual: freedom from want, freedom from fear, freedom of speech, freedom of religion *and* freedom from bureaucracy.

Nancy had seen her father plead for a gun to end the indignities he suffered with prostate cancer. She also knew her bedridden mother had tried to electrocute herself. Nancy vowed she would never let herself reach that stage. 'If I can't skip when I'm seventy,' she wrote, 'I'd rather be dead.'

Eldred's ideal choice of exit was to use his racing car and a solid cliff face. His fast-speeding cancer had immobilised him at age fifty-seven. Bravely individual to the last, he wrote farewell letters to his children, and settled upon taking a large number of barbiturates. He ate them with a spoon, like his favourite Crispies, because he couldn't keep water down. Nancy held his hand while Eldred slipped gently from sleep into coma and beyond . . .

My brothers and I were denied the chance to say goodbye to Dad because what Mum did for love was technically a criminal act, necessitating secrecy, even though Dad's suicide was *not* a crime in our eyes. Mum and I joined Exit to help legalise what we both passionately believed is our moral right to the peaceful and dignified death of our choice.

In 2000, aged eighty-three, Mum was hospitalised for four weeks. With her mind distorted by horrific morphine hallucinations and bedridden, incontinent, and unable to read, she decided it was time to go. But, after saying her goodbyes, she was *furious* to keep waking up in her tortured body, so she stopped eating and only sipped proffered drinks. Nearly two weeks later I brought her frail, wasted body home from hospital.

Before she died, in brief moments of lucidity she reminded me, 'You promised you'd help!' I told her I wanted to keep that promise, but Mum worried that I might suffer legal consequences. 'Damn bureaucrats!' she muttered. A few weary nights later, she slipped gladly from sleep into coma and beyond.

The human rights of the living are enshrined by a United Nations charter, but what about the rights of the dying?

Treating the symptoms

The decision to treat a patient's symptoms instead of attempting a cure is a radical notion in traditional medicine. Indeed, historically, medical discourse has been almost entirely concerned with disease, its diagnosis and its cure. This disease-oriented approach positioned the patient as the unknowing victim of a condition that was beyond their control. To shift the focus away from cure and toward the provision of symptomatic relief only is, for some doctors, to admit the unacceptable: that not everyone can be cured; that not everyone *should* be cured.

How do I justify that last statement? End-of-life treatments can be intrusive and traumatic experiences, especially for patients who are lucid and aware of what is happening to them. From the insertion of tubes and connection of monitors to pharmacologically induced stupors, the last days and weeks of a person's life can be downright miserable.

The symptom that is most commonly addressed by palliative care is pain. While it is commonly held that pain can be controlled for 95 per cent of patients,[9] for many the side effects of the treatment can often be more objectionable than the original pain. And while there is a huge range of strategies for pain control, many of the other symptoms experienced such as nausea, weakness, itching, incontinence and breathlessness have far fewer treatment options available. Weakness, for example, can be burdensome and untreatable.

The treatment of symptoms also means that palliative care is often concerned with the bandaging and mopping up of 'leaky bodies'. According to University of London academic Clive Seale, this may be what the term 'palliative' really means. The word palliation, writes Seale, derives from the Latin *palliatus*, meaning 'covered', 'cloaked' or 'disguised'.[10]

Death in the course of palliative care can also be disguised, especially when the drugs are upped, and the time that a person takes to die is regulated. Here, time is of the essence. If death is too fast we have active (illegal) euthanasia; but if we slow things down we're left with good symptom control and a 'natural' death. Who's fooling who?

Janet Mills' story

The second person to make use of the Northern Territory's ROTI Act was Janet Mills from Naracoorte in South Australia. Janet came to Darwin with her husband Dave in early December 1996. For nearly ten years, Janet had suffered from a rare disease known as mycosis fungoides. Slowly the cancer had broken down her skin, leaving extensive scarring, constant infection and ever-present itching that went on day after day. This is the same disease that the well-known British actor Paul Eddington from the series *Yes Minister* died from in 1995.

Over the years, Janet had received every known treatment for her condition and in her first phone call to me, she stated she had simply had enough. There was no further treatment to which she wished to be subjected. It seemed that the experts were out of ideas, and the future – according to Janet – looked pretty bleak.

When I first met Janet that December I was taken aback. Mycosis fungoides is a horrible, disfiguring disease. She was in pain, uncomfortable, restless and constantly scratching at her skin. The smell of infection filled her darkened motel room. She answered all my questions, telling me of treatment after treatment tried to no avail. When asked, she had reluctantly agreed to do what she thought was the right thing and show her body to medical students so that they might witness first-hand this rare condition. And, always, there was hope and the promise of a new treatment just around the corner. But late in 1996, she again said, 'I've had enough.' She spoke softly, deliberately, and all the time Dave sat by her side, supporting her.

Shortly after arriving in Darwin, Janet was admitted to Darwin Private Hospital and given a palliative care bed. While the admission went smoothly, the paperwork required in order for the ROTI law to be used could not be completed. One signature – that of a specialist who would confirm the diagnosis – we just could not get. No Territory specialist was prepared to confirm that Janet was terminally ill, despite there being documentation brought by Janet from South Australia to confirm this. An Adelaide oncologist, the delightful Jack Russell (the man, not the dog), had given his opinion; she was terminal and should be allowed to use the law. But the final signature had to come from a Territory-registered specialist.

After days of ringing around and a chorus of 'noes', my list of potential signatories was looking smaller and smaller. Husband Dave, a hardworking shearer, was a fish out of water in the hospital environment. But he refused to be deterred by the recalcitrance of the medical establishment and lobbied long and hard for Janet's right to use the ROTI legislation. I admired his tenacity and loyalty to his wife.

In desperation, I organised a media conference for Janet and her husband during which she appealed for a Territory specialist to come forward and assess her. It is hard to overstate the bravery shown by Janet that day. This sad, sick, disfigured woman sat in front of a bevy of television cameras and lights while a phalanx of journalists questioned and questioned her. The venue chosen for the conference – since the hospital would not cooperate – was the house in which Bob Dent had died just three months earlier.

While Janet's public plea for assistance made world news, it did little to encourage a specialist to break professional ranks and confirm she had terminal mycosis. There was a deathly silence following the press conference and so my phone calls to the dwindling list of Territory specialists continued. Not surprisingly, orthopaedic surgeons, those medically farthest from a disease such as mycosis fungoides, were at the bottom of my list of those to call. So in desperation I finally rang Darwin orthopaedic surgeon Steve Baddeley.

I began the call in my usual way: 'Steve, would you please

see my patient Janet Mills to provide a professional opinion about the nature of her illness. I will understand if you feel you are unable to undertake this request,' etc., etc. To my total surprise, Steve said yes immediately. My response was stunned silence. Just when Dave and I were about to give up and Janet had resigned herself to being unable to use the law and returning to South Australia, this courageous doctor saved the day.

The following day, Janet visited Baddeley's consulting rooms and underwent an extraordinarily thorough examination. Steve had quickly read up on the disease and consulted widely. He knew he would face a backlash for what he was doing, and there soon was one. In an attempt to thwart Janet's request to die, Dave told of how Adelaide dermatologist Dr Warren Weightman criticised her, stating that there was a range of treatments she had not yet tried. Janet was unimpressed. And she had a point when she replied that it was strange that a doctor who had been closely involved in her care and who had previously run out of ideas, could suddenly list a raft of treatments that were previously unknown to her. What Janet was seeing was a graphic example of the profession's inability to accept that people want end-of-life decision-making power. Dr Weightman was the rule; Steve Baddeley was the exception.

Luckily, the ROTI Act's definition of terminal illness was 'an illness which, in reasonable medical judgement will, in the normal course, without the application of extraordinary measures or of *treatment unacceptable to the patient*, result in the death of the patient'. Janet found all of Weightman's newly discovered options unacceptable. Plus Janet made an additional pertinent point – she had helped in the training of young doctors by going out of her way to visit medical schools for students to learn about her condition, and now she felt it was the medical profession's turn to help her. She was deeply hurt by the attitude of doctors like Weightman.

Once Janet's paperwork was finally complete, she and Dave booked into the Botanical Apartments in Darwin and on 2 January 1997 Janet died. She passed away in Dave's arms with one of her sons close by, on one of the wettest days that Darwin had ever seen. Despite how the movies try to portray it, death is rarely beautiful, but Janet's, when it finally occurred, was as good as it gets.

The influence of the Church in palliative care

Given that Cicely Saunders, the founder of modern palliative care, is a deeply religious woman, it is not surprising that her form of treatment continues to carry strong religious overtones. In the early days, hospices were almost always operated by religious institutions. These were mostly Catholic, but the Lutherans and the Uniting Church were active in the area too.

While there is nothing inherently wrong with religious-based care, especially not where quality care is provided, my question is this: At what point does religious ideology influence patient care? This question is especially pertinent given the primacy of patient choice within palliative care discourse. Let me explain. If palliative care is truly patient-centric, a patient's request for slow euthanasia or hastened death needs to be taken seriously and, within the confines of the law, acted upon. Yet what if that request contravenes the religious doctrine of the institution involved, or the personal religious convictions of the individual employees or volunteers? By that I mean, what is to be made of a request for hastened death if such a request is morally repugnant and unacceptable on religious grounds? Where does the palliative care ethos rest then?

Indeed, the lack of a conceptual framework within which to understand requests for hastened death is responsible for the common assertion that people who make such a request must be depressed, or in some way mentally ill. This is despite the fact that in Oregon, where physician-assisted suicide is legal, symptoms of depression have been found in only 20 per cent of patients who requested PAS.[11] Furthermore, one needs to remember that having 'symptoms of depression' is not the same as being clinically depressed and unable to give informed consent. With such a simplistic understanding, it is easy to see how a patient's wishes can be disregarded, and how the much-lauded 'wholistic' care of a patient, including the patient's right to participate in the decision-making process, can go clean out the window.

Finally, it is important to recognise that a patient's wishes can be overridden in ways that are barely discernible. Even the patient themselves may not be aware of what is being done, especially in those vulnerable days immediately prior to death. Doctors have many ways of choosing not to hear what is being said by a patient. When the circumstances are right, a patient may be coerced into staying alive and more or less oblivious to the course of events taking place, with little said or acknowledged.

In addition to the risk of a clash of ideologies and beliefs and the resulting conflict of interest between the patient and the institution providing the care, I have a second concern to do with palliative care. When a particular religious belief prevails, what guarantee is provided to patients that those who care for them will not use their position to promote the Christian message? Seriously ill people are vulnerable and the days and weeks before death are normally full of reflection. People are understandably apprehensive of the dying experience and the unknown that is to follow. I am not alone in questioning the extent to which palliative care staff, particularly those charged with pastoral care, may use the moment to try to 'convert' the patient.

Call me cynical, but I have been witness to too many instances where the palliative care professionals' personal religious convictions have affected the care of a patient. It was no accident that cab driver Max Bell found a priest at his bedside in Broken Hill Hospital moments before they began the final sedation. Did he ask for the priest? I doubt it. Who could tell at that stage? Did he die a Catholic? You bet.[12]

Dying at Grace

The issue of religious involvement in dying was brought home to me in a recent documentary called *Dying at Grace* by well-known Canadian film-maker Allan King. King's film followed five patients in the palliative care unit at Grace Health Centre in Toronto. The unit is run by the Salvation Army and Salvo officers figure largely in the daily lives of these patients, regardless of their religious beliefs.

In one scene we see Major Phyllis Bobbitt asking if there is any chance of a dying woman giving God one last go. The hapless victim reasserts her lack of religiosity, only to have the same major praying over her dying body at a time when the patient concerned was clearly too close to death to do too much objecting. In other scenes, when patients express a particular feeling about their situation, we see staff unable to engage with what is being said to them. 'I'm embarrassed because I'm incontinent,' a patient says. 'No, you're not,' she gets told by the major.

When I asked King if he intended his film to be an indictment of the palliative care system, his reaction was one of great interest to me, for he revealed he thought his film an honest depiction of a humbling and admirable field of medicine. Indeed, he said that a member of his film crew had already booked into Grace for when his time came in the future. I am still trying to make sense of this film and the difference between my interpretation of it and that of the film-maker.

My third concern with the influence of the Church in the provision of palliative care is its view on the meaning and significance of pain and/or suffering. In his 'Declaration on Euthanasia' in May 1980, the Pope explained this point at great length:

> According to Christian teaching . . . suffering, especially suffering during the last moments of life, has a special place in God's saving plan; it is in fact a sharing in Christ's passion and a union with the redeeming sacrifice which He offered in obedience to the Father's will.[13]

This type of ideological stance is to be found throughout the entire discourse *and* practice of palliative care. In 2000, the movement's founder, Saunders, reiterated the Pope's views on suffering, stating 'the final moments of darkness or weakness can open a window'.[14] Like others of a religious or spiritual persuasion, Saunders argues that there is *meaning* to be found in pain, and that pain or suffering can in and of itself be a worthwhile experience.

When I debated Bishop Anthony during the Catholic Church's Life Week at Sydney University in August 2003, this belief again emerged. A question from the floor went as follows: 'Is there any human value in suffering?' My answer was:

> It's more your [Fisher's] domain I would think. Personally I think not; I don't think it prises the doors of heaven one bit wider, and if a person makes a decision that their suffering is at such a level that death is preferable, and if that person is a rational individual, I agree.

Bishop Anthony's reply:

> I don't think that in itself, suffering is a thing that we would want for ourselves or wish for anybody else. But how we respond to suffering when it comes certainly goes to the heart of what we are as human beings and possibly our whole destiny. I think that when we face suffering, we hope to face it as people of courage and love, to bring that to the suffering when it comes either for ourselves or for each other. And in that sense you might talk of suffering being

redemptive or suffering in various lives being a point of
conversion or a point of insight, a point where people display great virtue . . . I do think that people can transcend
their suffering and in one way or another show something
of what is most noble about the human spirit.[15]

This type of belief also emerged when the House of
Representatives was debating the Kevin Andrews bill back in
1996. At the time, the Liberal Party MP for Wakefield, Neil
Andrew, was not alone in his thoughts when he said, 'I have a
dilemma with euthanasia. My dilemma is that it allows us to
escape that reality that life is the richer for the confronting . . . '[16]
Try telling this to a dying patient who has no desire to continue
suffering and for whom life has lost all meaning. This roman-
ticisation of pain and suffering is highly problematic for many
patients and their families. Most people, quite rightly, fear pain
and resent suffering. To suggest that there is personal growth
to be had from these things is hardly a comforting thought,
especially for those of a non-religious persuasion. To the non-
believer, this type of indoctrination can be downright offensive.

In summary, if the Church's role in the provision of palliative care was more transparent, I would be a lot less concerned.
The fact is, it isn't. Palliative care continues to be influenced and
directed by a particular set of ideological beliefs. A conflict of
interest is therefore unavoidable. However, on a more optimistic note, in recent years discussion of religion in the context of
palliative care has been expanded to include spirituality. In this
regard, spirituality is being defined more broadly as a 'search for
meaning'.[17] Preachings from the Bible have been replaced with

'listening and narrative reconstruction', as patients' life stories and tales have begun to be used as a means of making sense of their present and future.[18] In addition, therapies that involve music, art and even pets can make a positive contribution for some patients, especially those not yet in the last stages of their disease and for whom life still has meaning.

The cost and availability of palliative care

It is interesting to note that overall funding levels for this sector have risen since the issue of VE has been on the Australian political agenda. Palliative care has indeed been a clear healthcare winner in recent years. And just as the funding for palliative care has increased, so has the level of care provided. I certainly don't object to this increase in funding. After all, receiving high-quality care when seriously ill should be the right of every patient.

Interestingly, it was an alleged *lack* of palliative care in the Northern Territory at the time of the ROTI Act that was said to make such a bill permissible and acceptable in the first place. Critics said that if the Territory had had decent palliative care, VE legislation would never have been required. They argued that it was because the Territory had limited palliative care services that Territorians thought that they needed a law to enable them to die. This, of course, misses the point that a person's quality of life can depend upon things that have no relation to a medical condition, its symptoms or the palliative care that is provided. (See Valerie's story later in this chapter as an example of this.)

It is telling that the only amendment to the Andrews bill passed by parliament at the time the ROTI Act was overturned concerned palliative care funding. On 24 March 1997, it was WA Greens Senator Dee Margetts who moved the following amendment. She stated:

> the Senate calls on the Government to provide adequate funding for:
> (a) the development and implementation of national guidelines and standards in relation to palliative care;
> (b) increased levels of training for health care professionals in all aspects of palliative care;
> (c) an integrated approach to palliative care, including:
>   (i) co-ordination of care delivery, with the support of volunteers, whether in the home or in institutions, for maximum effectiveness, and
>   (ii) provision of respite care as an essential component; and
> (d) improved and expanded research into palliative care, especially pain control and symptom relief.

The amendment passed, thirty-eight ayes to thirty-four noes.[19] To this day, the palliative care movement continues to benefit from the Kevin Andrews private member's bill.

But there is another angle to palliative care and the funding debate. In almost all areas of Australian society, especially when a conservative government is in power, it is the economic rationalist model that prevails. Politicians usually feel if there is a way to save money, then they should do it; if it is possible to be more economical with the public purse, then changes should be made. Generic brand pharmaceuticals? You got it. Early discharge from hospitals? You can have that too. But where life and death are concerned, the logic seems reversed. Indeed, society's justification for willingly spending millions of dollars on end-of-life care – think the now-defunct Medicare Gold as an example – is such a touchy subject that in countries like Belgium where VE is legal, free access to palliative care drugs is mandated. The Belgians, just like Australians, believe that no one should die because they cannot afford the care they need to live.

But the high cost of palliative care is not just about the type or quantity of the drugs provided. It is also about the *type of care* being provided. Dying people often want to talk and palliative care counselling addresses this need. Intensive one-on-one counselling can be expensive, so while palliative care is often described as the low-cost cousin to high-tech, curative medicine, this is not necessarily the case. Palliative care is clearly the exception to the economic rationalist rule. But this alone does not explain why our politicians celebrate the relatively high cost of palliative care compared to costs involved with voluntary euthanasia. The question few have yet dared to ask concerns the logic and benefit of forcing expensive treatment upon a person who does not want to live.

The cost of dying

In the course of the second reading of his private member's bill, Kevin Andrews took strange pride in just how expensive end-of-life health costs can be. Here, Andrews boasted about the average amount of money that the government spent on a terminally ill patient, and compared this to what would be spent if VE were to be allowed. Andrews' argument implied that it was better to spend 'some $5000 to $6000 on average for a person in the terminal stages of their life in a palliative care hospice, than $25 for a lethal injection'.[20] That is, Kevin Andrews believes it better to spend thousands of dollars forcing a person to remain alive *against their wishes* than to allow them to hasten their death by a few days or weeks. In any other area, this type of saving would have governments jumping with joy. When it comes to VE, an expensive, forced existence is seen as preferable. Even more puzzling is that Andrews thought this wasteful expenditure was somehow associated with the common good of society.

The issue of end-of-life funding is clearly a contentious one. Indeed, it is so controversial that the debate has hardly begun. No one has yet attempted to explain why it makes good sense from both humane and economic standpoints to *not* allow a person the right to die. Instead of engaging with such arguments when discussing the issue of hastened death, anti-choice advocates spend their time scare-mongering. They adopt the political dogma of the right-to-life lobby and talk only of a feared imaginary world in which they believe it would become government policy – and not individual choice – that dictated who lived and died, and where *all* end-of-life decisions would be cost-driven.

At the current time, the Australian Institute of Health and Welfare estimates that around 30 per cent of the health expenditure for people sixty-five years and over occurs in the last year of life.[21] In Canada, more detailed research has recently become available. In the year 2000–2001, 1.1 per cent of the population of Manitoba in Canada died. Nearly half of these deaths occurred in hospitals, with a further 24 per cent occurring in long-term care facilities (for example, nursing homes, hospices). In terms of healthcare costs, this 1.1 per cent of the population consumed 21.3 per cent of the budget. The AIHW suggests that the Australian situation is comparable.[22]

This means that the last six months of life are an expensive affair. If the person who is dying is being kept alive against their will, then this expenditure is nothing short of scandalous. Yet the government is steadfast in their refusal to pass legislation that would allow the elderly and those seriously ill to end their life at a time and place of their choosing. And – ironically – they seem only too happy to see the 9.5 per cent of GDP that is currently spent on health services in Australia set to increase as a direct result of their selective public policy interests.[23] To top things off, the Productivity Commission has recently reported that by 2044, healthcare will consume a full 5 per cent more of the GDP, leaving a $2200 *billion* hole in Australia's ability to fund such care. One can but wonder when a government will have the guts to stop digging the fiscal black hole that is their ever-deepening legacy for future generations. While the enabling of end-of-life choices will not fix the economic woes of the next forty years, it would not hurt, given half a chance.[24]

So the next time you hear a government minister trying to argue why this or that payment or welfare program for single mothers or war veterans must be cut, counter their argument with their fiscal irresponsibility on end-of-life choices.

Can someone tell me what is ethical about telling a dying person, someone who is in pain and is suffering and wants to die and has asked to die, 'No. Sorry, mate. You've got to live. But don't worry about it, we've got these really good drugs that will have you so doped to the eyeballs you won't be able to shower yourself, you won't be able to toilet yourself and you won't recognise anyone that walks in the room'? And they are still expected to pay for this.

This is torture. When someone wants to sleep and wants peace, let them. If there is no choice, why prolong it? When I first saw the Andrews bill, to me it was democratic vandalism. This is democratically popular legislation. I doubt whether Andrews would spit on an Anzac's grave, but why desecrate what they fought for: our right to choose, the same way we choose who represents us.

– Audience member submission, Euthanasia Laws Bill[25]

Requesting death in the context of palliative care

Research shows that seriously ill people often request a hastened death in their last days of life, or would at least like that option to be available to them. A recent survey in Oregon found that of 429 hospice nurses interviewed, 157 had had patients for whom death had been hastened by either discontinuing food and fluid, or by using 'legally prescribed narcotics'. The main reasons given for why some patients stopped taking food and fluids included readiness to die; poor quality of life; and the wish to die at home. Patients requesting physician-assisted dying were described as more likely to want 'control' over their death.[26]

A different, larger survey looked at nurses' experience with terminally ill patients. Of the 2333 oncology nurses questioned, 23 per cent had been asked by a patient for a lethal prescription, while 22 per cent had been asked by a patient for a lethal injection.[27] Closer to home, during the recent attempted murder trial of New Zealand nurse Lesley Martin, defence witness Professor Roderick Macleod of Otago University's Medical School confirmed that patients often ask him to kill them. When cross-examined by Crown prosecutor Andrew Cameron, Professor Macleod said there were striking similarities between a conversation Martin describes in her book *To Die Like A Dog* where Lesley's mother asks her daughter to help her when the time comes and conversations he regularly had with terminally ill patients.[28]

A request for hastened death is common enough where seriously ill patients are concerned. But despite the widespread nature of these requests, the formal palliative care movement remains hostile to our right to die and to both VE and PAD. Beginning with Balfour Mount, the doctor credited with coining the term palliative medicine, specialists still fear that legitimising – let alone legalising – a patient's request for VE could make a slippery slope even more slippery.

The question that is always posed whenever VE legislation is discussed is how doctors would know how to avoid going too far, and how could society provide adequate safeguards? Almost every time a VE bill is considered by a parliament somewhere in the world, the image of uncontrollable doctors killing patients willy-nilly is used to instil fear among politicians and the community alike. One argument used by palliative care advocates and others who oppose VE is that of the slippery slope.

The slippery slope

Broadly speaking, the slippery slope argument contends that in time there will always be a deterioration in standards, an erosion of controls. Applied to voluntary euthanasia, those predicting a slope see it as inevitable that if one person is allowed the right to die, everyone else will want to do likewise. Or when people are comatose or suffering from dementia and are unable to say 'No, I want to live', they will be killed off all the same. The flood-gates will open and there will be no turning back. Voluntary euthanasia will inevitably become *non-voluntary*. This stance is social determinism at its worst.

The slippery slope theory is often utilised to justify why society needs to impose the strictest safeguards on VE laws. In short, it is employed to explain why the medical profession must regulate who gets to die. Fortunately, however, there are those who argue against the existence of an inevitable slope. Take Tristram Engelhardt, Professor Emeritus at Baylor College of Medicine in Texas. Engelhardt uses the example of happenings in his state to argue against the concept. He notes that even though the aiding and abetting of suicide was not prohibited in Texas until 1973, there was never any evidence of a slope existing. The populace in Texas has never undertaken assisted suicide to force death upon people who did not want to die. On the contrary, says Engelhardt, 'there is no evidence that such a legal vacuum [leads] to an increased frequency of suicide or of murder'.[29]

Similarly, when Derek Humphry first published his best-selling book *Final Exit* in 1991, its critics were hell-bent on finding an immediate increase in the suicide rate as a result of its publication; this would prove their slippery slope theory. They argued that everyone would buy the book, go home and top themselves that very night. Needless to say, despite a microscopic analysis of the suicide statistics by Humphry's detractors, no changes were found. And as Huib Drion has pointed out, 'a century ago opium was freely for sale but it never led to massive suicides.'

And then there is the Netherlands. In that country, with its twenty-year history of gradually decriminalising compassionate acts by doctors – acts that help seriously ill patients to die with dignity – the claim is repeatedly made that there is evidence of a creeping decline in standards. But is there? Let's look at the facts. The Dutch have always been concerned about the possibility of a slippery slope. That is why they commissioned a close investigation of VE practices. The first of the Remmelink Reports was carried out in 1991. Published in *The Lancet*, these reports have provided the first close examination of this issue anywhere in the world. And they were only made possible because of the Dutch decision to decriminalise VE. Only then were doctors prepared to talk about their practices and experiences.

The statistic that worried everyone when the reports were published was the percentage of total deaths that had taken place where a doctor was involved and where no explicit consent had been sought or given by the patient. In 1990, opponents of VE inaccurately claimed that these deaths – cases of *non-voluntary* euthanasia – were the result of the tolerant Dutch climate. To determine evidence of a slope, though, at least two points on a slope are required, and the Dutch repeated their study in 1995 and in 2001. The 1995 investigation was also published in *The Lancet*. Again, a group of people appeared who were helped to die without their consent. Opponents once more claimed that the evidence was there – people in Holland were being put to death by doctors against their wishes. For them, this was proof of the dreaded slope.

The problem for slope proponents, however, was that each time this category was examined in the reports, the numbers grew smaller. So if the slope existed, the trend was heading the wrong way. Non-voluntary euthanasia was certainly occurring in Holland, but despite the tolerant climate it was becoming less frequent. Was this only a feature of Dutch society? Other researchers began to repeat these studies in countries where strong legal sanction against VE made the research harder to perform. What these researchers found, however, was that the group of people being helped to die without consent existed in all surveyed countries, irrespective of whether there was an environment of decriminalisation or harsh legal sanction. Indeed, Peter Singer and his colleagues found that in Australia, where such sanctions are in place, a slightly higher percentage of total deaths reported was the result of non-voluntary euthanasia.[30] The evidence was beginning to mount that a tolerant environment *decreased*, not increased, this non-voluntary group of deaths. The editorialist of the *New England Journal of Medicine* put it best. Comparing the second Dutch report to the first, some five years between them, it was said 'it would be very hard to construe these findings as a descent into depravity'.[31] No slope. But the Church and the right-to-life lobby keep clinging to the argument.

Then there is the claim that with enough palliative care, VE would never be required. When New Zealand First MP Peter Brown's Death with Dignity bill was narrowly defeated in their parliament in July 2003 (sixty noes to fifty-eight ayes and one abstention), it was the palliative medicine consultant at Christchurch Hospital, Kate Grundy, who took the opportunity to promote her profession. Grundy argued that:

> what those in the pro-euthanasia camp really wanted was the right to die a peaceful, dignified death when the time came. With proper palliative care services, that could be achieved in the vast majority of cases without resorting to euthanasia.[32]

According to Grundy, the issue is simple. Provide proper palliative care and no one will want or need a VE law. While this argument is old, it is still effective and the challenge remains for death with dignity advocates to expose the lie upon which it is based. It is the same line that was put forward by the then president of the AMA, Kerryn Phelps, when I spoke at their national conference in 2002. At the press conference afterwards, Phelps reaffirmed this view, saying, 'I do not think that we will hear the demand for euthanasia, provided that we have sufficient palliative care resources in the community.'[33]

Babies and euthanasia

When we discuss euthanasia, we are almost always talking about voluntary euthanasia for seriously ill or elderly adults. But it's worth considering the possible role of euthanasia where severely deformed newborn babies are concerned. Any discussion about euthanasia for seriously ill babies is largely taboo because we are talking about non-voluntary euthanasia, as the baby cannot give consent. So who would make such a decision – parents, doctors, or both?

This is the question that caused such controversy for philosopher Peter Singer. He has written extensively on the issue, and has long advocated that the rights of the parent should override the baby's right to life. To many people, this is hardly a radical belief. Yet because babies are so symbolic (think love, warmth and the future), rational debate on this issue has been stymied from the start. This is mainly because the right-to-life lobby pounce on the issue whenever possible, skewing Singer's philosophical approach and alleging that he advocates infanticide being carried out willy-nilly.[34]

The issue of euthanasia for severely deformed newborn babies is, of course, much more complex. According to Barbara Smoker, a former president of Britain's National Secular Society, the euthanasia of a newborn baby can be usefully understood as a very late abortion.[35] Just as a woman can, in many jurisdictions, choose to terminate her pregnancy if deformities are detected prior to birth, so she should have that option in the period immediately post-birth. As Professor John Harris – a member of the British Medical Association's Ethics Committee – has put it:

People who think there is a difference between infanticide and late abortion have to ask the question: what has happened to the fetus in the time it takes to pass down the birth canal and into the world which changes its moral status? I don't think anything has happened in that time.[36]

The argument here is that a newborn baby does not yet have the rights of personhood. The baby has 'very limited awareness, no idea of any future, and no real stake in life'. And then there is the issue of the child's possible quality of life. On this, Smoker asks, 'Why should the child be forced to endure an intolerable life until he or she is old enough to choose suicide or until natural death finally brings relief?' This viewpoint is expounded in the writings of Peter Singer and Helga Kuhse in *Should the Baby Live?*[37] They argue:

When the life of an infant will be so miserable it would not be worth living, and there are no 'extrinsic' reasons – such as the feelings of the parents – for keeping the infant alive, it is better that the child should be helped to die without further suffering.[38]

In Australia, as in other Western countries, the birth of a severely deformed baby is often a negotiated affair, with the medical staff, parents and the law all stakeholders. A range of situations can result. For example, the parents might want the child to be allowed to die, but the religious beliefs of the medical and nursing staff involved could preclude this, and they might use the Hippocratic oath and anything else they can think of to justify keeping the baby alive. In other situations, medical staff can be sympathetic to the parents' point of view and a baby can be gradually allowed to die from lack of fluids and nutrition, while sedated. However, as Smoker has pointed out, this is not 'as merciful as a quick, lethal injection, if only the law allowed it. Starvation may take about ten days, and though the babies themselves, being sedated, are unlikely to suffer much, their parents and nurses certainly do'. Another scenario is that a compassionate paediatrician in a special care nursery might decide that the baby's pain and suffering are so great that only a large morphine dose will suffice. In these instances the parents may even be able to hold the baby as he or she dies.

The difference between the second and third scenario is largely one of timing. The former invokes the use of all modern technologies to sustain life till a point is reached where the stricken baby is left gasping intermittently for a death that may well take hours. The whole affair is likely to have the special care nursery team on edge, and to deeply traumatise the parents. But it is lawful. The latter scenario, letting the parents hold their baby as the doctor administers a large dose of lethal morphine, is illegal. However, parents who have gone through this experience tell me that they admire their doctor's courage for the rest of their lives.

Whatever approach is taken depends for the most part on the attitude of the specialist paediatrician who runs the nursery. If you have a seriously disabled baby, you may do well to enquire about your paediatrician's religion before having any discussion about what sort of death your baby can expect.

Never the twain shall meet

The hostility that those within the palliative care movement have against right-to-die advocates was made clear at the 2003 conference of the National Palliative Care Association in Adelaide. At this conference, the rather sedate South Australian Voluntary Euthanasia Society (SAVES) requested permission from the organisers to set up a display/information booth. By all reports, there were fifty or so other booths erected for the duration of the conference, yet permission was denied to SAVES, for reasons that remain unclear.

To me, such an overt exclusion of this VE society is further evidence that the palliative care movement continues to have trouble countenancing the concept of requests for hastened death. It is ongoing proof that VE and PAD remain antithetical to the discourse *and* practice of the palliative care profession. They still believe, as Balfour Mount has noted, in the possibly 'catastrophic' effect of VE laws.[39]

Between voluntary euthanasia and palliative care

In the midst of these opposing sides on VE, there are some academics and practitioners who are trying to make sense of the disjuncture between palliative care and one's right to die. Australian palliative care specialist Dr Roger Hunt, who coined the term 'rhetoric–reality gap', is one. Hunt suggests that as the palliative care discipline matures and the profession starts to recognise the limitations that it currently places on the autonomy of the patient, VE will eventually be embraced. The best palliative care option, he believes, is one that 'serves the interests of the patient, provides effective relief of suffering, accords ample respect for the patient's autonomy, and, ideally, has the support of those people who are close to the patient. Active voluntary euthanasia may be the most compassionate and best option'.[40]

Canadian sociologist Russell Ogden provides a similar framework of understanding, saying that a request for hastened death can helpfully be seen as part of a broader continuum of palliative care. There are occasions, he says, when a patient's pain and suffering cannot be eased. 'What comfort does palliative care offer to patients who say that they have simply had enough?'[41] This is why, as was stated in the Zurich Declaration on Assisted Dying of October 1998, 'excellent palliative care should not exclude the right to choose assisted dying'.[42] It is not an either–or situation.

The right-to-die and the palliative care movements *can* work together. A request by a seriously ill patient for a hastened death need not simply mean that more palliation is required or that the patient is depressed. This leads to the rather bizarre idea that if one is 'palliated' well enough, there will be no requests for help to die. And in one sense, this is true. If a patient insists loud and long enough for help to die they might find themselves 'palliated' to the point of unconsciousness, at which point these troublesome requests cease.

The knowledge that one has the ability to choose the time and place of one's death could provide an enormous sense of empowerment to the individual concerned. A request for hastened death needs to be seen less as an affront to the efficacy of this branch of medicine and more as just another aspect in a continuum of patient-centred care. It could become an accepted part of end-of-life care, in which the patient's wishes actually have some currency.

> Australia has just thrown away an opportunity to show the world that we have a compassionate and caring society which allows our terminally ill people the right to choose how and when they will die. To deny this right to anyone in pain and without hope is the ultimate act of obscenity.
>
> The point that these meddling minders have apparently missed is that palliative care does not work for many patients and even when pain can be alleviated there is another equally important aspect to their suffering to consider – dignity.
>
> I ask this: have any of you who so vehemently oppose voluntary euthanasia ever watched someone you love die in mental and physical agony, inch by inch? Well, I have, and it is a predicament that even the most blasé of us never forget. Certainly, if it happened to the family dog, it would not be tolerated.
>
> – Letter to the Editor, *Sydney Morning Herald*, 25 March 1997[43]

It's about more than just symptoms

The alleviation and treatment of a patient's symptoms remain the predominant concern of the palliative healthcare profession. If a patient's pain can be eased or eradicated, then palliative care is said to be working. If diarrhoea and nausea can be controlled, again the outcome is classified as 'successful'.

But what about symptoms that can't be controlled? What about weakness? What about shortness of breath? What about the meta-symptom of all combined symptoms? And what about the secondary conditions that are a by-product of the drug treatments that are busy addressing the primary symptoms? Finally, what about a patient's self-judged quality of life? What if the meaning of life has disappeared for them – what use is palliative care then? Are antidepressant drugs for mentally healthy patients the answer? I don't think so. To date, there is no cure for what Canadian writer Rita Daly calls 'existential suffering'. Daly is right to ask, 'what do we owe [the patient] as their caregiver?'[44] This last question has not yet been answered and I am not sure it ever will be. For these reasons, I believe it's time someone called the palliative care profession's bluff and challenged their claim that they possess all the answers for end-of-life care. Despite their best attempts, they clearly do not.

What also needs examining is the issue that for some patients the decision to end their life has nothing to do with their symptoms. The story of Valerie – the fourth and final patient of mine who made use of the ROTI law – is a good case in point.

Valerie's story

Valerie came to Darwin to die in 1997. She was stricken with breast cancer that had spread to other parts of her body. She was a very sick woman, and her arrival north was to prove a complicated affair.

Valerie was so sick, she couldn't sit up and needed to travel by stretcher. Travelling by plane is always difficult for stretcher patients. To begin with, a minimum of six seats must be purchased to enable the stretcher to be secured at the rear of the plane. And with five adult children accompanying you, it is not hard to imagine the logistical challenge involved.

Valerie flew into Darwin from her native Sydney, her three daughters and two sons by her side. I had organised an ambulance to collect her at the airport to take her straight to admissions at Darwin Private Hospital. There we would begin the necessary consultations with specialists and associated paperwork and Valerie could rest while she undertook the forty-eight-hour cooling-off period that was mandated by the legislation.

Yet upon arrival in Darwin, Valerie's transfer became increasingly complicated. Darwin's two ambulances were both called to an urgent multiple vehicle road accident elsewhere. Some time went by as we waited on the plane, and Valerie began to flounder in the heat. The airport engineers were contacted and asked about getting emergency airconditioning onto the plane. They hesitated; this was a big ask. And, anyway, the ambulance should arrive any minute, they said. But Valerie's condition was worsening, and everyone was getting tense.

The airport operations manager and I kept watch for the first sign of arriving flashing lights. As agitated as I was, it was the manager who was to say, 'Jeez, mate, you wouldn't want to be fucking dying in this place, not with this ambo service.' He was clearly unaware why Valerie had come to Darwin.

Several days later, after recovering in hospital from the trip, all Valerie's tests and paperwork were complete. This time, I had no trouble obtaining the requisite signatures. The law was beginning to work. Valerie and her family then booked into the Mirambeena Motel, the place she had chosen to die. When the time came, I prepared the Deliverance Machine and inserted the needle into her arm. I moved away from the bed, and Valerie's children drew near.

For the next half hour, the children formed a circle around their mother, holding each other's hands and holding her. After Valerie pressed the last button, the machine's characteristic 'tick tick tick' noise filled the room. Within a few minutes, Valerie died peacefully while her children held her and spoke softly to her. I did not hear what they said; I was well away from the bed, as I should have been. As her doctor, I had served my purpose by ensuring that Valerie had the means of her death within her control. Her passing itself was none of my business. At around midday, I certified Valerie's death and quietly removed myself from the room.

Valerie's story is unique and differs from those of the other three people who used the ROTI Act. This is why. Like the others, Valerie had received a large amount of palliative care. Unlike the others, however, she had responded exceptionally well to that care. In the phone calls made to me before she decided to travel to Darwin, Valerie told me that she now suffered no symptoms. She spoke proudly of her doctors in Sydney and their palliative care abilities. She initially had considerable pain and nausea as the cancer spread, but the doctors had skilfully dealt with all of her symptoms.

Not long after Valerie made contact with me, I rang her doctors to discuss her request to die. They were taken aback at the news she desired this, let alone that she was making the arduous trip to Darwin. These doctors considered Valerie a shining example of just how effective modern palliative care could be.

She was their crowning glory. Valerie's desire to die, given their success in her treatment, so irked these doctors that in what turned out to be acrimonious conversations, they went so far as to describe her as ungrateful. Their feeling of betrayal was obvious.

Yet Valerie was never ungrateful. She was the first to admit that life without pain and nausea is a whole lot better than life with those symptoms. But is it good enough to want to keep on living? The issue for Valerie was not her illness per se, but the alteration to her quality of life brought about by the breast cancer. Prior to her illness, Valerie had been a real golf buff. She lived for the game. Since becoming ill, golf had become but a distant memory. Once ill, her days were filled with 'waiting', she said – 'waiting for family or friends to visit'. She could not get out and about any more. She said this was 'no type of life' and she wanted out.

It's quality, not quantity

Like Valerie, many patients voice concerns about their loss of quality of life when they become elderly or ill or both. In this regard, decisions to keep on living or to die are based not so much on the extent of their pain or other physical symptoms, but on a complex mixture of considerations. One woman who wrote to me recently stated:

> Dear Doctor,
> I rang Exit about information on the Peaceful Pill. How can I obtain it? I live alone – six flights of stairs. When the

time comes and I can't manage I need to have something
here – something on hand – does the Pill keep?

I will pay for it. I am seventy-nine. Please let me know.

Thank you for all you are doing.

Jocelyn

For these people, I often argue and suggest that the feared
nursing home might be better than they expect. And sometimes
Exit members do go into a nursing home, and occasionally it
is better than they imagined. But not always. Perhaps a more
common statement I hear is 'The minute someone has to start
wiping my bum, I will know the time is right'. Again, I point
out that there are places where that level of intimate care is provided by staff who don't mind. The response I receive is almost
always 'Well, they can do what they like and clean up who they
like, but it's not for me, I don't want it'. And that's the point.
It's horses for courses. Some people will want to lie on a rubber
sheet, squeezing the last seconds out of a failing life – and they
should be able to. But for those who don't want to, are they to
be made to lie on that rubber sheet?

There are no prizes for forcing our end-of-life opinions onto
those with their own clearly thought-out positions. We need to
acknowledge and respect the views of others. They are no less
valid. More than a few of my patients have criticised palliative
care specialists, saying 'The doctors just don't understand me'.
Given that most palliative care professionals have little conceptual framework within which to make sense of a request for a
hastened death, the attitude of Valerie's attending palliative care
doctors is perhaps not surprising.

On the one hand, palliative care doctors pride themselves on treating the whole patient – mind, body and spirit – and of being nicely and respectfully patient-centred. Yet on the other, the philosophy of palliative care is compromised once a request to die is made. The point that many doctors seem unable to understand is that a patient's request for a hastened death does not necessarily reflect poorly on the palliative care profession. Rather, a person's ability to make decisions, to participate fully in life and to know that if it gets too bad they can say 'I've had enough now, let's end it', is as individual as it is complex. With a little more flexibility and less professional rhetoric, palliative care may be able to make its current contribution to end-of-life care even more effective. But it will need to try harder.

Like most Australians, I am a strong supporter of palliative care as a distinct discipline within modern medicine. The efficacy of palliative care is not the main point of concern here. Rather, it is that palliative care practitioners must acknowledge the double standard of the theory and practice of their discipline: the theory that says 'palliative care is patient-centred' and the practice that ignores and discourages requests for hastened death. These requests will only increase, and palliative care professionals must face the challenge of developing strategies that acknowledge, respect and act upon such requests, or risk being marginalised by the dying.

As many people attending Exit clinics now say, 'I've got good palliative care, the best symptom control possible. What I didn't tell the doctor was that I still wanted the means to end it. Anyway, he made it clear he wasn't having any of that. That's why I've come to you.'

Chapter 6

What's Wrong with Slow Euthanasia?

Slow euthanasia is the only form of euthanasia that is currently legal in all states and territories of Australia. It is the only way a caring doctor can help bring about the death of a suffering patient while escaping any legal consequence. Indeed, slow euthanasia is the 'doctor's loophole'.

Making use of the 'doctrine of double effect', or 'terminal sedation', as the practice is also known, a doctor helps a patient to die by slowly increasing the amount of pain-killing drugs until death occurs. While the practice is common, it is difficult to get doctors and other health professionals to admit their involvement. Nevertheless local and overseas studies continue to report high levels of the practice. In one Australian study, 70 per cent of 1112 doctors surveyed – doctors who had the opportunity to make a medical end-of-life decision – reported that they had hastened the death of a patient.[1] The same study also found that one third of all deaths in Australia followed an explicit medical decision to hasten death. Other studies confirm these trends.[2]

A bit of background

With its roots in Catholic moral theology, the doctrine of double effect states that it is 'morally justifiable to cause evil in the pursuit of good'.[3] Seen this way, death becomes an acceptable and an expected side effect of pain-relieving treatment with doctors, rather than patients, firmly in control of the process. All the decisions about if and when help will be offered are made by doctors.

What defines slow euthanasia is the doctor's *intention*. The doctor must have as their prime goal the treatment of the patient's pain. And if the patient should die, well, that's just the 'double effect'. Unlike active voluntary euthanasia or physician-assisted dying, the doctor is not – at least technically – said to be assisting the patient to die.

With its emphasis upon pain relief, the drugs used for slow euthanasia must be 'pain drugs' or analgesics like morphine. It would be indefensible to use an effective euthanasia drug like Nembutal. Nembutal is not an analgesic, so how then could the doctor argue that pain relief was their prime objective? The focus on morphine is the reason why, in lay circles, this drug is considered the 'best' drug to end life. But morphine is not the best – it's just the drug that doctors who want to help their patients die must use if they are to exploit the double-effect loophole.

> We extend our sincere thanks for the devoted TLC you [the doctor] gave so freely to Sam during the years of his fight, particularly this last week when you allowed him to blissfully pass away without that enduring pain he had suffered for so long.
>
> – Obituary notice, *Herald Sun*, 2004

How does slow euthanasia work?

At a chosen time (determined by the doctor, not the patient), and generally in an institution (a hospice, hospital or nursing home), the dying patient will be given strong pain relief (usually intravenous morphine) and a sleep-inducing sedative (usually midazolam). The plan is simple. The doctor starts by administering a low dose of morphine. A few hours later this is reviewed. On finding that the heavily sedated, sleeping patient is still 'in pain', the dose of morphine is increased.

Several hours later the process is repeated and so on it goes until, inevitably, lethal levels of morphine are reached and the patient dies. With luck, the patient will sleep through the entire procedure. The incremental process is absolutely necessary if the practice is to go unquestioned. The key word is *gradual* – gradual increases in the amount of morphine administered, and a gradual death, over a period of days.

If the doctor simply gave one large lethal dose of morphine 'for the patient's pain', there would be no defence for the doctor. The doctor needs to be able to demonstrate that the morphine is being adjusted – 'titrated' – to meet the patient's pain needs. A slow euthanasia death may take a week or more. In institutions, a number of medical teams may be involved in the assessment and the determination of morphine levels. This further clouds the link between cause and effect and further protects the doctors.

That is how it works, and this is what you should know:

- No one will ever clearly state that slow euthanasia is happening or is being used to bring about death. Doctors speak obliquely, referring to 'making the patient comfortable in the last stages', and patients and their families must play the game.

- Slow euthanasia will be *slow* (that is, it will take some time before death is brought about). The slower the death, the safer it is for the doctor.
- Morphine (or some other analgesic) will be the drug used to bring about death.
- The doctor will be in control. Doctors will determine if slow euthanasia is to be initiated, when, and how long the process will take.

Norma Hall's story

I met Norma Hall for the first time in August 2000. She had contacted me soon after being diagnosed with lung cancer. Married to a Canberra academic and mother to three adult children, Norma was an independent, strong-willed woman who knew her mind. From her cliff-top home in Coogee, she had come to accept her illness as her fate. What she wanted was control over when and how she died.

At our first meeting, Norma asked about her options. She joined Exit and requested a subsequent clinic visit. At that visit she asked about lethal drugs and we talked about slow euthanasia but she showed little interest in it. However, four months later when she again contacted me, her position had changed and she asked specifically about it. What had happened in the meantime was that despite Norma's two daughters pledging to secure the drugs she would need if she were to suicide, Norma had decided she could not expose them to any legal risk. Norma felt that, with current laws, slow euthanasia was her best option, and she wanted me to make this happen. But this was no easy request. I could not become Norma's treating doctor without upsetting the whole constabulary of palliative care professionals that were now involved in her care. And, as an outspoken doctor on one's right to die, I knew any interest I expressed in Norma's case would attract close attention. The Kevin Andrews bill was still fresh in all our minds. So I agreed to advise Norma, not as her doctor, but as a friend, and to not advise her on suicide, but on the best way of initiating the process of pain relief that would put an end to her life.

What had been intended as only a five-day visit to Sydney turned into a stay of almost three weeks, as no one could have foreseen the difficulties we were to encounter. When I had agreed to support Norma's request and advise her on how to obtain slow euthanasia, I naïvely thought that this would not be hard. How wrong I was.

To get the ball rolling, I rang Norma's treating specialists at the Prince of Wales Hospital in Sydney. Her oncologist, Dr David Goldstein, was not pleased to hear from me and was even less pleased with Norma for requesting my involvement. It was clear from our conversation that he would not help. He claimed there were other treatment options that Norma had not yet tried and he expected her to give them a go. Norma, however, was quite adamant that she didn't want any more treatment. She had had enough of hospitals and of her disease. The vomiting, the diarrhoea and the constant pain she experienced had dragged her down and she wanted out. And she wanted to die in a way that would cause the least trouble – by slow euthanasia in her own home. She wanted to be sedated until she died. She wanted to die in her sleep, peacefully.

Norma's request for slow euthanasia reflected the reality of the day. If the ROTI Act had still been in operation, Norma would have easily satisfied the criteria. She could have flown to Darwin, undertaken the required consultations, obtained the signatures, completed the cooling-off period and returned to Sydney, lethal drugs in hand. She could have taken the drugs, if and when she wanted to. But in the absence of any VE law, the questionable practice of slow euthanasia was her only legal option.

There are very few people who request slow euthanasia outright. Almost no one comes to an Exit clinic saying 'Doc, I want to spend four days dying'. When people make the decision that it's time to die, they want a swift and peaceful process. But that wasn't on offer for Norma. At the time, I thought that Norma's experience would advance the debate on VE and would be useful in explaining the practice of slow euthanasia to the public. I talked to Norma about this and re-established contact with ABC journalist, Murray McLaughlin.

McLaughlin was well versed on the right-to-die issue, having filmed stories for *Four Corners* about Max Bell and Esther Wild and he was keen to come to Sydney to film Norma's story, this time for the *7.30 Report*. Over a period of a week Murray followed the negotiations that were taking place, interviewing Norma and filming when she wrote an open letter about why she had requested slow euthanasia:

I, Norma Hall,

suffering from lung cancer that has spread through my body, intend to end my life by stopping eating and drinking.

I ask my doctors to take away some of the suffering I may have to endure with appropriate sedatives.

This is my own decision made freely and without pressure from family, friends, or treating doctors.

On camera Norma handed this letter to Professor Peter Baume, the patron of the VE Society of New South Wales and chancellor of the Australian National University. Baume was once federal health minister and explained the issues as he saw them clearly. He was supportive of Norma throughout this period.

To make it clear that Norma was of sound mind, I organised a private psychiatric consultation with Dr Rod Milton. His review confirmed the opinion of Prince of Wales Hospital staff psychiatrist Dr Richard Perkins. Norma was mentally fit and her request to die was, therefore, a rational one. In addition to organising consultations with the specialists, I visited Norma's Coogee GP, Dr Chris Eliades. I could have stated and restated the fact that slow euthanasia is legal – this GP would still have declined to act. He simply did not want to be involved. Next, I contacted Norma's palliative care team. Norma had been seen by palliative care nurses, then by a palliative care registrar, and eventually by department head Dr Richard Chye. The meeting between Norma, her family, Dr Chye, the nurses and myself was strained. Chye made it very clear that slow euthanasia was *not* an option that Norma could request. Her plan to initiate the suffering necessary to prompt sedation by refusing food and drink was also flatly turned down. She could stop drinking, she was told, but there was no guarantee the doctor would treat this induced suffering with the necessary terminal medication. Norma's experience confirms the rhetoric–reality gap noted by Roger Hunt of so-called patient-centred palliative care medicine.

It was becoming clear that my attempt to facilitate Norma's slow euthanasia was floundering. With the media involved, no medical professional wanted to be seen to grant Norma the death she so desired. This is another characteristic of the practice. Slow euthanasia invariably goes on behind closed doors, with a nod and a wink. And that's just the way many doctors like it. It is the medical practice that dare not speak its name. Slow euthanasia is common, but as soon as it is named or requested by the patient, the cone of silence comes into effect.

Finally, Norma stopped eating and drinking, and then took matters into her own hands. For her pain, Norma had been prescribed oral liquid morphine by her palliative care doctors. She had a new 200 mL bottle and asked me whether she would die if she drank the lot. At around 10 p.m. on 18 January 2001, with goodbyes to family said, she wrote a last letter and drank the entire morphine bottle. It was her decision alone. And it was her act of desperation:

> 18 January 2001
> I would like the end of my life to come by drinking my morphine.

Being off food and fluids is much too slow. It has been something over a week already.

Best wishes,

Norma Hall

As is so often the case with morphine, Norma did not die straight away. At 8 a.m. the following morning, though deeply unconscious, she was still breathing and we decided to call the palliative care doctor. There was no other choice. We could not just sit there, waiting until Norma's breathing stopped. On examining Norma, Dr Chye stated blankly that he did not think it appropriate to attempt resuscitation. Later that morning, Norma died. The police soon arrived and the house was quickly taped off as a possible crime scene. Daughter Julia, a lawyer, took charge.

The *7.30 Report* ran Murray McLaughlin's story on Norma the next Monday, and a debate on slow euthanasia followed on the Tuesday night. The *Sydney Morning Herald* devoted its front page to Norma's death the next day. The police began their investigation, requesting interviews and asking questions of family members and myself. Late in 2001, the New South Wales coroner dropped the investigation.

Norma Hall wanted to undergo slow euthanasia because it would not place her children in any legal jeopardy. Neither she nor I expected that her end-of-life plans would be frustrated in the cruel ways they were. Her death did, however, bring to the public's attention in a most profound way the details of the bizarre medical practice called slow euthanasia.

I agree completely with people having end-of-life choices. They should be the right of every responsible human being. I formed this idea in theory (via reading and writing about human rights) and in practice from watching my mother take thirteen days to die of starvation after she had a stroke.

In regard to Exit's DIY approaches, I deplore the fact that these 'technologies' are necessary because of the perversity of the law. In the circumstances I think that (a) they are effective, and (b) they help to draw attention to the need for the law to be changed. Most people are pro–voluntary euthanasia. Why should the prejudices of a few determine its unavailability?

– Dr Dale Spender AM: author, feminist, educational futures thinker and researcher, and all-round boundary pusher

Slow euthanasia and the medical profession

For many within the medical establishment, slow euthanasia is normally the only type of killing that is palatable. The reasons are understandable and logical. Slow euthanasia is safe for doctors to practise because it keeps them well within our current moral and legal frameworks. Treating pain is, after all, the core business of a palliative care doctor.

It seems ludicrous that as long as doctors chant – in mantra-like fashion – that they are treating a patient's pain, then they run very little legal risk. If doctors dare to be honest, however, they can expect to experience the full force of the law. While we might be critical of doctors who practise slow euthanasia, we do well to remember that that they are caught between a rock and a hard place.

The doctrine of double effect, a doctrine which is enshrined in the current version of the Hippocratic oath, remains the only real means doctors have to safely skirt bad laws that prevent people from seeking a death at a time of their own choosing. These bad laws force doctors into what, in any other profession, would be considered unconscionable conduct. This is *not* the fault of the medical profession. It *is* the fault of politicians.

In the United Kingdom in recent years there have been several celebrated cases where doctors have called upon the doctrine of double effect to avoid prosecution. Given that some 100 000 deaths a year in the UK are believed to be hastened by the double-effect loophole, it is not surprising that some of these cases have made it to the courts.[4] One of these occurred in 1999 when Dr David Moor was charged with murder after helping a patient, George Liddell, to die. George was eighty-five years old and seriously ill with cancer. Moor admitted in a media interview within days of George's death that he had administered slow euthanasia to him. At his trial, Moor's line of defence was that he had not intended to kill George. Rather, the huge dose of morphine he administered was only supposed to address George's pain.[5] The jury took sixty-nine minutes to acquit him.[6] David Moor is one of a number of doctors in the UK and elsewhere who has admitted publicly to practising slow euthanasia. Without such a confession, however, it is rare for a doctor to be 'caught out'.

In Australia, another instance of this type of admission being made publicly was in an open letter published in *The Age* on 25 March 1995. On this occasion seven Melbourne doctors wrote to the then premier of Victoria, Jeff Kennett. The

doctors who penned this important letter were general practitioners Norm Roth, Darren Russell and Andrew Buchanan;
cancer specialist David Bernshaw; urologist Rodney Syme;
anaesthetist Pat Scrivener; and the now late GP Sam Benwell.
In the letter, each doctor admitted to having broken the law
by deliberately hastening death using morphine. All argued the
need for law reform:

> Each of us who has signed this letter has personal experi-
> ence of treating terminally ill people whose condition has
> moved them to ask for assistance in suicide, and each of
> us has, on occasion, after deep thought and lengthy discus-
> sion, helped such a patient to die.
>
> We declare this now in public, knowing that this
> declaration may be construed in the State of Victoria as
> an admission of a criminal offence. We do this because we
> believe passionately that this State's law on the assistance
> of suicide is wrong, and because those who continue to
> support the law have failed to recognise the reality of our
> work.
>
> The assistance of suicide by doctors is already a recur-
> rent reality in the State of Victoria. We have assisted
> patients to end their lives and we know others who have.
> We believe we have acted in the best tradition of medical
> ethics, offering our patients relief from pain and suffering
> in circumstances when it would have been an act of cruelty
> to deny them.
>
> We respect life. All of our professional training and
> work deepens that respect. However, the reality is that

there are some patients who are beset by physical and mental suffering which is beyond the reach of even our most sophisticated efforts at control. When such patients clearly and repeatedly express a rational plea for help, it is out of respect for them that we have felt compelled to act.

What was the outcome of this letter? Well, there was almost no outcome. In the course of that week, Jeff Kennett stated that he would not act unless the majority of doctors in Victoria wanted him to do so. At the time, Kennett was being lauded as 'the nation's most high profile supporter of euthanasia'.[7] Yet when the Voluntary Euthanasia Society of Victoria approached the AMA with an offer to share the costs of conducting a State-wide survey to answer Kennett's question, the chairman of the Victorian AMA Council, Dr Clyde Scaife, rejected the offer. When the Victorian Medical Practitioners Board failed to take action against these seven doctors the issue died, as is so often the case with attempts at law reform.

Incidentally, when Jeff Kennett was approached for an interview for this book, he declined because he stated in an email that he does not agree with the way I have conducted the debate.[8] It seems *Age* journalist Ewin Hannan was right when, in 1997, he wrote 'social reformers should not hold their breath waiting for Jeff Kennett to act'.

In the absence of a VE law, slow euthanasia continues behind closed doors, unacknowledged by our politicians and doctors alike. However, things could be set to change if a 2001 court case in the United States is anything to go by. In a landmark decision, a California jury awarded $1 000 000 compensation to the family of a California man after finding that his doctor was negligent in treating the patient's pain. Commentators have noted that this decision has set a precedent, at least in the US, as it is the first time a jury has 'determined that inadequate treatment of pain translates into abuse of an elderly person'.[9] Death by omission may well become just as legally risky as death by commission.

While Australia does not share America's litigious culture, this decision may impact upon the way in which a request for hastened death is dealt with in the future. And, paradoxically, it may just improve one's chances of getting access to the dubious practice of slow euthanasia.

To all the senators who voted in favour of the Andrews euthanasia bill: you disgust me. You have shown that in Australia, as in the United States, the 'moral majority' is on the rise.

You seek to impose your religious and moral beliefs upon the wider community. You missed the point. You can't stop me gassing myself, or driving my car off a cliff. It's my life and I will control it, thanks very much.

All you have done is to remove a humane and merciful option. In doing so, you have run rough-shod over public opinion and the rights of the individual. Thanks to your vote, euthanasia will continue to be practised in secrecy every day in every major hospital in Australia.

When society matures further, a euthanasia law will be passed. As with most issues, I doubt that Australia will be in the vanguard of change.

– Letter to the Editor, *Sydney Morning Herald*, 25 March 1997[10]

The plight of Esther Wild

Darwin woman Esther Wild qualified for, but narrowly missed, the opportunity to use the Northern Territory's ROTI Act. Esther first contacted me in January 1997. She was dying of carcinoid syndrome, which is a rare form of bowel cancer. Having spent her working life as a nurse, Esther was under no illusions about what lay ahead of her. She was plagued by ongoing vomiting and diarrhoea. When I met her, she looked frail and emaciated. Esther knew she was wasting away.

With partner Martin Williams at her side, Esther asked for my help to use the ROTI law if and when the time came. But she didn't want to die immediately. Esther was an avid gardener and very much wanted to watch her Humpty Doo garden – in Darwin's rural area – spring into action as that year's Wet came to an end, just one more time. By contacting me when she did, Esther was simply planning ahead.

As with all of my patients who used the law, Esther had to undergo a number of tests and consultations in order to qualify. These would demonstrate (a) that she was terminally ill; (b) that she had had palliative care; (c) that she was not mentally ill or depressed; and (d) that she had to undertake the mandatory cooling-off period.

Several weeks passed and Esther completed the consultations and tests. Yes, she was dying; had had palliative care options explained; was not mad; and had undergone the mandatory cooling-off period. When Esther eventually qualified, it was the happiest I'd seen her for months. And this is one of the upsides of having a law. Laws provide choice, and choice gives dying people options: options that can make them a whole lot happier in their final days.

By March, Esther's health was deteriorating rapidly but she wanted to hang on. She was well aware of the risks she was running. The time was drawing near for the Senate's vote on the Kevin Andrews bill, a bill that would ultimately strip her of the choice she had fought for. She was in a catch-22 situation. On the one hand, Esther did not want to be forced into dying prematurely, before she was ready. On the other, she did not want to miss her window of legal opportunity.

Esther, however, was quietly confident that even if the Senate did pass the Andrews bill, it would make an exception for her to use the ROTI law, given that she had already qualified. With the assistance of Greens Senator Bob Brown, Esther tried to gain this assurance, writing to all Senators, outlining her situation. She requested that they let her follow through with her plans. But only one Senator bothered to reply. That person was Democrat Natasha Stott Despoja. Bob Brown then tried to move an amendment to the Kevin Andrews bill that would still allow Esther to use the law.

Senate Hansard, Parliament House Australia, 26 March 1997

SENATOR BROWN (Tasmania) (Midnight) – The letters columns in today's newspaper started to reflect the feeling of the Australian people about the failure of this parliament to uphold the voluntary euthanasia laws. I do not wish to hold the chamber for long at this point but I have circulated –

SENATOR CHRIS ELLISON – Why not; you've done it all week. You're a disgrace.

SENATOR BROWN – The honourable senator...I want to incorporate into *Hansard* the page of letters in today's *Sydney Morning Herald* published under the heading 'Senate's night of shame'. I seek leave, having circulated this page, to have it so incorporated.

Leave granted...

SENATOR BOB BROWN – The letters speak for themselves. They are a consistent barrage of vitriol, disappointment and disgust with the fact that the rights of individuals in this country have been overridden by a majority of people in this parliament not reflecting what the people themselves think...

SENATOR KAY PATTERSON – I find that offensive; you are appalling.

SENATOR BOB BROWN – You may find that offensive, but I find what you did offensive in the extreme. The difference between you, Senator Patterson, and me – through you, Madam President – is that I have not voted to override the right of individuals. If you want to get up to defend your position, you do so, but I stand here on the point I take and I stand defiant of your point of view.

ALP Senator Bob Collins spoke passionately of Esther's right to follow through with her use of the law. I've long admired Collins' commitment to arguing this on Esther's behalf, especially given his hostility to VE legislation. But it was not to be. The ROTI Act was overturned and the Brown amendment was lost. In a last desperate effort, Esther wrote to the then Governor-General, Sir William Deane. In that letter she begged Deane not to ratify the bill until after the impending Easter holiday. Esther thought that way she would have the four days of Easter to use the law. But Esther hadn't counted on Deane's strong Catholic convictions. Like a good Catholic, Deane signed the bill at 4 p.m. the day before Good Friday. Esther couldn't believe it and neither could I. And we found it gutless of Deane to pass it off onto his press secretary to call Esther to inform her of his decision.

While most people think Sir William Deane was an admirable Governor-General and a fine, upstanding human being – especially where human rights are concerned – I believe this act of weakness detracts from his integrity. And I can well understand why Esther's partner Martin Williams confronted Deane with such vigour on one of Deane's subsequent vice-regal trips to Darwin. Pushing through a throng of people outside the Darwin Art Gallery, blue-singlet-clad Martin yelled, 'You bastard, you're the one who didn't have the guts to help my Esther have a decent death.' Deane was shaken and Martin was roughly shuffled sideways by security. I looked on, glad that Martin had had the chance to confront Deane with his heartfelt and deeply personal experience. Martin did this because Esther did *not* have a good death. Rather, she died by slow euthanasia – the only option left to her by the Senate. And I narrowly avoided prosecution for my role in her passing.

With the ROTI Act overturned and very few options available to her, Esther had little choice but to undertake the gradual process of slow euthanasia. By then I was officially her treating doctor. Esther was lucky in that she was able to stay in her own home. This was made possible by the help of a number of close nursing friends. For most people, the logistics and expense of slow euthanasia at home means it is often an impracticable option.

With Esther's time drawing near, I tried to involve other doctors in her request for slow euthanasia. None wanted to know about it. But Steve Baddeley, the Darwin orthopaedic surgeon who had courageously helped Janet Mills a few months earlier, agreed to see Esther and help share the responsibility. The image of Steve driving his new sports car along the rough bush track to Esther's home in Humpty Doo has stayed vivid in my mind. But there is nothing pretentious about this man. His commitment to Esther, and previously to Janet Mills, impressed me enormously. Steve Baddeley is a man of integrity and a doctor I respect greatly.

Esther's slow euthanasia process began at around 10 a.m. The plan was that she would be given gradually increased doses of morphine. The claimed 'aim' would be that we were alleviating her pain. The expected outcome of the treatment was that Esther would die. She would remain unconscious until she died and, while not ideal, it was acceptable to her. As Esther herself knew all too well, she had run out of options. If only this plan had worked.

Esther turned on the tap on the cannula that I had inserted into her arm and as the drugs flowed, she quickly lost consciousness. But I was soon alarmed at how much morphine was needed. Her long illness had made her emaciated body surprisingly resistant to the drug. When she was sedated and deeply asleep, Esther's nursing friends took over, keeping a watchful eye on the drugs and expecting to turn her every few hours. Yet I swiftly found myself running out of morphine. When it became obvious that we would soon be out altogether, I dashed home to collect more of the drug. On my return, I couldn't believe my eyes. As I walked into the house, far from finding Esther prostrate and in a deep sleep, she was sitting up in bed, smoking a cigarette. I could hear her friends clattering about in the kitchen.

I approached the bed with enormous trepidation, whispering to myself 'Oh my God, oh my God'. Esther had said her goodbyes to everyone and waking up was definitely not part of the plan. I finally stuttered, 'What happened?' She replied quickly, and with a hint of humour, 'You fucked it up, didn't you?' At that moment her friend Cathy came in and explained that while I was gone, the drip had tissued (blocked) and that they had been unable to get it restarted. The whole process would need to begin again. With a new batch of morphine now secure by her bedside, Esther repeated her goodbyes, hugged Martin and, with the cannula positioned in the other arm, the process was started again. As I watched, I remember clearly thinking, This process has got nothing to do with medicine; this process is an obscenity.

As the hours passed into days, I thought that finally, Esther would not wake up. Yet in the middle of the second night I was awoken, this time by Cathy's whispered plea, 'Philip – get in here.' Again the drip had blocked, and Esther was waking. In her semiconscious state she recognised her friend, asking, 'Cathy, have I died? Am I dead yet?' There was no choice other than to continue administering the morphine. I relocated the needle as fast as I could before she fully regained consciousness.

This is what slow euthanasia means. This is the death our politicians had condemned Esther to. By day three, Esther was still alive and Martin was getting increasingly agitated by her plight. He demanded repeatedly, 'Just give me the bloody drugs. If you don't do something, I'll bloody do it.' It took all my powers of persuasion to stop him from taking the law into his own hands. If I stuck to the protocol, I was protected. Martin was not.

Finally, on day four, Esther died. The ordeal that should never have taken place was finally over. And I was left to reflect on the comparison between the quick, painless death available to the four people who used the ROTI Act, and the slow, macabre process Esther had to endure. There *is* no comparison.

Again, the ABC covered the death. Murray McLaughlin had filmed the time leading up to Esther's passing. His production, 'The Dying Game', appeared on *Four Corners*. Again, the power of the program was significant, and letters of dismay and anger poured in to newspapers around the country. For the first time, many Australians realised just what their Federal Parliament had done. 'How could a civilised country allow this to happen?' people asked. I still don't have that answer.

Exactly one year ago today, my husband died from lung cancer that had spread to the right side of his brain. He had never smoked in his life, and prior to this was always fit and well. He suffered unsuccessful surgery for the tumour in his lung and this left him with many painful side effects. He also had an unsuccessful radical combination of radiation and chemotherapy treatment. When it became clear that the lung cancer was terminal, he told me he was going to commit suicide. He thought it was just a matter of driving off somewhere, connecting a hose to the exhaust of the car and switching on the engine.

We attended one of Philip's Exit workshops and it soon became clear that it was not that easy – modern cars have cleaner exhaust, and the possibility existed of the attempted suicide failing and my husband ending up in a vegetative state. This was at the time when Nancy Crick had ended her life and the police where threatening her friends and raiding Philip's office and taking his computers, etc.

I suggested that if my husband chose to use a sleeping pill and Exit Bag to end his life, I would lie in his arms until he had gone, then go to my own room and come in in the morning and 'discover' his body. But he could not bear the thought of my having to do this, or that I might have trouble with the police, and therefore chose to sacrifice himself to conventional slow euthanasia in hospital.

He apologised to me several times during the course of his illness for causing me so much trouble. This was heartbreaking, as I would have done anything for him without regard to the consequences. Over the course of several months, I watched my tall, proud, handsome husband die by inches, subjected to every indignity that he had so hoped to avoid. The brain tumour caused him to become paralysed all down his left side, and he could not move, speak or write. My only memory of him now is lying in a hospital bed with his mouth hanging open from the effects of morphine and his eyes glazed over.

I know there were things he wanted to tell me because he would try to write but all he could manage was my name, and then the writing just became a scribble. Now I will never know what he wanted to say. Had a Peaceful Pill been available (preferably legally) for him, this fine man would have been able to make the dignified exit that he deserved, instead of a horrible, long, drawn-out death forced on him by current legislation. I curse any politician who lets the Church or any other pressure group prevent people from making a free choice.

– Melody Stewart, eighty-seven years, 20 January 2004

We *can* do better

For doctors of integrity, there is little difference between killing by omission (passive euthanasia) and killing by commission (active euthanasia). This point was well made by the world-famous heart transplant pioneer Dr Christian Barnard. More than twenty years ago, Barnard argued that 'when death is the goal or purpose sought', the two acts (passive/active) are 'morally indistinguishable' and 'ethically they are the same'.[11]

But the law in Australia does not agree. According to the law, there is a difference; a difference that can be enforced. While doctors might not be keen to expose the hypocrisy of slow euthanasia, academics such as Sharon Fraser and James Walter of Loma Linda University in California are. Writing in the *Journal of Medical Ethics*, these researchers suggested that the 'double effect' should really mean 'double standard'.[12] Is slow euthanasia intentional killing or isn't it? This medical emperor clearly has no clothes.

In a recent edition of *Nursing Standard*, Janice Moody, a lecturer at Napier University in Edinburgh, has argued that traditional attitudes towards euthanasia need to be reviewed, starting with an acknowledgement that intentionally letting someone die and helping someone to die by active means are morally and legally the same.[13] Moody argues powerfully for honesty to become part of a medical doctor's toolkit.

In my mind, however, transparency will not be possible as long as the artificial distinction between active and passive euthanasia is maintained, at both a philosophical and practical level. We all need to come clean. Melbourne broadcaster Neil Mitchell is one commentator who has sought to expose this hypocrisy. In an interview on his morning radio show in 2001 with the then vice-president of the AMA, Dr Trevor Mudge, Mitchell took Mudge to task:

MITCHELL: . . . a survey reported today that shows that one-fifth of the nation's . . . or more than one-fifth of Australia's surgeons effectively indulge in euthanasia . . . On the line is the Vice-President of the Australian Medical Association, the Ethics Committee Chairman, Trevor Mudge. Good morning.

MUDGE: Good morning, Neil.

MITCHELL: You don't trust the findings. Why not? . . .

MUDGE: It's not euthanasia. What the surgeons are saying in response to the questionnaire is that there have been times when they have given treatment to relieve pain or improve the quality of remaining life in a terminally ill patient, and that that treatment has had the effect of shortening the patient's life.

MITCHELL: And why is that not euthanasia?

MUDGE: It's a matter of the primary intent. It's exactly the same difference as between murder and manslaughter . . .

MITCHELL: But that is really semantic, isn't it? I mean, would you really doubt that there are regular occurrences of doctors prescribing, whether it be pain-killers – I suppose it is usually pain-killers – prescribing pain-killers to a level they know – they *know* – will hasten death?

MUDGE: No, I wouldn't deny that for a minute . . .

MITCHELL: Okay, well, this is the point of it. People have been denying it.

MUDGE: That's right and proper, because no, what they're doing is improving the quality of that patient's life knowing that it will shorten the time-course of it. And that's good medical treatment.

MITCHELL: But that . . . to shorten from days to minutes. I mean, that happens, doesn't it?

MUDGE: No, I don't think it does at all. I don't think . . .

MITCHELL: You really don't?

MUDGE: No, no, I don't. I absolutely don't.

MITCHELL: I'm astounded . . .

MUDGE: The principle is one of improving quality of life, and not taking it. And I think that if, in improving the quality of life, we shorten it, then that's a secondary effect. It's not a primary intention . . .

MITCHELL: See, I think it is an issue because I believe it is one of the great undiscussed issues of this world . . . I can't believe the number of doctors I speak to privately who admit to me that it regularly goes on . . . But nobody will actually stand up and admit it publicly . . .

MUDGE: They are talking to you of examples where treatment they have given has shortened life. No question. But they're not . . .

MITCHELL: Deliberately.

MUDGE: . . . talking about . . .

MITCHELL: Deliberately. They see somebody suffering, they know, 'If I give them this extra morphine' . . .

MUDGE: Their suffering will be reduced.

MITCHELL: What, by dying earlier?

MUDGE: No, by the treatment given . . .

MITCHELL: Well, I disagree, and I think a lot of people would have seen it happen and would disagree . . . [14]

In this interview, as in others, the AMA promotes a professional double-speak based on the principle of double effect: of intention versus effect and all that grey area in between. With a professional association so wrapped up in maintaining slow euthanasia as acceptable, it is little wonder that doctors want their actions kept out of sight. Like Exit member Melody Stewart, I too curse any politician who lets the Church or any other pressure group like the AMA prevent people from making their own end-of-life choices.

> I am a supporter of end-of-life choices. My mother lingered on with uterine cancer for nearly a year of pain. The night she was death-rattling the rest of the family couldn't bear it, and had to leave. So I got into the bed with her and rocked her while she died. It shouldn't have happened that way.
>
> – John Bryson, author of *Evil Angels* and *To the Death, Amic*

The future looks bleak

After four years of the AMA trying to have me deregistered as a doctor, the association finally invited me to speak at their annual conference in Canberra in 2002. For the conference I was scheduled to take part in a debate with the Professor of Medical Ethics from Canada's McGill University, Australian expatriate lawyer, Professor Margaret Somerville. After the debate, AMA members would be asked to vote on whether or not they would support a 'neutral' position on the issue of voluntary euthanasia. This would see the AMA adopting the same position for VE that they currently have for abortion. And it would mean that the AMA recognises that, like abortion, VE is an issue for the individual to decide, and not one that the profession should be imposing their views on.

The motion that the AMA adopt a neutral position on VE was defeated seventy-nine votes to thirty-four. The group could not bring itself to do it. They still could not relinquish the conviction that it is doctors who should make up society's mind on this issue. The reluctance of the AMA to engage with the VE issue became even clearer at the post-conference press gathering on the Sunday afternoon. With the journalists trying to get a toe-hold of an understanding, the association's officers took pride in preventing them from infiltrating the semantics of primary and secondary intent and effect that permeate the VE issue. I felt sorry for the enquiring minds who were trying to make sense of the barrage of words and theories that masqueraded as replies to some fairly insightful questions. With the anti-euthanasia Somerville running the AMA party line, the press conference exposed the complacency of the association and its ready acceptance of the status quo. Given the AMA's hostility to all forms of euthanasia, the hypocrisy of the widespread practice of slow euthanasia seems unlikely to change.

While in some countries medical associations have sought to create guidelines that attempt to clarify the murky division between palliative care and slow euthanasia, the debate in Australia is one that the AMA would prefer to just go away.[15] Meanwhile, the seriously ill are left with few end-of-life options. Doctors who would like to help patients end their suffering have to do so in ways that patients often don't want, or they must take the inevitable serious legal risks.

In Exit's recent Peace in a Pill report, less than 1 per cent of the people surveyed said that they would prefer to die using slow euthanasia than any of the other methods listed (for example, the Peaceful Pill, or traditional drugs such as Doloxene). What this means is that slow euthanasia is one of the least preferred methods of death when a range of options is given. Provided with a choice, people almost always prefer dignity and control over the travesty of the human spirit that is slow euthanasia. In this regard, no one wants to spend the last hours and days of their otherwise proud lives in a drug-induced stupor – humiliated, demeaned and out of control. When people decide that their suffering is so great that they want to die, they want this to happen quickly. So let us be clear.

Slow euthanasia has absolutely nothing to do with medicine or good patient care. Rather, it has everything to do with skirting bad law. In the current legal climate, it is the only way a caring doctor can safely help a dying patient. And while we may be critical of those doctors who provide this form of assistance, we should remember that they are using the only safe means they can to help. The fault clearly lies with the politicians and legislators that leave in place laws that provide such a loophole. When patients are desperate enough, and nothing else is on offer, they will, of course, grasp this straw. But we can do better.

Chapter 7

Tired of Life

> The great, usually unexpressed, worry of many old people is that there will come a moment for them where they can no longer look after themselves in the most elementary aspects of life because of physical or mental decline. It seems to me an essential obligation for society in which the number of old people increases very strongly, to take away that threat.
> – Huib Drion, Dutch Supreme Court Justice, 1917–2004[1]

Providing end-of-life options for those who are seriously ill, with no hope of recovery, has long been Exit's aim. However, in addition to the seriously ill, there is a growing number of elderly Australians for whom the right to die is of utmost importance. These people are not sick. They simply believe they have reached a stage in life when they are ready to die. In this chapter I introduce you to these people: those who want not only to be well informed about death and dying, but to be equipped with real and practical choices. One of these people was 79-year-old Lisette Nigot, the subject of the feature-length documentary film *Mademoiselle and the Doctor*:

I don't like the deterioration of my body . . . I don't like not being able to do the things I used to be able to do . . . and I don't like the discrepancy there is between the mind, which remains what it always was, and the body, which is sort of physically deteriorating.

Perhaps my mind will go and I would hate that. And certainly my body will go and I wouldn't be very happy with that either. So I might as well go while the going is good.[2]

For some time now, my daily work at Exit has made me aware of the increasing need among older people to have end-of-life choices available if they decide they are tired of life. However, I think my eyes were only really opened to this when I came across the writings of the late Dutch judge, Huib Drion. More than a decade ago, Drion wrote a letter to the editor of the Dutch newspaper *NRC/Handelsblad*. Drion bemoaned the fact that while his doctor friends would know what to do and how to access the right drugs when the time came, he did not. He questioned the logic of why he, a retired judge, should not have the same knowledge and the same ready access to a peaceful death as his friends.

In writing the letter, Drion opened a can of worms. His ideas struck a chord among readers and generated hundreds of letters in response. It seems there was something to be said for Drion's innocent-enough question.[3] Why should older people, of sound mind, be denied end-of-life choices to enable their suicide just because they do not share the knowledge and the privileges of doctors or vets? Drion's writings and my subsequent

Above Philip in the Faraday cage of the physics laboratory at Flinders University in the early 1970s

Below left Max Bell in Darwin, 1996, shortly before having to drive his cab back to Broken Hill after being unable to use the Rights of the Terminally Ill (ROTI) Act

Below right Bob Dent, the first person to use the ROTI Act, when he still had a life worth living

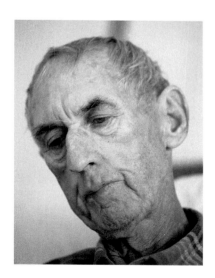

Above Philip at Parliament House, Canberra, burning the *Rights of the Terminally Ill Act 1995* and the Constitution of the Northern Territory as a symbolic protest in the early hours of 24 March 1997, after the Act had been overturned by the Senate

Opposite top Marching with the Western Australian Voluntary Euthanasia Society at a pro-voluntary euthanasia rally in Perth, September 2002

Inset Kevin Andrews – the politician responsible for the private member's bill that would eventually overturn the ROTI Act

Opposite below Philip with former Northern Territory chief minister Marshall Perron on Bob Dent Memorial Day, 22 September 2004, Maroochydore, Queensland

Above Nancy Crick and Philip at a voluntary euthanasia public meeting on the Gold Coast, shortly before her death in May 2002

Below Bottles of Nembutal purchased by Exit on a trip to Mexico in January 2004

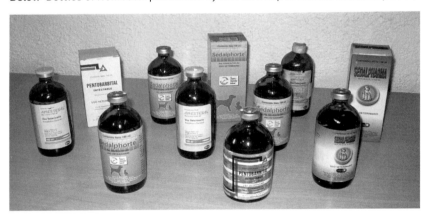

Opposite top Philip with Lesley Martin outside the Wanganui Courthouse in New Zealand, during her trial for the attempted murder of her mother, July 2004. Lesley was found guilty and served seven months of a fifteen-month jail sentence

Opposite centre Philip talking with Lisette Nigot (the subject of the documentary film *Mademoiselle and the Doctor* by Janine Hosking), December 2002

Opposite below Philip with motor neurone disease sufferer Sandy Williamson at her home in Melbourne, July 2002

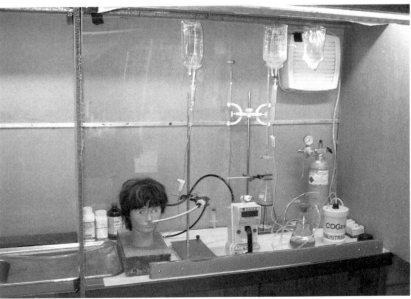

Top Exit members inspecting the CoGenie at Exit's national conference in Sydney, May 2003

Above The Exit laboratory fume cupboard

Above Philip holding the original laptop Deliverance Machine, now on display in the British Science Museum

Below Exit's first practical workshop, held on the Gold Coast in October 2003

Above Philip shaking hands with the then AMA president Kerryn Phelps at the association's national conference in Canberra, May 2002

Below Philip with co-author Dr Fiona Stewart

conversations with him at his home in Holland are the inspiration for much of my thinking in this book. They have helped me make sense of the needs of the older, relatively well Australians who join Exit every day. Huib Drion has assisted me enormously in gaining a future perspective into ageing, and the need for end-of-life choices to be much more widely available. The news of his death in April 2004 at age eighty-seven was cause for sadness and reflection.

A short history of suicide

Suicide is generally defined as the act of deliberately taking your own life. The act of suicide is morally laden and subject to extensive social censure. With few exceptions, suicide is seen as a negative and destructive act. Anyone who seeks information about suicide can find their motives or their mental health called into question. This is why the quest for information about suicide – the ability to choose the place and timing of one's death – remains a closeted affair. Yet the annals of history show our dismay about suicide to be a relatively recent phenomenon. To fully understand suicide, knowledge of its history is essential.

Over the centuries, the ways in which suicide has been viewed and understood by different societies has varied enormously. Indeed, it has not always been seen negatively, nor has it always been associated with the depressed or mentally ill. Before Christianity's influence spread through Western society, self-destruction was more often considered a virtue than a sin. In Egyptian society, for example, suicide was a neutral event.

Death was simply seen as a passage from one form of existence to another. Self-destruction was considered a humane way of escaping intolerable hardship and injustice.[4] In ancient Greece, Athenian magistrates kept a supply of poison for anyone in society who wanted to die. All that was needed was their official permission. In Roman times, suicide was only punishable under certain circumstances – for example, if it was irrational, or if it was used to escape prosecution.[5] For the Stoics, suicide was considered an appropriate response 'in accordance with nature' if pain, grave illness or physical abnormalities became too great.[6] However, they also believed that suicide should never be a rash act.[7] And the Stoics allowed suicide to be a part of the state-sanctioned execution process. The death of Socrates is a good example. In 399BC, Socrates was found guilty of corrupting the minds of Athenian youth. In front of a jury of 500, he was sentenced to death. History now tells us that 'Socrates' suicide was a triumph'.[8] A victim of a corrupt justice system, Socrates' execution by suicide led to great admiration of his bravery at standing up for his beliefs and not retracting his teachings. In each of these pre-Christian societies, suicide was more likely to be seen as the act of a martyr and as a rebellion against authority than the act of an immoral or mad person.

With the rise of Christianity, however, all this was to change. Suicide became universally condemned. It was Saint Augustine in the fifth century who first formed the Christian case against it. From this time, suicide was banned on the grounds that it violated the sixth commandment, 'Thou shalt not murder'.[9] (This is despite the fact, as Jesus proved, that you could be a martyr in your dying.) In her book *Leaving You*, Lisa Lieberman argues that Saint Augustine was responsible – almost single-handedly – for 'supplanting the Roman ideal of heroic individualism with a platonic concept of submission to divine authority'.[10] He turned suicide into a sin of the very worst kind. At this point in history, the posthumous punishment of the suicide also began.

Regardless of the reason behind the death, the families of those who suicided would usually have their belongings confiscated and their relative would be denied a Christian burial. Burial usually took place beside a public highway, or the body would be impaled on a stake in a public place.[11] In the French Ordinance of 1670 it was stated that the 'body was to be dragged face down through the streets on a hurdle and hanged by the feet as a public example'.[12] Although, according to the English law writer Henry de Bracton, if the suicide had resulted from 'weariness of life or impatience of pain' then the loss was limited to the goods of the family only.[13]

From the Renaissance to the eighteenth century, suicide was again given new meaning, with prominent scholars bravely publishing treatises against the Church's position. Best-known among these were those by Sir Thomas More, the English writer John Donne, and the Scottish philosopher David Hume. Hume wrote: 'When life has become a burden both courage and prudence should engage us to rid ourselves at once of existence'.[14] At the same time, however, French philosophers including Jean Jacques Rousseau and Alex de Tocqueville wrote that suicide was a sign of personal irresponsibility and a national failing respectively. Both saw suicide as a threat to communal solidarity.[15]

The late 1700s to the mid-1800s is known as the Romantic

period and suicide was again reinterpreted during this time. For the Romantics, especially the writers and the poets, suicide was a way by which to create their identities. Angst-ridden compositions were a precursor to the death of many a famous writer. Seventeen-year-old Thomas Chatterton is one of the best known of these. To this group of artists, death had a purpose and a goal. It could be the culmination of a career. While this acknowledgement of suicide did not apply to all classes or social groups, suicide was a 'marker of cultural refinement, the privilege of great lovers and gifted but fragile souls of the young and talented especially'. As such, suicide was a prominent theme in the books, poems and lives of writers and artists of this time.[16]

In France, the liberal attitude to suicide was largely a result of the Napoleonic Code that regarded civil liberties as a central tenet. However, after Napoleon's defeat at Waterloo in 1815, suicides and suicide survivors were again punished. As Glen Evans and Norman Farberow tellingly note in *The Encyclopedia of Suicide*, 'when liberty and democratic government reappeared, the rights of the suicide also reappeared and were respected'.[17]

The meaning of suicide changed again with the emergence of the profession of medicine in the nineteenth century. With new specialties such as psychiatry gaining a toehold, suicide was to prove a rich field of study. It was at this time that suicide first became linked – in a sustainable way – to mental illness and depression. The 'medicalisation' of suicide allowed the medical profession a powerful stranglehold over the ways in which suicide was understood by society. Viewed as either a sociological or a biological phenomenon, debate about suicide during this period oscillated between whether a person was born with a genetic predisposition to it, or whether the act was a reflection of our experience in the world – our alienation, or *anomie*, as French sociologist Emile Durkheim would have put it.

As history now shows, psychiatry proved a powerful and lasting force in the redefinition of suicide. Concepts such as personal autonomy, liberty, self-determination and free will – values cherished by contemporary Western society – became increasingly sidelined.[18] Medicine's interpretation of suicide still largely prevails today. If you want to kill yourself, you must be mentally unwell, and the illness needs to be treated – even in the case of those with a debilitating physical illness. This is also despite the fact that studies continue to show that 'sadness and despair are normal responses to the news that one is gravely ill'; that only one in five people who are seriously ill go on to develop major depression;[19] and that older Australians are less likely than other groups to suffer from depression.[20]

In spite of these findings, suicide in the West is still seen as a health problem in need of a medical cure. It is talked about as a 'national tragedy'. Campaigns like Beyond Blue exploit this concern, making much of the statistics of the cost of depression, social and financial.[21] Yet I want to argue that not all people who take their own lives are sick. Nor are they necessarily depressed. Some people may even have legitimate reasons for doing so.

The statistics of suicide in Australia

At the current time, less than 2 per cent of all registered deaths in Australia are attributed to suicide. In 2002, this meant that around 2300 people took their own lives, 124 less than in 2001.

To be classified as a suicide, the death must be recognised as due to 'other than natural' causes and a coronial inquiry must establish that the death resulted from a deliberate act of the deceased.[22] Within this definition, it is easy to see why an accurate suicide rate may be difficult to obtain – that is, the real rate is probably higher, but proving the deliberate nature of a death makes detection of suicide all the more difficult. This is particularly the case if the means of death are hidden. *Final Exit* author Derek Humphry has referred to these less obvious deaths as 'silent suicides'. Humphry suggests that around '40 per cent of elder suicides' may not be reported for these reasons.[23]

In terms of methods employed to commit suicide, the most common by far is hanging. This is the favoured method in Australia for both women and men. The second most common method is poisoning (including the inhalation of lethal gases) for both men and women, but the type of poisoning for the sexes differs. Men are more likely to use a substance other than drugs (for example, car exhaust fumes), while women tend to use drugs. Firearms is the third most common suicide method for men, while for women it is poisoning by a liquid or a gas, which includes carbon monoxide (car exhaust fumes).

These figures, however, pose a question. If hanging is so popular, why do the sick and elderly *not* come to Exit clinics and say to me 'Doc, what I really want to know is how to hang myself'? No one does this. On the contrary, sick people invariably ask questions about drugs. So why the discrepancy? If people want to use drugs, why aren't they doing so in greater numbers? The answer is two-fold. First, finding out on your own about which drugs work is difficult. Second, locating these

drugs is almost impossible, unless, of course, you're a doctor or a vet, or a doctor or vet's wife or husband. Yet people
who are suffering and who want to put an end to it – but who
have no information – will listen to rumour and gossip. These
people will try various drugs because they think they will work.
But they don't. It's actually quite hard to end your life with drugs
unless you know exactly what you're doing. Finally, these same
people will become desperate, and desperate people do desperate things. Rope is always available, and hanging works. The
ABS statistic on hanging speaks for itself. And it damns a society that prefers to see our elderly and sick die this violent death,
rather than making peaceful, reliable options a possibility. Exit
plans to challenge and to change this.

In addition to the variety of methods used, specific age
groups show different rates of suicide. In this regard, teenagers
are least likely to deliberately take their own lives. This is perhaps surprising, given the media hype surrounding the concept
of the 'troubled teen'.[24] Such statistics weaken the arguments
of my critics who try ceaselessly to associate the phenomenon of
teenage suicide with the quite different question of the suicide
of the elderly and seriously ill. These two social groups live
in very different worlds, face different issues in their everyday
lives, and have different priorities for the future. Because the
issue of suicide is context-dependent, any comparison between
them is like comparing apples and oranges. In 2002 in Australia,
the suicide rate for teenagers was 13.9 per 100 000 for males
and 4.1 for females. This compares with 16.8 per 100 000 for
people aged seventy to seventy-four years, and 22.5 for those
aged seventy-five and over.[25] The suicide rate is highest among

men aged twenty-five to twenty-nine years, and for women aged forty to forty-four years. The ABS reports that the Australian suicide rate has been relatively steady since the early part of last century.

In terms of mental illness, in 1998 the ABS reported that only 15 per cent of men and 18 per cent of women who suicided had 'an associated or contributory diagnosis of a mental disorder'.[26] Given how frequently the link between suicide and mental illness (particularly depression) is cited, it is clear that there may be many other reasons why a person might choose to end their life. To assume that suicide is always the result of depression or some other psychiatric condition is to fall into the biomedical trap.

I now want to present some alternative ways of thinking on why a person might want to take their life and why their decision to do so should be respected.

Do we have a right to die or are we asking the wrong question?

The bottom line in any discussion about end-of-life choices is the issue of personal autonomy. And, as this book has made clear, autonomy is not exercised in a social and cultural vacuum. Rather, our ability to make choices about our own life (and death) needs to be understood against a background of social forces and constraints. As discussed in chapter 4, these include the medical profession, the Church, the state and, of course, the media, through whose eyes contemporary life is played out. Each of these social institutions impacts upon an individual's choices and options, throughout life and especially at life's end. More than this, these institutions form the background against which our attitudes and opinions are formed. They create the world as we know it; a world that gives us a sense of identity, purpose and place.[27] They help generate the choices before us.

Earlier I quoted Professor John Harris of Manchester University. Harris argues that euthanasia should be permitted because to deny a person control over their death 'like all acts of tyranny is an ultimate denial of respect'.[28] Until now, 'respect' is a term that Right to Life has sought to claim as their own: 'respect' for human life; 'respect' for the sanctity of God's creation. But what about respect for the individual, their choices and their decisions, even when they differ from ours? It is time the concept of respect was reclaimed and put to better use.

The importance of respect for a person's ability to make key decisions – for example, which vocation to follow, who to marry, how to raise one's children – is widely acknowledged by social researchers and public policy makers. Here, the concept of respect is tied to a notion of dignity, central to which is a person's right to their own decision-making. As the American philosopher Professor Margaret Battin says, dignity is a 'fundamental human right not to be overridden'.[29] Closer to home, Associate Professor David Clark of Monash University concurs, arguing that suicide may best be considered in terms of 'respect for the person'.[30] Writer Lisa Lieberman makes a similar argument. Far from being an act of self-destruction, 'a passive succumbing to grief or despair', suicide can be 'an active assertion of identity. "I die, therefore I am".'[31]

Who am I?

In contemporary society, personhood – that is, one's sense of identity, our sense of who we are – is based upon our ability to make decisions. According to the former Director of the London School of Economics, Professor Baron Anthony Giddens, a person's sense of order is influenced by the events in which they participate and their everyday experiences.[32] We all find meaning in our daily actions. 'All such choices . . . are decisions not only about how to act, but who to be.' It is through the decisions we make that we come to have a sense of who we are.[33]

Our ongoing need to make decisions, says Giddens, contrasts with pre-modern times where life was more about fate and fortune; when personal decision-making was less a factor of everyday life, and the Church had a much greater influence on people's lives. This was a time when the law of God provided the signposts of how one should travel life's road. This was – and is – what is so attractive about religion. The need for personal decision-making is minimised as the teachings of the Church lay out a framework of conduct to which the faithful unquestioningly adhere. But for most people in modern society there is no signpost pointing one way or another. Instead, we have to make our own decisions. 'We have no choice but to choose'.[34]

So where does death fit in?

For older people and those who are seriously ill, the approach of death can be difficult to ignore, especially once one's body becomes marked as dying; whether it be weak, leaky or racked with pain (sick); or whether it be stiff, wrinkled or slow (old). In this respect, it is the body that gives the living game away. As sociologist Erving Goffman puts it, the dying body 'spoils our identity'.[35] It disrupts who we know ourselves to be.[36]

When our body shows signs of illness or age, we are forced to confront the possibility of our death head-on. This is no easy task. After all, our knowledge of ourselves is about living, not dying. Although, as David Menadue has pointed out in his book *Positive*, the concept of death can also become a necessary part of the dying process. For example, writes Menadue, gay men with HIV came to include their expected death as part of their individual and collective sense of self. When the 'new range of life-saving drugs arrived in the mid-nineties', Menadue writes, 'it was not unheard of for some people to tell their counsellors "Give me back my early death". Death was a promised part of the process of living with AIDS'.[37] To remove death was to take away a part of these men's identity.

For most people, though, death is not part of the game plan. For this reason it is not something that is easy to talk about. Rather, the deterioration of our body drastically serves to undermine our ability to know ourselves and, therefore, our place in the world. This can cause both frustration and fear as the individual is presented with a direct challenge to their ability to create meaning.[38] Regardless of whether death is desired or not, control over one's death represents the final instance in which our sense of self is confirmed. It is verification that we still exist. It matters little if we are suffering from disease or old age – the ability to choose the time and place of one's death allows a victim to become an avenger. To take control of one's decision-making – as we have done all our life – for this one last time proves the point.[39] Given that we spend our lives creating meaning about ourselves and our place in the world, to suddenly be deprived of this power can amount to an annihilation of self, and feels like a personal affront.

This is why, for some people, to be denied the ability to decide how to die is to already not be alive. Worse than this, it is to have been stopped being *you*. This point is confirmed in recent medical studies where it has been noted that requests for euthanasia and assisted suicide are seen by patients as a final means of limiting one's 'loss of self'.[40] Deciding on the time and place of one's own death is nothing short of integral to one's integrity and (self) respect.

> I have a very strong view that we should not be encouraging healthy people to take their lives, no matter what age they are. I'm appalled to think that we may have reached a situation in this country where any aid or assistance or encouragement is given to a healthy person . . . and I have quite strong views about euthanasia generally.
>
> – Prime Minister John Howard, 27 November 2002[41]

Lisette Nigot's story

In 2000, at seventy-seven years of age, French academic Lisette Nigot joined Exit and attended one of our introduction workshops in Perth. On a number of subsequent occasions over the next two years, I made clinic visits to Lisette at her home. Her story was always the same. She told me that at some point in the future – regardless of whether she was sick or well – she would want to end her life. Like the character of Maude in the 1971 movie *Harold and Maude* (the one with the fantastic Cat Stevens soundtrack), Lisette told me that eighty years of age was her cut-off point:

> I'm going to be eighty in a couple of months, and that's the limit I had given myself. I decided long ago that I would not become too old. At that time I didn't really know what too old might be.
>
> But lately I have said, you know, that's enough. I want to go and I decided that, okay, I'm going to be eighty, that's a good age. I don't want to be in my eighties . . . I don't take to old age very well.[42]

For Lisette, the right to die was a given. As she said:

> I have always taken care of myself and paid my taxes. I'm not a burden to anyone . . . But I would be a burden to myself if I was in a place where I can't move, where people make it their business to keep me alive against my will.[43]

The fear of being a burden to oneself is the most telling of insights into Lisette's attitude to her eventual suicide, and one that reaffirms the importance of her ability to make decisions for herself. Lisette Nigot had a profound sense of who she was: a strong, independent woman who never married or had children. 'I couldn't stand to have a man ask me, "Darling, what's for dinner?" Now anybody who said, "Darling, what's for dinner?" – they got a plate in their face. I couldn't possibly have put up with a man, night and day.'

Lisette's views about her right to die are not unusual among Exit members. While our members come from all walks of life and across all social classes, many have a personality – an identity – which is used to doing, acting and living in a world of their making. For older people, suicide is morally prohibited, as for the rest of us. Yet for a woman like Lisette, who has taken responsibility for herself her entire life, any attempt to stop her from dying would be almost unconscionable. And her thinking on the issue is not that uncommon. Take Teresa (a pseudonym), a 68-year-old former nurse from Melbourne. She was one of 1000-plus Exit members who completed our Peaceful Pill survey in 2004. At the end of her survey she offered the following reflection on her right to die:

> I'm expected to make my own decisions during my lifetime, and am held responsible for those decisions – legally and morally. I believe no other person should impact on the way I choose to end my life; I intend to do what I consider is in my own interests when the time comes to make my own decision. I also believe if and when I choose to 'Exit' I can do it in a dignified manner.

Being a highly organised and strong-willed woman, Lisette Nigot was full of the need to know about her end-of-life options. She sought out and obtained the best drugs she could. The barbiturates Soneral and Seconal were her choice, and she had taken years to stockpile them. But what Lisette needed to know was what amount would be lethal, whether drugs that were long past their use-by date would still be effective, and what side effects – if any – she would suffer. I answered her questions bluntly; I gave her the facts. But I also used these opportunities to try and convince her to stay on and I felt compelled to try. Why not write a book? I suggested. Why not travel? Why not?

Lisette was an important patient to me. She was the first person to call my bluff. Finally, she had enough of me and my protestations that she should live. She told me to 'stop patronising' her. I was mortified to hear her allegation that I had become the type of doctor I despised. Lisette noted that I preached one thing in theory – that a person of sound mind has a right to end their life at a time and place of their choosing – and another in practice. As a doctor, I was still taking it upon myself to 'know best', treating this well person as a 'patient'. Upset, but also indignant that Lisette had begun to see me that way, I took a step back and stopped trying to frustrate and thwart her plans. That was very hard to do, however. I really liked Lisette – she was a gutsy, intriguing, vivacious woman from another generation – and I didn't want her to leave.

On 22 November 2002, Lisette Nigot suicided. The front-page headline of the *Sydney Morning Herald* the next day read 'She didn't want to turn 80'. Speaking on ABC radio, the then president of the AMA in Western Australia and now head of clinical studies at the Catholic Notre Dame University in Perth, Dr Bernard Pearn-Rowe, was particularly vocal about her actions. When host Liam Bartlett asked if there was anything

Pearn-Rowe would have done as a doctor to help Lisette, he replied: 'If she had been a patient of mine . . . I would relieve any suffering . . . [and] I would help [her] move into some kind of institution . . . It is very sad that this lady could see no future . . .' Bartlett concluded the interview stating, 'I couldn't agree more.' They just didn't get it.

Upon her death, Lisette had left a friend a handwritten note. In it she said, 'Please tell Philip that it took more than an hour to swallow those capsules,' and she added, 'I do hope I will get there. There must be an easier way.' And there should be.

Reflections on suicide

There are clearly many reasons why people might be tired of life and wish to die. Whether or not you or I see these reasons as 'rational' and 'legitimate' is, in many respects, of little consequence. What is important is that individuals and their choices on matters as fundamental as their own death be respected. It is nothing short of hypocritical for contemporary Australian society to push individual rights and responsibility in everything from employment to parenting, to only renege on the big question of death. Why we as a society do this needs further interrogation.

The powerful influence of the Catholic Church and its attitude to suicide within politics and the medical profession as discussed in chapter 4 explains to a large extent why suicide is still so frowned upon in our society. During the Life Week Debate with Bishop Anthony at the University of Sydney in August 2003,[44] the questions were stacked and dealt with just about every conceivable Catholic criticism on the death with dignity debate. One of them was: 'You do not ask to be born, so therefore why should you decide to end it [life]?' My answer was:

> It's true, I did not ask to be born . . . if one believes in the so-called 'sanctity of life', that this is a God-given gift and you have no right to interfere with that process, God gives life, God takes life . . . that could be your belief. But it's not my belief; I don't believe in God.
>
> [You] can adopt and live in accordance with those beliefs and I will sanction and support your right to do so. But . . . I believe that my life is mine to assess and when I think that the scales tilt and death is preferable, I want to know that . . . I've got my bottle of Nembutal in the cupboard. The people who come to me say that 'I want to be like you, Doc, I want that option', because they don't believe that argument that you're putting . . . I'll personally protect that right of yours to die in any way you like, but don't *you* tell me how.

It is little wonder the Pope doesn't agree with those of us who fail to recognise a godly jurisdiction over our own bodies and lives. But the role of religion in broader contemporary society is too easy an answer on its own as to why suicide is such an affront and subject to social censure. Probing more deeply, Lisa Lieberman's writing is especially illuminating on the dynamics at work in how we view suicide. In *Leaving You*, Lieberman suggests several reasons why we are so hell-bent on denying the fact that some people want to die; people who are not 'mad' and who may not even be ill.[45] She says one reason for our inability to understand why a person may want to die is that we are frightened by suicide. The fact that slightly more than 2300 Australians deliberately take their own lives each year is enough to send many of us into a panic. We find it entirely unpalatable that some, if not many, of these people have personal – and, dare we say, legitimate – reasons for wanting to die.

A second and related reason in explaining our discomfort about suicide, according to Lieberman, concerns the utility of mental illness. Confronted with the suicide of a person we knew, most of us are inclined to seek a psychological explanation for the act. Were they depressed? Did something happen to upset them? Did they show signs of emotional turmoil before taking their life? It is more consoling to regard self-destruction as a passive act than to consider the possibility that someone we cared about wanted to leave us. In this regard Lieberman's theory goes to the crux of our collective dismay about self-destruction. And it is here that the linkage of suicide to mental illness becomes so convenient. All of a sudden we can stop interrogating ourselves, both individually and collectively; we no longer need to take the rejection of the person who suicides at a personal level. If we believe that person was mentally ill, we are all let off the hook. If we think this way we also need not confront the awfulness of disease and its ability to destroy our sense of self. And we need not confront the realities of old age, where an ageing body can spoil the treasured image. The image in the photograph taken many years before is usually the one we want to remember.

And then there is the issue of how little control one individual can have over the life of another: how far short we fall in

cajoling others to see the world as we do. On this, Lieberman
notes that 'It is easier to live with our powerlessness in the face
of mental illness than to acknowledge how limited we are to
influence the behaviour of another human being.' Lisette Nigot
adds:

> Nobody has tried to talk me out of it. I mean, they just
> don't believe it . . . Well, some people have said, 'Don't you
> realise how lucky you are? You are in relatively good health
> and there are people who suffer a lot' . . . also they com-
> pare me with people who are much older than I am because
> they know that old age is one of the reasons why I want to
> knock off. And they say, look, my aunt was ninety-five and
> she was still doing this, and that person is 120 and he is still
> playing tennis. And I say, good for them. I think if people
> want to live, that's marvellous. You know, really. I am not
> saying that people should think what I think.[46]

Trying to make sense of our collective pity for the suicide
and our abhorrence for their actions is indeed a difficult challenge. While the Australian government has baulked at the idea
of legalised voluntary euthanasia, even for those close to death,
in countries such as the Netherlands, there are some politicians
who – albeit cautiously – consider the 'tired of life' concept
to have legitimacy. Els Borst, the former Dutch Minister for
Health, is one such person. Borst raised the issue of the Peaceful
Pill soon after the Dutch parliament legalised euthanasia. 'Being
tired of life,' said Borst, 'has nothing to do with the euthanasia
law, with medicine and doctors. You may be releasing someone

from their suffering, but it is a suffering that has no link with illness or handicap.' Rather than being a matter for the Health Minister, Els Borst said, 'it could well be that a Justice Minister says: "I want to allow people to end it all"', although she added that there would still need to be 'a test to check they fulfilled the right criteria'.[47]

Would Lisette Nigot have fulfilled Borst's criteria? We don't know. What we do know, though, is that attempting to establish standards by which everybody's life can be judged a life worth living is a futile exercise. As retired British neurosurgeon Ramanand Kalbag wrote in a recent edition of the *British Medical Journal*:

> A robust moral framework, which dictates how a sentient rational adult should think, let alone face incurable illness, has ominous connotations for what most of us believe is a free society.[48]

The Crofts' story

In the years before their joint suicide in 2002, elderly Bundaberg couple Sydney and Marjorie Croft attended three Exit introduction workshops. Each time they came, they would sit together, holding hands throughout. They were clearly a couple in love. And each time they would take the opportunity to ask questions about the characteristics and availability of various drugs, despite the fact that they were not ill. When their suicide note arrived in my mailbox in Darwin, I was as surprised as anyone. It read:

To Whom It May Concern

Please don't condemn us, or feel badly of us for what we have done.

We have thought clearly of this for a long time and it has taken a long time to get the drugs needed.

We are in our late 80s and 90 is on the horizon. At this stage, would it be wrong to expect no deterioration in our health? More importantly, would our mental state be bright and alert?

In 1974 we both lost our partners whom we loved very dearly. For two and a half years Marjorie became a recluse with her grief, and Syd became an alcoholic. We would not like to go through that traumatic experience again. Hence we decided we wanted to go together.

We have no children and no one to consider.

We have left instructions that we be cremated and that our ashes be mixed together. We feel that way, we will be together forever.

Please don't feel sad, or grieve for us. But feel glad in your heart as we do.

Sydney and Marjorie Croft

The Crofts' note is a plea for society to try to understand them. They knew their decision to die together was right for them. But their note asks us to try to understand the un-understandable. And this we *should* do – if for no other reason than out of respect for these people and as a sincere attempt to treat with seriousness their reasons for wanting to die. What other choice do we – a modern, civil society – have? Are we to confiscate people's drugs, stop them from attending workshops and asking questions? Are we to 'section' them and put them in a psychiatric hospital? Take away their belts and shoelaces? Imprison them because we can't understand their decision to leave? Or do we owe them the respect that all rational elderly Australians deserve? Allowing people dignity not only in dying but in making this choice should be the obligation of us all.

Chapter 8

Legal Constraints and Legal Opportunities

As it is with all areas of our lives, the process of dying is strictly regulated by a range of laws at both a federal and a state level. While voluntary euthanasia is currently illegal in all states and territories (except for slow euthanasia), a dying person does have some limited end-of-life options. Suicide, for example, is lawful. If you can end your life by yourself, no crime is committed. But heaven help anyone who might 'advise, counsel or assist' you in that endeavour.

As it is defined under the *Commonwealth Crimes Act (1914)*, assisted suicide is a crime throughout Australia. However, there continue to be numerous grey areas and much debate about exactly what constitutes 'assistance'. What is clear, however, is that we do have the right to refuse medical treatment: no pills, tests and transfusions and no sitting in a hospital bed if that is not what you want – even if such a refusal may result in your death. It is your choice and no one else's.

Bear in mind, though, that *refusing* treatment – even if it causes death – is not the same as *asking for* treatment that will bring about death. And if you lose the ability to speak through unconsciousness, coma or dementia, this is where problems can really occur. It's hard to refuse treatment if you can't speak. And there are further difficulties in relation to definitions. For example, what exactly is the medical treatment that one can legally refuse? How is it different from something called palliative care which a person is stuck with, whether they like it or not? For example, you can say no to penicillin, but not necessarily to the glass of water it comes with. Further confusion results when a person is deemed to be mentally incompetent. An incompetent person is unable lawfully to refuse treatments that are considered to be in their 'best interests'. In this case, you can be forced to take the medicine.

In this chapter I discuss the minefield that characterises the existing legislation and the traps one can easily fall into when someone you love asks for help to end their suffering. This chapter also examines the limited options provided by living wills, the appointment of a medical power of attorney, and the difficulties that can result if one is found to be in need of compulsory psychiatric treatment. In short, there are myriad legal challenges to be overcome if we are to have any real control over our end-of-life choices in Australia today.

The refusal of medical treatment

All of us have an absolute right to refuse medical treatment. But, as is so often the case in the intense medical climate of a hospital or ICU, this is not always easy to do. One can find oneself offered – even compelled – to take various treatments, including life-saving options. It can take a brave person indeed to put up a hand and just say 'No'.

While the critics of VE legislation often focus on the risk of a patient being coerced into dying, what is often overlooked and equally damaging is the pressure a patient can receive to go on living. Partners, families and doctors often join forces to convince those who are sick that they should take the treatments and strategies on offer. It doesn't matter that the chemotherapy has a 100 per cent chance of making you feel sick if it has a 10 per cent chance of arresting the cancer. Take it. Do the right thing. Fight the disease.

How often have I sat in a church listening to a eulogy as those left behind wax lyrical about how hard their loved one had 'fought' the disease? Often these people 'fought' as futile treatment after futile treatment was foisted on them, the unwilling patient. A patient too weakened by the disease and the pressure applied to do what is often the most courageous – to say 'No more'; too weak to exercise their right to refuse.

Is the person of sound mind?

Like all rights, the right to refuse treatment comes with important caveats and qualifications that can severely constrain patient autonomy. The most obvious of these is that the person must be of sound mind (that is, sane). While this may sound simple, it is not. There is a persistent view within the medical profession that if a patient seeks to refuse medical treatment or, worse, asks for help to die, that patient must be depressed. This is a classic catch-22 situation.

If you ask for help to die, you risk being classified as insane. And an insane person cannot be taken seriously. Any doctor can invoke the Psychiatric Treatment Act. While the name of the exact legislation varies from state to state, the underlying intent of the law remains the same. This set of laws allows a doctor to force a patient to be taken to a psychiatric hospital and constrained there for up to three days while a compulsory psychiatric assessment is made. Once 'sectioned', a patient loses their right to refuse medical treatment.

At the end of the assessment period, a patient has the right to put their case to a magistrate, and perhaps regain freedom. But in every case I have ever witnessed, it is the view of the assessing psychiatrist – not the patient – that prevails. So the risk is clear. If you insist on your right to refuse treatment, you may find yourself sectioned and constrained. In many ways, agreeing to undergo the chemotherapy on offer might be the easier course of action.

David Kissane, the psychiatrist with whom I co-authored a paper about the ROTI Act for the medical journal *The Lancet*, was of this opinion. Kissane thought that each of the four of my patients who used the ROTI Act showed 'elements of depression'.[1] Kissane thought that none should have been given access to the law. To me, the 'elements of depression' shown were normal and understandable reactions given the suffering those people were enduring. Their behaviour and their elements of depression were a rational reaction to the dire circumstances in which they found themselves. None of the people who used the ROTI law was mentally ill. All were correctly allowed the option to end their lives with medical assistance. However,

Kissane's approach – and that of many medical profession-als – is to use their professional privilege to strip a patient of their most fundamental right. And this is done under the guise that the underlying disease – the depression – is so subtle that only the most experienced of psychiatrists can detect it.

Sam and Steve's stories

In 1999, two people contacted me, separately, asking for help to die. Both had become quadriplegics as a result of serious acci-dents. Both had gone through exhaustive rehabilitation processes to help them adjust to their greatly changed worlds. But for both men, despite the passage of several years, neither found satisfac-tion in their new lives and they continued to request help to die on several occasions.

Although Sam and Steve were similar in many ways – both were in their twenties, from upper-middle-class backgrounds, and with traumatic fractures to their neck – there was one vital difference. Sam's fracture was at a slightly higher level than Steve's. Because of this, Sam needed a ventilator to help him breathe. Steve, on the other hand, had a somewhat 'better' frac-ture, lower in the neck. While he still could not move his arms or legs, he could breathe without the use of a respirator.

I talked at length to both men, their families and their car-ers about their options and what came to pass provides a clear example of the injustice of existing legislation. Sam, who had the more serious injury, thought himself luckier than Steve who, while paralysed, could breathe unaided. This was because Sam was kept alive by breathing with a ventilator and because the ventilator was classified as 'medical treatment', he could exercise his right to have it switched off.

Eventually, Sam made this choice. He died peacefully, in accordance with his wishes. Steve, on the other hand, had no such option. Steve would have needed help to die that no one could lawfully provide. I remember vividly the time when he looked at me and, with great sincerity, told me how much he envied Sam, someone with a more severe injury. 'If only I'd been luckier and had a worse [higher] fracture,' he lamented, 'then at least I'd have a choice. As it is, I'm just trapped.'

Despite this, Steve's desire to die was eventually fulfilled. He began to refuse food and water, became weaker, and died slowly. He was lucky that no one involved in his care forced fluids or food upon him under the guise of palliative care – care he would not have been able to refuse. He was lucky, too, that no one decided he was in need of compulsory nutrition because of his mental state, and had him moved to a psychiatric hospital.

Can the person speak?

While a patient may insist on their right to refuse medical treatment, no matter how necessary the treatment may be, this right can be seriously compromised once a patient loses the ability to speak. A person brought into casualty unconscious will be given a cannula into a vein and fluids will be commenced. If the patient is awake they could simply say 'No cannulas, no needles'. But if you are unconscious, you can't say a word.

It has long been argued that the right to refuse treatment

should not depend on a patient's ability to speak. One could imagine, for example, a situation where an unconscious person is hydrated till consciousness returns, at which point they insist on their right to remove the hydrating line, and they lapse back into unconsciousness and the cycle is repeated. It was to address such a situation that the concept of a living will came about.

Living wills

A living will is a legal document that extends a person's absolute right to refuse medical treatment into circumstances where the ability to communicate is lost. Thus even if that person is unconscious or demented, the living will ensures the person's wish to refuse treatment is respected.

The living will document – or advance directive, as it is also known – usually contains a list of the various treatments that a person has decided would be unacceptable to them. A living will does not, however, extend to requesting physician-assisted dying. A living will cannot, therefore, include a request for hastened death in any form.

Some famous people have made use of living wills, including former US President Richard Nixon and former first lady Jackie Kennedy Onassis. Nixon died four days after suffering a stroke. This stroke was said to have robbed him of his ability to speak and see. Following his instructions, doctors implemented the wishes specified in his living will and did nothing extraordinary to keep him alive. For Kennedy Onassis, the living will served a different purpose. At the time of her diagnosis with lymphoma, Kennedy Onassis had already signed a living will that stated her wish to die at home, rather than in hospital. She also wanted to be surrounded by her family and friends. Her living will ensured that her wishes were granted.[2]

In Australia, a living will document can be drawn up by anyone. What is most important, though, is whether the document has any legal status. Not all states and territories recognise living wills. At the current time, a living will or advance directive applies in the ACT, the Northern Territory, Queensland, South Australia and Victoria. (Some of these states have express recognition for interstate advance directives.) There is no legally binding living will/advance directive provision in New South Wales, Tasmania or Western Australia.

Are living wills foolproof?

While living wills are important, they are far from foolproof and there is considerable evidence that suggests they are often overlooked by treating doctors. Their implementation can be haphazard. In the US, for example, where more than 20 per cent of Americans have living wills, recent research shows that the wills are not always considered, despite that country's national register of living wills (and their easy access by medical staff). The study documented that doctors discuss the contents of a patient's living will in as few as 12 per cent of all cases.[3] Other studies confirm this trend.[4] There are plenty of stories about how hard it can be ensuring previously recorded wishes are respected and treatments stopped. One dutiful daughter described her family's difficulties when her father was dying, even though he had a living will:

We got to the point that we were barring the nurses from coming in, saying, you know, 'He has said he wants all treatments stopped'. And they would come in and try to take blood tests or do insulin, and he finally got out of it enough so that he couldn't say 'no' for himself any more.[5]

The dying person's bedside can be an adversarial environment and this is not always the fault of the individual doctors. Modern medicine must accept some of the blame. This is because medicine maintains that a living person is a success in terms of medical treatment. Death is still seen as an incidence of failure. Doing nothing or withdrawing treatment is not something that comes easy to all doctors. As one palliative care specialist has put it: '[Palliative care practitioners] have a twisted psychology whereby they push death away . . . I sometimes wonder if palliative care work is a death-denying phenomenon.'[6]

Ensuring your living will is noticed

For your living will to be respected, you must reside in a jurisdiction that has such a legal provision. But even then there are some traps one can fall into. The one most important to note is the exemption that is currently provided for ambulance officers – they need not comply with your wishes. This is of particular importance for a person who has attempted suicide by taking lethal drugs. Depending on the drugs chosen, there will always be some time from the ingestion of the medication until death results. If an ambulance is called to a scene and finds an unconscious person, the ambulance officers will resuscitate that person, even if a legal living will exists. Ambulance officers do not have the time to sort out the validity of documents of this nature. And their justification is genuine. The living will may be a forgery; perhaps the officers have stumbled on an attempted murder and the document has been strategically placed to fool the authorities.

In all cases, though, the effect is the same. If an ambulance is called, your living will – requesting that resuscitative measures not be carried out – will be ignored. The officers' usual response is that you can 'sort it all out later at the hospital'. But this is cold comfort for someone wanting to end their suffering by using lethal drugs.

Thus, for good reason, people often go to great lengths to ensure that everyone knows about their living will and their lawful request that they not be subject to medical resuscitative procedures. There are cases I know of where people have filled out a living will and pinned a copy onto their pyjamas before taking lethal drugs. Others have drawn attention to a living will's existence by writing about it on their forehead in lipstick. In one well-publicised case, 85-year-old British nurse Frances Polak was found to have the words 'Do not resuscitate' tattooed across her chest. When interviewed about this, she said, 'It's not the dying I fear, it's being kept alive when I should be dead.'[7] This is a sentiment echoed by some of my patients.

To avoid being resuscitated when you have no wish to be, the advice I give in all Exit workshops is to do what you can to ensure that no one arrives until after death has occurred. If the unexpected does happen, try to ensure that your doctor is called, not the ambulance. Your doctor knows of your living will and will be less likely to initiate treatment. But things can still go wrong.

The best laid schemes o' mice an' men/Gang aft a-gley

In early 2002, two of my patients decided to end their lives while they still had the ability. Both had motor neurone disease and were worried if they left it for too long, they would find themselves trapped in bodies that were slowly becoming paralysed. First, there was Sandy Williamson (Sandy's story is discussed at length in chapter 10) and there was Bill from Newcastle. Both Sandy and Bill had contacted me to ask about lethal drugs they might obtain and administer themselves if they were to avoid their most feared fate – dying badly and with no dignity. In 2002, both took their drugs and hoped for the best.

The worst phone calls I receive usually come in at about 5 a.m. These calls are often from desperate family members who are anxiously watching the light gathering in the east as their seriously ill loved ones lie there, still alive, hours after taking drugs to end their life. The question asked is always the same: 'What do we do now?' Bill and Sandy's cases deviated at this point.

When Bill's wife could leave it no longer and had to make a phone call to protect herself – she knew the legal consequences, and feared Bill might stay in a coma indefinitely – she rang the family doctor. The doctor knew of Bill's condition and of his living will. The doctor arrived at the bedside, and did little to establish the cause of the coma. He reassured Bill's wife, pointing out that he knew that Bill's condition was terminal and of his wish not to be resuscitated. He provided some morphine 'to keep him comfortable' and Bill died that morning. The death certificate said that the cause of death was 'complications from motor neurone disease'.

Sandy's case was different. When Sandy did not die hours after taking lethal drugs, the doctor was called. But with the media that had surrounded Sandy's story – she had appeared on TV and talked to the papers about her experience with MND – the doctor was nervous and he called an ambulance. And then he, presumably, also called the police, as they arrived soon after. Despite protests from her sisters, the comatose Sandy was taken to hospital. There, extraordinary measures were undertaken to keep her alive. It would be another four days before Sandy died, after she was returned home and the fluids that were keeping her body alive were finally turned off. So even with the best laid plans, things still do go wrong.

The economics of a living will

In recent years, living wills have come to the attention of economists who have noted their clear benefits for a country's health budget. From a financial point of view, the budget has much to gain if we have quicker and cleaner deaths – if we don't hang around against our express wishes in comatose states in hospital ICUs once nothing more can be done for us. So powerful is the economic argument for living wills that in the United States, hospitals are now required by law to provide living will education to staff. In turn, staff are expected to educate patients and encourage them to sign one. Given that more than 10 per cent of the States' health budget is said to be spent on care that is provided in the last thirty days of patients' lives, the logic is not hard to follow.[8] And, with an ageing population, future health costs in that country can be expected to dramatically climb.

In Australia, however, the debate about the economics of end-of-life care is only just beginning where living wills are concerned. The push is coming from right-to-die groups such as Exit and the state-based VE societies, but the Federal Government is largely silent on the issue. While there are some moves afoot to have living will documents incorporated into a person's car licence documentation in a way similar to that for organ donation, this process seems destined to take a long time.

In the meantime, some state-based VE societies are active in compiling their own living will registers. One reason for this is because living wills come under state, not federal, legislation. That said, it appears it will be a long time before Australia follows the United States' lead and establishes a national online register of living wills (see www.uslivingwillregistry.com) that provides a central and easily accessible reference for doctors, medical staff and ambulance officers.

Appointment of a medical power of attorney, agent or proxy

Another equally important strategy to ensure your voice is heard if you are unable to communicate is the appointment of a person to make medical decisions for you. While legislation again varies depending on the state in which you live, a medical power of attorney carries out the same function as a living will. This person's job is to ensure that if we lose the ability to communicate, our choice of acceptable medical treatments is respected. It is often much more effective to have an articulate person attempting to implement your wishes than a passive piece of paper.

Let me explain why. There is a chance that your living will (that clearly states that antibiotics are not to be given to you, for example) may not be noticed as you are fast-tracked into intensive care. You have a greater chance of being heard if your chosen advocate is standing at the foot of your bed, brandishing the living will document and insisting that the drugs be stopped. Clearly, both strategies are desirable and can complement each other. The medical power of attorney can argue – forcibly, if necessary – that your wishes, as recorded in your living will, are to be complied with.

Generally speaking, most people see a living will and the appointment of a medical power of attorney or agent as sensible. Families like to feel involved and the medical profession – by and large – supports the principle. These strategies make it easier for doctors who often find themselves second-guessing the sorts of treatments their comatose patient would want. And because doctors and patients often differ in their ideas about what is best in a particular situation, it is clear that the more safeguards an unconscious patient has in place, the better off they will be.[9]

State and territory legislation summaries

The biggest problem in regard to living wills and medical power of attorney is the range and variation of legislation across the nation. It is nothing short of a mess and leads to much confusion. Some states allow a living will but no medical power of attorney. Others allow medical power of attorney but no living will. Some states provide for neither. For example, Western Australia is a place where you cannot write an advance directive that has any legal validity, and you cannot appoint a medical power of attorney. As I often say to those attending Exit workshops, you would be better off *not* having your disabling stroke while holidaying in Perth if you want your medical wishes to be respected.

Why Australia cannot have uniform legislation on something as fundamental and non-controversial as living wills and medical powers of attorney is hard to understand. Nevertheless, as Queensland academic Dr Colleen Cartwright has noted, all states and territories do provide for some form of guardianship of one kind or another. But one needs to look at the fine print.

AUSTRALIAN CAPITAL TERRITORY

In the ACT a living will can be made. An agent can also be appointed, but only for a current illness (which does not have to be terminal). The *Medical Treatment Act (1994)* allows for the refusal of treatment, but only for current illnesses (as is also the case in Victoria). The agent can consent to both the withdrawing and withholding of life-sustaining measures. An information kit containing the relevant forms is available on the Canberra Connect web site: http://www.oca.act.gov.au/publications/pdfs/EPA-Form.pdf.

NEW SOUTH WALES

In New South Wales there is no legislation for living wills or for the appointment of an agent. However, the health department does have 'Dying With

Dignity Guidelines' that instruct hospital and other health employees to respect advance directives where possible. The department has recently released a 'Using Advance Care Directives' statement (available at http://www.health.nsw.gov.au/pubs/2004/adcare_directives.html) that states that a living will which complies with the document's requirements is binding in New South Wales. Also, an 'enduring guardian' may be appointed. The appropriate form can be found on the attorney-general's web site: http://www.agd.nsw.gov.au/opg.nsf/pages/enduring7a.

NORTHERN TERRITORY

In the Northern Territory, a living will can be written at any time as long as the person is aged eighteen years or older. The living will applies only to a terminal illness (as is the case in South Australia). While no specific medical agent or proxy can be appointed, you can appoint a general enduring power of attorney. The appropriate form is available on the Land Titles Office web site: http://www.nt.gov.au/justice/docs/landtitl/forms/pa/096.pdf. For the form to be valid, however, it must be registered and lodged at the Registrar-General's Office. A fee is payable.

QUEENSLAND

The *Powers of Attorney Act (1998)* in Queensland allows for a living will and an enduring power of attorney for personal/health matters. Amendments passed in 2001 allow proxies or agents to consent to the withdrawal and/or withholding of medical treatment if a doctor considers these to be futile. The *Guardianship and Administration Act (2000)* also allows for a guardian to be appointed. A tribunal can consent to the withdrawal/withholding of life-sustaining treatment. The living will form, called an 'Advanced Health Directive', is available at http://www.justice.qld.gov.au/guardian/forms/health.pdf and at newsagents.

SOUTH AUSTRALIA

In South Australia the *Medical Treatment and Palliative Care Act (1995)* allows a person over eighteen years of age to write a living will which is known as an anticipatory directive. This applies to a terminal illness only. An agent can be appointed in South Australia as a person who can consent to the withdrawal/withholding of life-sustaining treatment, but *not* the withdrawal of provision/administration of food and water or pain-relieving drugs.

An enduring power of guardian can also be appointed. The kit can be purchased at a cost of $14.95 at the Legal Services Commission web site: http://www.lawhandbook.sa.gov.au/index_shop.asp?action=view&id=5 &section=2. A basic form for a medical agent or proxy is available at http:// www.saves.asn.au/resources/advance/cmtpca2b.htm. A State Register of Anticipatory Directives is operated by Medic-Alert, 216 Greenhill Road, Eastwood SA 5063, ph. 08 8274 0361.

TASMANIA

At the current time in Tasmania there are no provisions for a living will or for a medical power of attorney or agent. I have recently been advised, however, that the government is reviewing the situation. In the meantime, 'Dying with Dignity' guidelines do exist, and an enduring guardian can be appointed. The relevant form is available on the Department of Justice web site: http://www.justice.tas.gov.au/guar/forms/e_g.pdf. The person named in this form can then make financial, property, lifestyle and health treatment decisions on your behalf.

VICTORIA

In Victoria the *Medical Treatment Act (1988)* allows a patient to write a 'refusal of treatment' certificate, but only for a current illness, and the

illness need not be terminal. The certificate form is available at http://
www.publicadvocate.vic.gov.au/CA256A76007E8265/All/CE8461B900F1
CD75CA256B20001EAD4C?OpenDocument. The *Medical Treatment (Enduring Power of Attorney) Act (1990)* allows for the appointment of an agent
or proxy, while the *Medical Treatment (Agents) Act (1992)* allows for the
appointment of an alternative agent as well.

The Enduring Power of Attorney (Medical) form can be found on the
Victorian Health Department's web site at http://www.health.vic.gov.au/
mta/downloads/mta88_sched02.pdf.

WESTERN AUSTRALIA

In Western Australia there is no current legislation for the making of a living will or for the appointment of a medical power of attorney, although
an enduring power of attorney can be appointed. Interestingly, a private
member's bill for refusal of treatment by terminally ill people (Medical Care
of the Dying Bill 1995) passed WA's lower house in 1995 but then lapsed
when an election was called. Subsequent legislation has never been introduced. A full information kit containing the relevant forms is available on
the Department of Justice web site: http://www.justice.wa.gov.au.

Palliative care vs medical treatment – what's the difference?

In recent times, definitions that outline the difference between
medical treatment and palliative care have proven controversial.
These definitions are important because in some states living
wills apply to medical treatment only. In Victoria, for example, medical treatment can be refused but palliative care cannot.
It took a recent high-profile case before the Victorian Supreme
Court to have the definitions legally clarified. The question

put to the court in the case of Mrs BWV in 2003 was whether artificial feeding and hydration – that is, feeding and hydration that is administered through a surgically inserted peg in one's stomach – is 'medical treatment'.

Mrs BWV was a woman in her sixties with Pick's disease that had resulted in a severe form of dementia. For the last years of her life she was comatose and in institutional care. Mrs BWV was unable to move or communicate, even with her husband. As a comatose patient, she was being kept alive through a peg in her stomach by which she was fed and hydrated. Yet Mrs BWV had previously verbally stated that she never wanted to be kept alive in this way. While Mrs BWV had talked about what she wished to happen to her if she were ever ill and unable to speak for herself, her wishes were never written down.

Mrs BWV's husband argued that her wishes should be respected and that she should not be kept alive. However, for her care/treatment to be stopped, the courts needed to determine if her artificial feeding and hydration constituted palliative care or medical treatment. If it was medical treatment, her husband could have it stopped. If it was palliative care, he could not.

In the court, the Catholic Archbishop of Melbourne and Catholic Health Australia argued that the feeding and hydration were palliative care. On the other side, the Victorian Public Advocate argued that the feeding and hydration were medical treatment. In the end, the court ruled that artificial nutrition and hydration are indeed medical treatment. The decision was based largely upon the fact that the peg had been surgically inserted into Mrs BWV's stomach. As these forms of treatment were then classified as medical, they could therefore be refused/withdrawn. Shortly after the verdict was handed down by Justice Stuart Morris, Mrs BWV stopped being fed and hydrated, and died a week later from starvation.

The full decision of this ruling can be read at http://www.austlii.edu.au/au/cases/vic/VSC/2003/173.html.

Assisting with a suicide – the legal issues

Nobody ever said that the law is logical. Nowhere is this lack of logic more obvious than in relation to suicide. While suicide is legal, assisting someone to die is illegal and something about which those close to a dying person – a person who has decided to end their own life – need to be very wary.

Assisted suicide is variously defined as assisting or encouraging a person to commit suicide although, as the table opposite illustrates, the wording and the crime varies depending on the state or territory. At the current time in Australia, helping someone to die carries a sentence that ranges from five to ten years in New South Wales to life imprisonment in Western Australia and Queensland.

Assisting a suicide is a serious charge and not one to treat casually. And while it might seem bizarre that it is a crime to assist someone to do something that is itself not a crime, that's just the way it is. There is no other example of such incongruity in our legal system. Nowhere else does assisting with a non-crime become a serious crime. Even though assisting in a suicide is more often than not an act of love, knowing whether you are assisting is not always easy to discern. That's

State	Name of statute	Wording of offence	Max. penalty
ACT	*Crimes Act (1900)*	s 17: 'aids or abets' or 'incites or counsels'	10 years
NSW	*Crimes Act (1900)*	s 31C(1): 'aids or abets' s 31C(2): 'incites or counsels'	10 years 5 years
NT	Criminal Code	s 168: 'procures, counsels or aids'	Life
QLD	Criminal Code	s 311: 'procures, counsels or aids'	Life
SA	*Criminal Law Consolidation Act (1935)*	s 13A(5): 'aids, abets or counsels'	14 years (s13A(6)(a)(i))
TAS	Criminal Code	s 163: 'instigates or aids'	*
VIC	*Crimes Act (1958)*	s 6B(2): 'incites, aids or abets'	14 years
WA	Criminal Code	s 288: 'procures, counsels or aids'	Life

* The judge has the discretion to impose punishment as the judge thinks fit. In exercising such discretion, the judge is constrained by s389(3) of the Code, which is a general sentencing provision and provides for a penalty of a maximum twenty-one years and/or a fine.

the problem families and friends frequently face – what exactly is 'assisting'?

Defining assisted suicide

The lack of clarity around the definition of assisting with a suicide led twenty-one people to sit with Nancy Crick when she died in 2001. These human rights activists, family and friends wanted it established – once and for all – whether being in the same room as someone who lawfully takes their life is defined as 'assisting' in a suicide. While not everyone wants twenty-one people to be present when they die, most people want someone. Almost no one wants to die alone and why should they? But without knowing what actions are classified as assisting and what are not, the answer to the question about whether you should act alone is not clear.

At the current time, no lawyer will answer the question. There is no case law to establish clearly whether sitting with someone is assisting. It could perhaps be argued, although it seems a long bow to me, that just sitting with someone about to commit suicide provides psychological encouragement. And perhaps there is a duty of care – maybe you should leap from your chair and grab the glass of lethal drugs from the person's lips. (But wouldn't that be an assault?)

This was the question 'the Nancy Crick twenty-one' posed for the Queensland authorities and it took two years for the police to come up with an answer. On 18 June 2004 Queensland Police Commissioner Bob Atkinson finally announced that the 'Crick investigation' had concluded, stating, 'At this point in time there is insufficient evidence to support any charge against any person in relation to the offence that is on the statute books of assisting someone to take their own lives . . . actually being present when someone takes their life does not in itself constitute an offence.'[10] Despite this long-awaited decision, I should stress that as this was not a decision made by the court, assisting with a suicide in Queensland is still illegal. And, as Commissioner Atkinson added at his specially convened press conference, 'any new information about the circumstances of Mrs Crick's death would be investigated'. In this case there was no crime, but there is little certainty of what might happen with future cases.

The death of Nancy Crick is not the only instance where the issue of assisted suicide has recently raised its head. In Tasmania there has been another significant case, this time concerning the suicide of 88-year-old TV chef and Exit member Elizabeth Godfrey and the charge that her adult son, John Stuart Godfrey, assisted. In this case, Godfrey pleaded guilty to assisting with his mother's death, saying that Elizabeth had 'lived her entire life boldly, and it was extremely important to her that she met her death with the same bold, independent spirit'.[11] Interestingly, what 'assistance' John was alleged to have given his mother was never actually defined, only that it comprised 'a recipe involving a plastic bag, medication and alcohol'.[12] In sentencing, Justice Peter Underwood said that because Godfrey's crime was motivated 'solely by compassion and love', and because he had the 'support of his family and gratitude of his mother', a twelve-month suspended jail sentence 'on the condition he be of good behaviour for one year' was deemed the appropriate legal response. The maximum sentence for assisting a suicide in Tasmania remains at twenty-one years.

Yet Justice Underwood went further, and raised an entirely new issue where the suicide of seriously ill people is concerned. Speaking of Elizabeth Godfrey's predicament, he said 'it might be said that those who wish to end their life but are physically unable to do so, are discriminated against by reason of their physical disability'. He went on to conclude, however, that 'it was for the community and parliamentarians to debate the appropriateness of the crime of assisting suicide, and not the court'. With such diverse circumstances surrounding suicide, it seems the law continues to be a grey and murky area. Is it assisting a suicide to provide lethal drugs to a terminally ill patient, knowing what they intend to do with them? Probably. Is it assisting a suicide to tell a patient that the drugs provided for their insomnia will be lethal if taken in excess? Probably not. Will you be prosecuted either way? Who can tell.

For a doctor, the safest course of action is to walk away from a patient's request for help to die. Despite the circumstances of the cases discussed above, below are some of the many other actions whose classification remains unclear:

- Telling a friend where to obtain lethal drugs.
- Answering questions about lethal drugs – names and quantities.
- Advising someone where to purchase/how to make a plastic bag.
- Answering questions about why a plastic bag causes death.
- Supplying someone with a plastic bag for their shopping.

- Advising someone where to buy parts to make a CoGenie device.
- Answering questions about why breathing carbon monoxide causes death.
- Collaborating with a group of people on how to make a Peaceful Pill.

Sensible legal clarification is desperately needed in all these areas. Without this, the families and friends of the person wishing to suicide will continue to be at risk; risk that often places unbearable pressure upon relationships and occasionally leads loved ones into the court room. Under the current legal conditions, some adult children come to resent a parent's expectation for their assistance to die, and this is easily understood. Others may unswervingly keep to the promises made out of a sense of duty.

The hesitance of a family member or friend to be too closely involved in this awful catch-22 situation is understandable, given the risks involved. In early 2004, *The Bulletin* reported the story of one of my patients, Peter. Peter is a medical specialist who – through a cruel twist of fate – is in the early stages of motor neurone disease. When *Bulletin* reporter Julie Anne Davies went to interview Peter about his experience with the disease and his thoughts about his right to die, Peter's wife brought the interview to an abrupt halt. Her ultimatum went thus: 'If you go public with your story, I will not help you when the time comes.' She realised that Peter's comments about eventually wanting help to die could possibly link her with his future suicide. Her anguish was unbearable, Davies wrote:

Her partner in life is dying and one day she will have to administer the drugs which will kill him. An act of love, she believes, but she does not want to endure a court case and possible jail term after he has gone.[13]

Modern, civil society can do better that this. It can do better than subject people – people who are already facing the loss of a loved one – to this type of quandary.

The Exit motor neurone disease LifeNet project

At any one time Exit has a number of people with motor neurone disease (MND) on its books. This disease presents these people with specific difficulties and, without access to VE legislation, many find themselves worrying about the ways by which it will be possible to end their life, should their condition become intolerable. With advancing paralysis, the problem concerns the person's ability to self-administer drugs. Sufferers realise that if they leave it too late, they will be in need of help to die, and in so doing they will expose those they care about to significant risk.

Exit has long pondered this problem. Recently Leo, an Exit member and MND sufferer from Perth, suggested a solution. Leo offered to help a more seriously ill MND sufferer to die. This would remove any risk from the family of the sufferer. As Leo put it: 'What are they going to do to me? Arrest me, push me onto the stand in my wheelchair and sentence me for the crime of helping someone avoid what I'm about to go through?' And Leo has a point. What government would want their public prosecutor to put a terminally ill man on trial for his life – for a 'crime' that has been prompted by the government's own failure to adequately address the issue? Once again, a legal problem has been turned into a political problem, and one much more difficult for the government to solve.

Exit established the LifeNet project in response to Leo's suggestion. The eight people currently on our books with MND are all interested in the project and are currently being put in touch with each other. It is a case of MND sufferers helping other MND sufferers and, in the process, keeping families safe and bypassing a government that has failed them so badly.

Knowing the risks of assisting in a suicide

Many who attend Exit workshops want to know what legal risk their possible suicide might present to those who are left behind. An important consideration in this question is whether the person wanting to die cares whether it is known that their death was a suicide or not. In my experience, people tend to fall into two distinct groups: those who do not want their death recorded as a suicide, and another group who are equally clear that they do not care if this is made known or not.

Those who fall into the first category believe that if a person is close to death and they choose to end their life to avoid additional suffering, they do not think it fair that the cause of death is listed as suicide on the death certificate, especially given the battle they have often had with the disease. Rather, these people feel that the death certificate should record the death as due to the lung cancer or whatever the disease was that prompted the patient to act in that way. But if the doctor certifying death is aware that intervention occurred, the death will not be recorded in this way regardless. In this situation the coroner must be contacted and suicide will be recorded as the cause of death. If this happens it is important to note that there are no legal implications and life insurance policies – by and large – are not affected (remember, suicide is not a crime). What most often concerns people, though, is the stigma associated with suicide and the concern that their chosen death might be seen to reflect badly on the surviving family members.

The other equally common standpoint is for the dying person to have absolutely no interest in what is written on the certificate. People put it just like that: 'They can write what they want on that bit of paper, it won't affect me. I'll be dead.' In many ways, this attitude is much simpler. The person ending their life need not bother trying to disguise the fact. They can leave the empty bottle of Nembutal by their bed, or they can have the CoGenie or the Exit Bag with them. If this is the case, the death will be recorded as suicide (even if you were only a few hours away from dying of your lung cancer). But the question of whether or not you were assisted could be raised and could implicate those close to you.

If, on the other hand, the decision has been taken that suicide is not to appear on the certificate, thought must go into picking a strategy or method that will disguise this. If the person ending their life is very sick, and this is known by the doctor who certifies the death, the assumption that they died of their disease will usually be made. That is unless the patient has an Exit Bag over their head, or empty packets of tablets by the bed, or a suicide note. If there is any evidence at all that this was not a natural death, the doctor must refer the death to the coroner. If this is to be avoided, nothing pointing to suicide can be found at the deathbed. Tablets and packaging must be cleaned up, and friends or loved ones agree to remove any other 'incriminating' items so that the assumption is made that the disease caused the death. This approach usually works well.

It is important here to clarify the legal distinction between cleaning up after a death and assisting in a suicide. For example, helping someone put on an Exit Bag is clearly assisting a suicide and, if discovered, could attract serious punishment. Alternatively, if you find a loved one has died using a bag, if you remove the bag and fail to mention it to the doctor so that the death is thought natural, this is also a crime, but one of far less significance. When this is detected – and it rarely is – the grieving loved one might attract a legal slap on the wrist. The usual defence is that they hid the bag as it was in the family's interest to conceal the fact that this was a suicide. Clearly, if the method used caused obvious marks or signs on the body, there is no chance that this will be recorded as other than a suicide.

If a diagnosis of natural death is desired, the most common methods of suicide employed are the taking of drugs by mouth or the use of an Exit Bag. Neither method leaves any obvious sign. If the doctor becomes suspicious, however, they will not sign the death certificate and the coroner will arrange an autopsy. Autopsies are by no means routine, though, and their use is becoming less frequent, as the New York Times reported recently:

Autopsies were once routine, performed in more than half of hospital deaths and, in some parts of the country, in a majority of deaths that occurred elsewhere. But over the last few decades, the number of such procedures in the United States and several other countries has sharply dropped.[14]

The determining factor where autopsies are concerned is usually cost. Autopsies are expensive. So unless there is an obvious medical mystery (why did this person die?) or legal mystery (what were the circumstances of this death?) they are often forgone. If an autopsy is performed, any drugs involved will be detected and if lethal quantities are found, the death will be identified as a suicide. The use of an Exit Bag, with or without helium (see chapter 9), is unlikely to be determined, however, even with an autopsy.

Whether you want a finding of natural death or suicide, with either scenario I always advise that a signed and dated note be left that states clearly that you acted alone, with no help from anyone. If you leave it beside you as you take the drugs to end life and it is found, suicide will be recorded as the cause of death. If this is not desired, hide the note or give it to a trusted friend or relative – if questions are asked about the nature of the death it can be 'found' later while dusting or going through drawers to protect anyone under suspicion.

In Australia there are a range of laws that structure our end-of-life choices. While it might be comforting to know that if it all gets too bad we can legally suicide, it should be kept in mind that for this to be legal you must receive no help, information or advice from anyone, and unless you want to challenge the law and have your loved ones possibly find themselves in court, you should probably die alone. Anyone who tries to help you could, in at least three states of Australia, find themselves in prison for life.

If there are people who wish to be present, to avoid them being implicated you could try to end your life in a way that obscures the fact that it was a suicide, so that the assumption of a natural death is made. This will, however, seriously restrict the method chosen, and in the event of an autopsy, the suicide could be discovered. And while it might be comforting to know that you can refuse medical treatment and, in some circumstances, obtain a peaceful death that way, you should also remember that if you find yourself 'sectioned' in a psychiatric ward, your right to have your say will fly straight out the window.

Similarly, if you think you can simply die by refusing food and water, remember that on losing consciousness 'palliative care' can be initiated against your will. In some states, you can appoint a medical power of attorney and/or leave a list of directions (your living will) about medical treatment for doctors to follow if you do lose your ability to communicate. Remember, though, your power of attorney can never help you die. As I've highlighted throughout this chapter, the legal and logistical minefield around current end-of-life issues is significant. Picking one's way through is no easy feat, and requires extreme caution.

Chapter 9

The Joys of Technology

Technology is widely acknowledged for its capacity to change the way we live. Broadly speaking, I see technology as the process by which we address our needs and solve our problems. According to Denice Denton, Professor of Electrical Engineering at the University of Washington (Seattle), society shapes technology as much as technology shapes society. Nowhere is this more obvious than with end-of-life choices. This is why Exit is shifting its operational focus to go beyond law reform and to explore the potential for new technologies as the most effective means of increasing an individual's choices in dying.

Our change in focus is significant and has been a long time coming. It was in 1998 at the conference of the World Federation of Right-to-Die Organisations in Zurich that I first set out my thinking about the role of new technologies. That talk was titled 'Euthanasia, a Technical Solution: The Politics and Evolution of the Suicide Pill'.

While some inventors concern themselves with creating the ultimate mousetrap, my aims are more modest. At the heart of all my efforts is a desire to fulfil the needs of Exit members.

Older people and those seriously ill make up the vast majority of our supporters. Since 1996 I have listened to countless stories of suffering and need. I have been privileged to have had access to these first-hand accounts of what elderly and very sick Australians think and why. These people tell me that they want choice about when and how they die. Curiously, many people assume that our inventions are readily available. This is not the case. 'Dear Dr Nitschke, please may I buy your Peaceful Pill?' is a request I receive in the mail each week. As the Exit International Research and Development (R&D) Program consumes more and more of our time, our work also presents us with an increasing barrage of legal challenges.

Exit's approach to technology

The association of new technologies with end-of-life choices tends to open a can of worms. And for this reason, the term 'technology' needs some further clarification. I like the idea that technology can be understood in the following two ways.[1] First, technology can be said to be 'intangible' in that it involves expertise and knowledge. To create a new technology, one must know what to do. Second, a new technology depends on 'show-how'. That is the skill, the tangible means by which a device is created. The tangible side of technology also involves the sourcing and use of equipment, tools, software and often machinery. To build something – anything – a person must know what to do and how to do it.

Take lethal drugs as an example. A person must not only know which drugs are lethal, but they need to know where to get them, how much to take of them and in what combinations.

To this end, Exit's R&D program also includes research into new and existing drug combinations, natural and synthetic, prescription and over-the-counter. We are testing what is lethal and what is not. We are asking how normal people can acquire them. Is it possible for Exit members to make them themselves? What are the effective ingredients, and in what combinations? These questions are all currently being answered by Exit's R&D work.

As end-of-life options, Exit's CoGenie and the Peaceful Pill have aspects of know-how (intangible) and show-how (tangible). Without both aspects, neither device can be prepared. For example, to build a CoGenie you not only need to know the right chemical ingredients, but you also have to acquire pieces of piping or plastic containers. In addition, you will need to know how to put them together. To make a Peaceful Pill, you not only need to know where and how to source the ingredients, but you require the knowledge of what to do with them. Most importantly, it is in the know-how and the show-how that built-in safeguards lie, safeguards that make the rash use of such devices very difficult indeed. You can't just conjure up something that will help you die. You need to know exactly what you are doing.

Exit is all about sharing information.[2] Our practical workshops are based on a collective approach, one that sees ideas and information exchanged between members on a regular basis. The development of the CoGenie was the result of the hard labour of many Exit members, all working together. And this is what our R&D program is all about. For a device or drug to be of use, the technology must be in place so that the item can preferably be made at home, with no external assistance, from readily obtainable objects or ingredients.

Technology and ageing

Older people make use of technology in myriad ways, and this is going to increase. Indeed, there are now even groups such as the Dutch-based International Society for Gerontology that is committed to researching and creating technology that is specifically targeted at 'independent living and social participation of older persons in good health, comfort and safety'.[3] This sort of technology is represented in my 83-year-old mother's electric scooter, which allows her the independence of going to her local post office, shops and hairdresser unaided. Telecommunications are already widely used in remote-care giving – for example, home alert systems. Then there are access devices such as stair lifts and no end of gadgets that assist with independent living. Technologies have even been developed enabling micro-sensors to be embedded in a toilet seat in order to provide daily monitoring of vital medical signs. Indeed, you could say that technology has become so user-friendly that it is largely invisible. Just think how many of us:

> use technology with minimal comprehension of how it works, the implications of its use, or even where it comes from. We drive high-tech cars but know little more than how to operate the steering wheel, gas pedal, and brakes.[4]

In a 1999 study of the future needs of baby boomers, it was reported that this generation will have particularly high expectations of technology as they age. Indeed, this research predicted that boomers will 'expect technological genius to respond to their needs in old age'.[5] The field of gerontology is surely set to explode into action. Yet while our expectations of technology are increasing, our ability to deal with the issues that relate to their use is lagging behind.[6] This is perhaps why technology that assists with dying is still so controversial. My use of technology has led to accusations of morbidness. The Deliverance Machine – a controversial new form of technology – is a case in point. This machine was the laptop computer (with syringe driver and cannula) used by my four patients who qualified to utilise the ROTI Act to die in 1996. The machine now sits in the British Science Museum. Why it is not on display in an Australian public institution is testimony to the controversy that surrounds it. How this happened makes an interesting story.

In early 1997, after the ROTI Act was overturned, the Sydney Powerhouse Museum approached me, wanting to acquire the Deliverance Machine for their medical collection. Shortly after this, the then curator of health and medicine, Megan Hicks, seemed to come under extraordinary political pressure to rescind the offer. The risk – as I understood it – was that the machine would prove so controversial that it would most likely never be displayed. Instead, it would probably languish for decades in the museum's basement and not be seen by anyone.

It wasn't until I consulted the Hansard record of Federal Parliament that the politics of the museum's invitation were revealed. Not long after I received the invitation from the museum, the Senator for the Northern Territory, Bob Collins, accused me of having gone 'one step too far on this [VE] issue'. In Parliament, Collins stated:

> Will it be a ghoul's gallery at the Powerhouse Museum?
> . . . What is being proposed is ghoulish. . . . It is just appall-
> ing that a medical practitioner would even contemplate
> handing over a piece of his medical equipment, particularly
> this one.
>
> It is Dr Death and his killer computer . . . For a medical
> practitioner to even contemplate doing this is appalling . . .

Collins then called upon the Powerhouse Museum not to acquire the machine. History tells us that the museum did indeed follow the Senator's advice. At the time I thought it astounding that the Territory's own Senator should be the one to block what I thought then – and still think now – is a good Australian invention. Looking back, it seems that Bob Collins's attitude personifies how, as a society, we lack the analytical frameworks within which to make sense of emerging technologies, particularly those that seek to open up new frontiers.

Interestingly, when the British Science Museum heard that the machine would not go to the Powerhouse after all, they expressed interest in its acquisition. My first thought on receiving their offer was that that they must be more enlightened than we are. But this was apparently not the case. Rather, the director of the Welcome Wing Project and head of science communication, John Durant, told me that the only reason the museum could countenance the presence of the machine in its hallowed halls was because it had been used some 13 000 kilometers away. This distance, I was assured, somehow sanitised the invention, making it palatable for a broader public audience.

In an email to me in 1999, Durant wrote:

One of the Science Museum's aims is to raise wider moral and social issues in the fields of science, medicine and technology; and our commitment to display your machine lies in the fact that it raises profoundly important ethical questions concerning the wider role of contemporary medicine.[7]

John went on to say that it is only once a society is mature enough to accept its own history that the icons of that history can be displayed in its national museums. It would seem that Australia has a long way to go before it starts to come to terms with the issue of voluntary euthanasia.

The medical profession and technology

The last half-century has seen profound breakthroughs in medical science on a number fronts, many of which concentrate at either end of life – birth and death. In regard to the former, technology has led to a significant reduction in infant mortality and an increase in survival rates of women during and post-childbirth in the developed industrialised West. At the other end of life, new technology has focused upon the treatment of life-threatening disease, sometimes at all costs. Indeed, our line of 'defense against death has been said to run the gamut – from ventilators and organ transplantation to dialysis and open-heart surgery'.[8]

Broadly speaking, discussion of medical technology is seen in the context of progress: progress that is infinite, and where things just get better and better. In some countries, progress is even understood as symbolic of a nation's maturity and sophistication. Take the South African surgeon Dr Christian Barnard as an example. In December 1967, Barnard performed the world's first human heart transplant at the Groote Schuur Hospital in Cape Town. Immediately after this technological breakthrough, Dr Barnard became a household name around the world. He was catapulted to fame as a media star and a public diplomat. South Africa's capability to perform heart transplants placed the country firmly in the ranks of the First World, belying its mixed developed and developing economy that grew out of separatist apartheid policies.[9] The ability of South Africa to perform this technological feat was said to symbolise the country's self-sufficiency and became a source of national pride.

The most important factor that continues to be overlooked in the application of life-prolonging technologies is the quality of the life concerned. In this respect it is all too easy for doctors to believe that it is their obligation to 'extract every possible moment of life' – thereby prolonging the bare biological existence.[10] However, as Lance Stell, Professor of Philosophy at Davidson College in North Carolina, reminds us, 'medicine is not horticulture'. Is it the right course of action for doctors to try as hard as they do, applying the tricks of their trade on everyone, especially those who do not want it? From where does our perceived responsibility to preserve life at all costs actually come? One scholar who has challenged the 'preserve life at all costs' belief system is Professor Haavi Morreim, from the University of Tennessee. According to Morreim, much of what passes for life support would be better referred to as patient cruelty. And I agree. But what do we mean by cruelty? And how does it involve the medical profession?

In a report for the American bioethics organisation the Hastings Center, Morreim argues that his cruelty argument springs from 'medicine's values as a profession: preserving life, curing illness, alleviating suffering, and ameliorating handicaps'.[11] Accompanying the increased availability of technology to prolong life is the pressure on doctors to use it. This pressure doesn't just come from the law and from the doctors themselves who fear accusations of negligence if they don't pull out all the stops to save lives. It also comes from family members who want the 'best' for their loved one. The indignity so often associated with the use of such technology is sometimes not thought about until it is all over.

Technology for death's sake

Discussion of the role of technology in hastening death is largely taboo, contrasting sharply with discussions about the role of technology in postponing death or prolonging life. While the latter specialty is drowning in choice, with the former there is no choice at all. Older people and those who are seriously ill continue to suffer. Yet if technology is applied smartly, real end-of-life choices can be created and things can change – not only for older people and the seriously ill but for those who, in medical jargon, experience 'profoundly diminished life'. As a society we deserve no less. In the medical profession, we owe no less.

'Profoundly diminished life' refers to patients whose condition is irreversibly poor. These are people who may survive for many years if provided with proper nutrition and nursing care. The case of Mrs BWV (discussed in chapter 8) is an excellent example. What she was undergoing made her a prime candidate for Morreim's argument of patient cruelty. There is no doubt that there is as much a role for new technologies in the hastening of death as there is in its postponement.

> The unrepresentative swill of the Senate have affirmed that though God may decide when we die and rest in peace, they may dictate how long we live in agony.
>
> But some good will come of this – it continues the exposure of their unworthy membership. Our glimpses of their cosy corruption and smug arrogance coupled with this latest failure to represent the wish of the majority will make us look very carefully at that long strip of paper next time we are in the ballot booth.
>
> No more ticking off the numbers according to the party ticket. We have learned the importance of appointing true representatives and we have learned that we cannot trust the two major parties' recommended candidates.
>
> The Ides of March have never been a good time for senators, and trust me – the knives are out.
>
> – Letter to the Editor, *Sydney Morning Herald*, 25 March 1997[12]

Where to for technology in end-of-life choices?

While controversial, the creation of technologies to die by addresses a need that is already upon us. Beginning with my generation – the baby boomers – the longer and more healthy the lives of successive generations, the greater the demand will be for end-of-life choices. Yet while the medical profession will likely be involved in developing new ways to prolong life, they are much less likely to involve themselves in ways to shorten it.

This is why I can envisage a time when our dying will be more technologically influenced than ever before. But instead of doctors – or politicians or legislation – calling the shots, dying will become democratised. By democratised, I mean that the process of dying will be more likely to be controlled by the person concerned. This heightened level of autonomy will open up new choices to the ordinary person. Just as the Deliverance Machine gave control back to my four patients during the time of the ROTI legislation, so future inventions and technologies will place control firmly in the hands of those in need.

Since 1996, Exit has developed a strong track-record in the area of new end-of-life technologies. The following highlights some of our achievements.

The Deliverance Machine

The Deliverance Machine was the device used by Bob Dent in the world's first case of legal voluntary euthanasia. I inserted the needle into Bob's vein, but it was he who answered the three questions that were presented to him on the laptop screen, and it was he who responded by tapping 'Yes' into the keyboard.

The Deliverance Machine enabled me to move out of Bob's personal space and allowed his wife Judy to be at his bedside with him when he died. Freeing this space was the right thing for me to do. It was the right privilege for me – as Bob's doctor – to pass up. Of this experience Judy Dent says:

Bob was fiercely independent. To him, the most painful aspect of his illness was the inevitable erosion of his independence. He was so pleased that Philip had made the Deliverance Machine so that he could control his death himself, with Philip standing by but removed from the actual process. He didn't want his death on anyone's conscience.

I shall forever admire and respect Philip for his commitment to Bob and to making ROTI work.

The idea of inventing the Deliverance Machine came to me after reading about American doctor Jack Kevorkian's device called the Mercitron. Kevorkian developed the Mercitron so that his patients could control their death. The device consisted of three holding bags of drugs connected to a single IV drip. The first bag contained a saline solution, the second a barbiturate for sedation, and the third contained a mixture of potassium chloride combined with a muscle relaxant. Jack or an assistant would start the saline solution. The patient would then flick a switch to start the barbiturates. Once asleep, a mechanical trigger would administer the lethal drugs.

My machine took Kevorkian's idea and added a computer to replace the switch. This made the initiation of the drugs an automated and interactive process. It also meant that a doctor was only needed to insert the needle and load the machine, although under the ROTI law a doctor was required to be present at the death. On the four occasions that the machine was used, I would insert the cannula into the patient's arm and then step back, leaving the laptop in the patient's hands.

The Deliverance Machine turned voluntary euthanasia into physician-assisted dying.[13]

My use of a computer extended Kevorkian's thinking in other ways. The Deliverance Machine ensured that the patient had full knowledge of their impending death. The patient needed to answer 'Yes' to three separate questions to initiate the process. The first question asked was: 'Are you aware that if you go ahead to the last screen and press the "Yes" button you will be given a lethal dose of medications and die?' The second was: 'Are you certain you understand that if you proceed and press the "Yes" button on the next screen you will die?' The third and final question was: 'In 15 seconds you will be given a lethal injection . . . press "Yes" to proceed'. If the wrong button was pressed or a button was pressed outside of a specified time limit, the program would stop and the process would need to begin again.

Although I built the syringe-driver that delivered the drugs, others were also involved in the machine's conception. Exit member Des Carne developed the software used by the laptop, and Ian Taylor of the psychology department at the University of Melbourne built the interface for the syringe-driver and the software. The drugs used in the machine were Nembutal (the barbiturate) and Pancuronium, a curare-like muscle relaxant.

The Exit Bag

The Aussie Exit Bag is another means of self-deliverance that Exit has focused upon. A simple, custom-designed plastic bag, when used in a certain way it results in a peaceful, low oxygen (hypoxic) death. The use of plastic bags to bring about a peaceful death is not new. Derek Humphry outlines the practice in his book *Final Exit,* but the use of a specific 'customised' bag for the purpose of ending life was first described in a brochure written by Canadian John Hofsess in 1997.[14]

The Right to Die Society of Canada was the first group to market the bag and an instruction booklet in 1997 and the bags have since been widely distributed around the world.[15] Many Australians have ordered them by mail, paying US$46 for the kit. But all this came to an abrupt end in 2001 when the US anti-euthanasia campaigner Wesley J. Smith visited Australia. With sympathetic front-page coverage from the Catholic journalist Denis Shanahan, *The Australian* revealed the importation of the Canadian bags into Australia was occurring.[16] Florid in style, Shanahan's article demonstrated a complete misunderstanding of the science of the bags: 'The suicide bags, reminiscent of the Khmer Rouge's shopping bag executions in Cambodia's killing fields, are mailed directly to applicants in a plain white envelope'.

Intended or not, the factual errors and sensationalist slant of the story were enough to create a moral panic, one that led Justice and Customs Minister Chris Ellison to call for an urgent report from Customs to determine whether there were grounds to prevent the importation of the bags. The very next day Ellison was quoted as saying: 'I would remind anyone considering the importation of these kits that aiding and abetting or inciting the killing of a person is a criminal offence in all states and territories'. All this occurred within a week of Shanahan's article, confirming that the government *can* respond quickly when it wants to. These moves by the Australian government spelt the end for the importation of the Canadian bag. While there was some doubt whether Customs could actually detect the arrival of such bags, the threat was enough to put an end to the trade as Exit advised its members of Ellison's warnings on the issue.

When Exit was contacted by a number of elderly members who said they had changed their minds about ordering the Canadian bag, we set about developing our own. Modelled on the Canadian version, the Australian Exit Bag is made of thick plastic and has an adjustable soft-neck opening consisting of material with elastic attached. It is important to note that while an Exit Bag may not look very attractive, it is a reliable method of 'self-deliverance'. A low oxygen death is peaceful. More common 'hypoxic' deaths are those caused by a lung infection (pneumonia – the old person's friend) or the sudden depressurisation of an airplane, where whole aircrews occasionally die as if in their sleep. This is not a violent death from a mechanical obstruction of one's airway. A person using an Exit Bag breathes easily with the oxygen concentration in the inhaled air decreasing until unconsciousness and death result. To suppress the arousal produced by the raised concentration of carbon dioxide in the bag and low oxygen levels, sleeping tablets are taken beforehand and the bag positioned so that it only functions once sleep comes.

For an Exit Bag to work as planned, skill is required. In the United States and Canada, the bag is often used in combination with helium gas. This gas improves the efficiency of the bag, since the helium displaces the oxygen so that hypoxia and death occur in a matter of minutes. In America, disposable helium canisters are readily available in supermarkets, but in Australia helium is only available in leased high-pressure cylinders. The resulting paper trail can legally complicate the process.

Evelyn Martens and the Canadian bag

The acquisition of helium is not the only legal issue that should be considered in regard to the use of plastic bags to cause death. In Canada – the 'home' of the customised Exit Bag – a prominent member of the Right-to-die Network (the organisation that distributes the bags) was in 2003 charged with two counts of assisted suicide.

Evelyn Martens, a 74-year-old pensioner, was formally charged with assisting and counselling two people to suicide in January and July 2003. They were a 64-year-old former nun, Monique Charest, and a 57-year-old teacher, Leyanne Burchell of Vancouver. The evidence gathered against Martens included the discovery of a supply of helium, plastic tubing and plastic bags to these women. Martens was charged following an undercover operation whereby a Canadian policewoman posed as the goddaughter of Monique Charest. The policewoman recorded Martens describing the death and how she had been present. In evidence presented to the court, Martens is alleged to have told the policewoman, 'I made sure that this was what she wanted.'[17]

Evelyn elected to be tried by a judge and jury, and it is well she did. In November 2004 she was acquitted of all charges. More information about Evelyn can be found on her web site: http://www.evelynmartens.ca.

At the most recent meeting of the NuTech group in Seattle in January 2004, almost all the Americans present thought that using the plastic bag with helium gas represented the method *par excellence* for a peaceful death. Indeed, the bag is the predominant method of 'self-deliverance' recommended by the US VE-support group, Caring Friends.

Despite this, however, many people consider dying with a plastic bag on their head to be rather undignified. This view is often heard at my workshops, even by those who have a clear understanding of the reliability and peacefulness of the method. 'I don't want to be found looking like that' is the common response. While these concerns are based on aesthetics, not physiology, they are powerful disincentives when it comes to using an Exit Bag. In the documentary *Mademoiselle and the Doctor*, Lisette Nigot discusses this point in some detail:

> I didn't invent it, but Philip had presented the plastic bag at one of his workshops . . . I looked at it with interest. I said, 'I would never use a thing like that' . . . but my interest had been awakened and I said, 'Mmm, I can make one' . . .
>
> The bag is one of the many bags I have in which I buy my parrot's seeds . . . I stitched a very large hem and I left an opening . . . Now, I don't like it at all. I don't think it's nice . . . it's not a nice way to die. But apparently it's a very good way and you never miss . . . [For me] the bag is really the last option.

And this is a common sentiment. While American activists continue to promote helium-filled plastic bags, members of Exit

International prefer to seek other means. Exit's own research shows that less than 1 per cent of our members would prefer to use an Exit Bag rather than the Peaceful Pill (89 per cent). You will find an in-depth discussion about Peaceful Pill preferences in chapter 11.

The CoGenie

Over the past two years, Exit has focused much of its research on the use of the gas carbon monoxide as a means of obtaining a peaceful death. Our R&D in this area has led to the development of the CoGenie, a device that generates carbon monoxide (CO), hence its name. Like the Deliverance Machine before it, the CoGenie is loosely based on the research work of Jack Kevorkian. Jack advocated the use of carbon monoxide, although he never created a device that would generate it.

According to the fan club web site of Kevorkian's high-profile lawyer, Geoffrey Fieger (see www.FansofFieger.com/mercitron .htm), Jack sourced carbon monoxide from pre-purchased cylinders. The patient then had only to connect a simple gas mask to a cylinder via plastic tubing and turn the gas supply on. Kevorkian found that carbon monoxide caused a peaceful death in about ten minutes, and was used by about half of the reported 130 patients he helped to die. Exit's version of such a machine – the CoGenie – is different in that it actually manufactures the monoxide itself. This avoids the not insignificant difficulty of finding a supplier of the compressed gas.[18]

The first CoGenie was built in Darwin in late 2002. The prototype was rough. Made of PVC piping and glass, and splattered with silicon and blue PVC glue, the original device looked quite unappealing. On testing the CoGenie in the Exit fume cupboard, however, it was found to produce pure carbon monoxide at the rate of 1 litre per minute, more than enough to be effective.

I had planned to demonstrate the first CoGenie at the national conference of the Hemlock Society in San Diego in January 2003 but my plans were interrupted. Australian Customs officials seized the CoGenie at Melbourne Airport, just as I was about to board my flight to the US. On this occasion I was ushered into a side room and my case – which I had previously checked in – had its contents spread out on a table. Three customs officers inspected the disassembled parts of the generator before confiscating them. I was then handed a piece of paper outlining recent changes to the Customs Act (prohibited exports); changes that had been gazetted quietly by the Howard Government only a few weeks earlier and that made it an offence to carry a 'device designed or customised to be used by a person to commit suicide'.

When I arrived in the States without the CoGenie, significant publicity about the seizure of my equipment ensued. This drew the attention of the international media to the Australian Federal Government's predatory approach to the issue. With the assistance of my good friend Neal Nicol (a long-time associate of Jack Kevorkian), I was quickly able to build and display a replacement CoGenie. Construction plans for this simpler device were then emailed back to Australia, bypassing the regulation that had netted the authorities a few pieces of plastic tube.

The intrinsic strength of this technological, rather than

legal, approach to end-of-life options was clearly demonstrated. While VE legislation can be overturned, it is futile to try to use Customs regulations to suppress ideas. Although laws can be repealed, ideas cannot be un-thought of and technologies cannot be uninvented. While individual CoGenies might be able to be seized, thousands of others can be made by those who need them. It is the know-how and the show-how of the design that matters, not this or that piece of plastic tubing.

In May 2003, the CoGenie got its first Australian demonstration at Exit's second biennial conference in Sydney. The device was shown to an eager audience that included thirty-odd Australian and international journalists who waited and watched as the gas detection stick changed colour, indicating the generation of pure carbon monoxide. While most of us associate carbon monoxide with the dirty exhaust fumes from car engines, in its pure form the gas is odourless and invisible. And, as Jack Kevorkian found, it is particularly suitable for a peaceful death.

Within days of the Australian conference, an American web site run by someone called 'Frog' appeared.[19] Frog's initial homepage lasted the best part of a month and described the CoGenie in detail, replete with instructions for its construction. Through word-of-mouth in the online and offline world, the know-how was being shared around. This is how the Genie – quite literally – escaped from the bottle. Since this time, information from Frog's web site (see www.geocities.com/monoxidemachine) has been shared among Exit supporters with small groups of members being active in building and refining their own CoGenies through our practical workshop program (see chapter 10 for a full discussion).

To date, well over 200 elderly people have attended workshops where the construction of the CoGenie has been discussed. These same people are all co-authors of the handbook that shows how to make one. The local hardware shop is still the most important source for materials, and there are now many better versions of the device in existence. The caustic liquids used in the first version have been replaced by semi-solid gels, and some acids by salts. Each of these changes has made the device easier to manage and simpler to construct. Now, there is even a ladies' version – created from kitchenware rather than hardware products like PVC piping. Women are normally more familiar with the supermarket shelf than the local hardware, and the substitution of such parts was a logical development. Some ladies' insistence on decorating their CoGenies with plastic flowers and coloured lids was unexpected, however.

The CoGenie is an example of an accessible and easy-to-assemble piece of technology that can ensure a peaceful death. Of equal significance, however, is the strategy that has allowed the CoGenie to be made and has enabled a good idea to become reality. Most importantly, this same strategy enables individuals to bypass the restrictions imposed by a hostile government. The practical workshop program is just such a strategy. The use of the Internet is another.

Beyond the Internet

Bill Gates once famously said that 'the Internet changes everything'.[20] And he wasn't wrong. Implicit in his remark is a belief that Internet technology has the potential to help us think and act smarter. Where choices in dying are concerned, the Internet is allowing us to share our ideas with other activists around Australia and the globe. Through the online publication of our monthly newsletter and the posting of press articles on our news lists, Exit members are better informed than ever. It seems the word is out and there will be no stopping it.

That national governments have no jurisdiction over offshore-hosted web sites – despite their best efforts at censorship and filtering – ensures that these lines of communication remain clear and open, and details about the design and construction of devices such as the CoGenie and the Peaceful Pill can still be circulated. This is what I mean by the transformative potential of technology. With knowledge at our members' fingertips, the need for a voluntary euthanasia law can be questioned. Why pander to a specific medico-legal criteria about whether or not you are permitted end-of-life choices when you have all the technology you need? The elderly and the seriously ill will have the information they require to choose when and how to die (and they won't need to drag friends and family into a legal minefield). This is what technology can provide.

Also, when considering the lifestyle of seriously ill and older Australians, the Internet is again the tool *par excellence* for information sharing. It is cheap and can be accessed from home or the local library. People with limited mobility can use it, and at any time of the day. As Nancy Crick wrote:

> My laptop computer has changed my life. Since the decline in my health, I have used the computer and the Internet to talk to my friends and family. My Internet diary has let me

talk to people I would never have met in real life. Talking to someone on the other side of the world using my computer is just amazing.

Nancy is a good case in point of someone who harnessed the revolutionary power of the Internet. The twenty-one people who sat with Nancy Crick when she died used the Internet to organise the night. Email was used to decide everything – from the time of the dress rehearsal to the transport arrangements. Even the catering for the evening was discussed via email. Much of this email was encrypted, however, and we were glad of this when, weeks after Nancy's death, the police executed search warrants in a number of Australian states and confiscated several Exit computers.

The benefits of using the Internet to share information about end-of-life choices are enormous. The movement's challenge is to now ensure that we remain one step ahead of governments who seek to control and restrict our right to information. While the Australian Federal Government is currently attempting to introduce Internet censorship legislation of the most restrictive type, it remains to be seen how effective these attempts at modern-day book burning will prove to be. (See the Conclusion for a full discussion about this legislation and its implications for end-of-life choices and for Exit.)

Nancy Crick and the Internet

Nancy Crick was sixty-nine years old when she died in May 2002, surrounded by twenty-one family members and friends.

In the last years of her life, Nancy suffered from bowel cancer and had undergone three operations in which most of her bowel had been removed. Prior to this she had been in good health and didn't think twice about agreeing to accompany her friend to a free Rotary screening for bowel cancer. However, after testing positive, Nancy soon found herself in hospital for what should have been a simple polyp removal. But simple it was not. As Nancy put it, 'I woke up five hours later in intensive care with a bag stuck to me and no arsehole.' Over the following few months Nancy's symptoms worsened and on two occasions there was further surgery to find out whether her weight loss and constant vomiting and diarrhoea were due to a resurgence of the cancer, or whether it was a consequence of the previous cancer surgery.

Nancy first contacted me in March 2001, joined Exit, and asked for a visit the next time I was on the Gold Coast. When I met her a few weeks later she gave me the most graphic account of how her quality of life had deteriorated since the surgery. She complained bitterly about the cold and the weight loss that she couldn't arrest. At frequent intervals she had to leave the table to go to the toilet. As Nancy put it, 'I spend most of my day in the smallest room in the house.'

Nancy made it clear that if things didn't improve, a peaceful death would be better than what she was going through. Nevertheless she agreed to pursue some further medical options that I suggested. I visited her on several occasions over the following few months as medical strategy after medical strategy failed. None of the palliative measures initiated by Nancy's bevy of treating doctors in those last months gave her any significant relief. A peaceful death was looking increasingly desirable. But if she went ahead and died, Nancy was adamant that she wanted her close family with her. And she wanted to die in her own home. I explained that it was not that simple: the presence of her family at the bedside when she died could be seen as a breach of the Queensland criminal code and could in theory attract a life prison sentence. She reacted angrily. Clearly Nancy was no ordinary patient.

A feisty, outspoken woman, Nancy had spent over thirty years as a barmaid in one of Melbourne's roughest pubs – the old Cumberland Arms in Sydney Road, Brunswick. And like so many other working-class Victorians, Nancy and her husband Jimmy had decided to move to the Gold Coast for their retirement. Tragically, Jimmy died within months of their move, leaving Nancy to her retirement alone, although her adult children and their families were by that time living in Queensland. Visitors to Nancy's modest Burleigh Waters home would usually find her in her dressing gown on the front porch, next to a doormat that read 'Make My Day – Piss Off'. She would welcome visitors with the same laconic humour and hand outstretched, saying 'G'day, the name's Crick – that's Crick with a "P"'.

Nancy and I discussed many ideas about ways for her family to be with her if she chose to die, and how they might be protected. But the main idea that grabbed her attention was my suggestion that she start up an Internet diary: a medium through which she could talk about her worries and have her voice heard, and from where she could condemn a system that would turn her and her family into lawbreakers if she went ahead with her plan. The idea appealed to Nancy's rebellious streak. As we discussed the idea she leapt ahead, suggesting more and more things she might be able to do with the diary. By the end of our conversation, www.nancycrick.com was born. There then remained only one more problem to solve – what about the legal risk for those she wished to have with her when she died?

Nancy wanted about seven close family members and friends present. I suggested she increase this number to include a broader, more representative community group – safety in numbers. Surely the police wouldn't arrest and charge twenty or more people, including Nancy's family, friends and supporters – some of whom would be in their nineties – with the crime of assisting in a suicide, a crime that in Queensland could put them in jail for life. The prospect may not have presented the Beattie government with unsolvable legal difficulties, but politically they would clearly have had a problem. Nancy jumped at the chance, making it clear to me that she very much wanted to make a difference to the VE debate. Her Internet diary and the planned gathering at her death, she thought, were the best ways for her to do it.

Nancy's diary (see www.nancycrick.com) was Internet use at its best. Through this daily log of her last weeks, she was able to bypass the traditional media and speak directly to those interested in her plans. The thirty-two diary entries, accompanied by photos that chronicled her last months, began appearing in February 2002.

> 6 February 2002
> Back in 1989 my husband of 37 years . . . dropped dead unexpectedly from a heart attack. I was naturally shocked

by this tragedy . . . At 60 years of age, fit and healthy, he was due to retire, to sit back, take it easy and enjoy the good life. I considered he was most unlucky to have died the way he did – that was until two years ago when I was diagnosed with bowel cancer and given 3 years to live.

Since then I've come to realize he was the lucky one. During the last two years I've formed a very close relationship with my toilet – so close I am never more than a few steps away from the smallest room in the house. Although I live in a sub-tropical paradise my body began to shrivel up and last winter was spent in front of heaters – not just feeling cold but frozen to the bone.

I made a promise to myself not to live through another winter. I intend to keep that promise. Whether it happens by natural causes or by my hand remains to be seen.

Nancy used her web diary to ask all manner of questions and raise many issues about voluntary euthanasia. When Premier Peter Beattie attacked her during a radio interview and suggested that her family might be behind her suicide plans (that is, encouraging her to kill herself), Nancy was able to respond immediately. In her diary she promptly invited the premier to have a cup of tea with her in Burleigh and talk about the issue. Of course, he never responded. In this diary entry, she also acknowledged how the Internet was changing her life:

13 February 2002

Transcript of Brisbane 4BC Radio News noon 8th February 2002:

Queensland Premier Peter Beattie says while he is deeply saddened by the plight of a terminally ill Gold Coast woman, there's no way the government will legalise assisted suicides [voluntary euthanasia].

The Premier went on to say 'who knows, for example, if you haven't [sic] got the wealthy grandma and the kids want the money . . . and ok they may . . . she may not be well but who is to determine at the end whether she was done in by herself or by someone in the family?'

I was sitting listening to the midday news on Brisbane Radio Station 4BC last Friday when this interview with the premier went to air.

At first I had a laugh to myself about the wealthy grandma claim. I thought, Mr Beattie, I am an aged pensioner, I live week to week – I will gladly swap bank accounts with you any day.

My humour turned to disgust when you went on to suggest my grand kids could do me in for my money.

Shame on you Mr Beattie, you have attempted to place a dollar value on my death, something my family would never do. The only way my family would contribute to my death is by smothering me with affection . . .

Mr Beattie, I rarely move out of the confine of my home, I am often confined for much of the day and night to the smallest room in my home. The room measures six feet by three feet – it's called a toilet – to me it has become a prison.

Mr Beattie, if your government confined prison inmates to an area this size they would protest – why shouldn't I protest, why shouldn't I tell the world that not all grand-mothers die peacefully in their sleep.

Mr Beattie, instead of going on radio talking about me, a woman you've never met, why not drop into my home? I'll make you a cup of tea and we can have a heart to heart chat. I'm always here.

To all my Internet friends enquiring about my health all I can say is, going on the Internet has put a spark back in my life.

Goodbye for now, Nancy Crick.

But the entry that was of most practical importance to Nancy was the one posted on 24 March 2002, just before she attended the Gold Coast VE rally that was to be her last outing. In this posting Nancy asked for help from the many thousands of people all over the world who were by then following her diary. She asked if anyone could help her get 'the premier drug for self-deliverance, Nembutal'. Nancy had found a way for the Internet to serve her interests. By speaking directly to her global audience she was able to obtain what few people with her working-class background can: she got her Nembutal.

24 March 2002

At 8.45pm on Friday evening two plain clothed cops came knocking on my door . . . one of the cops informed me he had heard I was going to kill myself at a rally on Monday. A similar story appeared in a major Sydney paper the next morning. Unless I die from natural causes I'll be here on Tuesday and Wednesday and so on. I'll go when I'm ready.

Thank you Karl Sadil [founder of Wales Right To Die] for your recent e-mail advice, I prefer the use of drugs. Derek Humphry in his book *Final Exit* identifies the drug Nembutal as the premier drug for self-deliverance; I understand Marilyn Monroe died from it. If it was good enough for Marilyn and other celebrities it's good enough for me.

I have temporarily postponed my departure in the hope that someone, any one, out there in cyber-space can help me out . . .

Goodbye for now, Nancy Crick.

Nancy's request was read all around the world and the answers she wanted came in. The more the media covered her story, the more her web site was visited. Media coverage of Nancy's plight extended from South America to Europe, the United States and Asia. Her guestbook received dozens of entries daily: a hospice patient in Venice, a farmer in the US, and even a fisherman from the Falklands contributed. Writing her diary entries and reading the guestbook became one of Nancy's fondest activities in the last months of her life. Although virtually imprisoned in her house by her poor state of health, her innovative use of the Internet allowed her to travel in a way this 69-year-old battler from Melbourne had never been able to do before. It changed her life – and her death.

Nancy Crick – postscript

Nancy's last diary entry was posted on 21 May 2002. That evening, with a large group of friends, family and supporters from several states gathered in her house, Nancy provided people with cake and cups of tea and made sure everyone was comfortable. Then, at about 8 p.m., she drank the Nembutal, and followed it with a Bailey's liqueur and a cigarette. She died twenty minutes later. The following is a diary entry recorded by Nancy shortly beforehand:

21 May 2002
This will be my last diary entry.

It's really a public statement and I've just recorded it so people can see that it's me that's saying these things. I want to thank all who have written to me from all over the world and all those who have helped me through this difficult time.

My name is Nancy Crick, I'm 69 years of age and I live in my own home here at Burleigh Waters in the Gold Coast.

Three years ago I found I had bowel cancer and I've since had 3 operations. Despite the best surgery and palliative care, my life has deteriorated to such an extent that I feel that death would be a blessed relief. But I could not legally get help to do this and the Premier, Mr Beattie says the law will not change . . .

I joined Exit (Australia) and asked how I could best draw attention to my situation so others would not have to suffer as I have had to. One way I thought I could make a difference was by an Internet diary nancycrick. com. The diary has given me a chance to explain to everyone why I think we've got to make changes to the law. I've been overwhelmed that my diary has been such a huge success and I've had letters of support from all round the world.

One thing I used my Internet site for was to get the drugs that would help me die peacefully, easily and reliably, when I decided it was time to go. Several kind people provided me with drugs which I know will put me to sleep and end my life.

The thing that most upsets me is that the law says I can kill myself anytime I want to, but no one can be with me because they might have helped me.

Well that's just rubbish and I don't see why I should die alone. I don't want to die alone.

Surely people just sitting with me, people I love, my friends, don't have to risk going to jail, just because they chose to be with me when I die. So I've invited relatives, friends and supporters of voluntary euthanasia to be with me – Nancy's Friends.

Under existing laws, here in Queensland and everywhere else in Australia, those who choose to be with me risk prosecution and a possible jail term of life imprisonment.

The law may decide to charge my friends who stayed with me. The law may say that simply being with me is the same as helping and assisting in my suicide.

THIS IS JUST NOT TRUE.

I have chosen to take my life at a time when I am able to do so myself, I am not asking for and do not need or want any help to die.

I am not being pressured or encouraged to take my

life, in fact everyone has been trying to get me to stay longer – but they're not going through what I am.

Let me be clear, no one has paid me, or my friends, family or supporters, any money to do this.

I am not depressed or unstable or mad I've simply reached a point where my life is done and now I want to die peacefully.

I tried all the medical options, gave all of them my best, but in the end it didn't work out. I'm not angry and I don't feel sorry for myself – it's just the way it is.

Nancy's Friends being with me when I die is meant to be a challenge – a challenge to an unjust law.

But I want to protect this group of people as much as I can, and this is the reason I'm making this tape.

If anyone out there is asked to serve on a jury that is called upon to judge those who bravely chose to be with me when I died, I want you to acquit these people who have stood by me.

They've done nothing wrong. I want you to find them NOT GUILTY of any ridiculous charge that tries to say they assisted in my suicide.

It's my death – I'm doing it – NO ONE else.

After Nancy died, it wasn't long before the Queensland police embarked on their lengthy and expensive investigation eventually leading to the execution of search warrants and the confiscation of computers, documents and videotapes from Exit premises in Darwin, Adelaide and New South Wales. At my home in Darwin, the police were particularly enthusiastic in their execution of their search warrant, seizing a great deal more material than the warrant permitted. This led to a successful legal action against the Queensland Government and their police commissioner by my legal team, led by the well-respected John Tippett QC, in the Darwin Supreme Court. The government was forced to pay our considerable legal costs, which came in at around $40 000 of Queensland taxpayers' money. You could say their enthusiasm got the better of them.

The leaking of Nancy's autopsy results

Nancy's death was bound to be a high-profile, political affair. Despite this fact, few could have foreseen the way in which the preliminary results of her autopsy would be leaked to the public in an attempt to damage my reputation. I learnt of the leak when I received a phone call from a senior journalist with *The Courier-Mail* newspaper just forty-eight hours after Nancy's death. His comments shocked me. 'Very reliable sources', he said, had leaked to him the news that a government pathologist at Brisbane's John Tonge Forensic Centre had reported he could find no trace of cancer in Mrs Crick's body. 'This,' he said, 'changed everything.'

What was most shocking about this report to me was that an autopsy had been arranged so quickly, and that the 'results' of what could only have been the most superficial of examinations were at *The Courier-Mail* before Nancy's body had cooled. In my experience, autopsies take time to arrange, time to execute and usually weeks for the microscopic, histological and biochemical examination necessary to accurately establish a cause of death. And, besides, test results are confidential until the coroner makes their decision about the need or otherwise for an inquest. So how did it happen that just three days after Nancy's death, the major papers across Australia all began running the headline 'Crick Died Cancer Free'?[21] There is a stench about what happened, and I suspect influence was exercised at the highest of levels.

To this day I still think it is of little importance that Nancy did not have cancer. Suffering is suffering. Nancy also saw the question of her cancer as being of little significance, and I think there is much media that saw it as convenient to ignore that even she was ambivalent about her actual cancer status. Two months before her death, in an interview with journalist Leisa Scott in *The Weekend Australian*, Nancy had said:

> I don't know what I've got and they don't know what I've got, but whatever it is, it's bloody well there. And they can't find it with their operations and in the end it comes down to quality of life and I've got none of that now. Those who keep telling me what to do aren't going through what I'm going through. It's not up to the politicians, or the church or the doctors, it's up to the people, and it's up to the patients. Why don't they ask the people?[22]

But for a government wanting to hide its own inadequacy, and a society preferring not to have to deal with the awful reality that life after 'successful' cancer surgery can be worse than cancer itself, truth is sometimes of little importance. Indeed, media report after media report came out at this time condemning me.

The AMA's deputy president, Trevor Mudge, sermonised that 'you have to look at the quality of the advice she's been offered', while other nameless 'leading surgeons' were said to have 'expressed concern' about my diagnosis.[23] I was being portrayed as a person who had used Nancy to serve my own wicked purposes and as having lied to the Australian public, to Nancy and to her family.

Of course, none of these accusations was true, as the article in *The Weekend Australian* had made clear some two months before. *No one* had known exactly what the situation was with Nancy's health. All we did know was that she had a problem and that she – not I – felt her life was not worth living as a result. Yet it was Queensland Premier Peter Beattie who really took the opportunity to sink the boot in, stating 'I just say to the learned doctor, you've got a lot of explaining to do'.[24] He then went in for some more scaremongering by suggesting that 'legalised euthanasia could be misused by some people to attempt to murder their relatives'.[24]

The stress of the attack from Beattie, the AMA and my many other enemies – not to mention the media itself – was huge, and it was during this time that I found Marshall Perron most helpful. A person with many years of experience with the head-kicking and back-stabbing that is Australian politics, he rang and simply said, 'Don't be too discouraged. You only cop this sort of flack when you're over the target.'

After this brouhaha, I spent quite a bit of time feeling sorry for myself and licking my wounds. In retrospect, I should have publicly stressed to a greater degree that it didn't matter to *Nancy* whether it was the cancer or the cancer treatment that had destroyed her life's quality. The point was, with no quality and no relief in sight, death had become the best option in her view. One lingering lesson from what occurred following Nancy's death is that I was again made to realise that when you tangle with powerful forces and people used to playing the dirty games of politics and power, you can get really hurt. What was also made crystal clear to me is that governments will do everything they can to destroy the integrity and credibility of those who show them up. And they will do anything but engage in the issue of our collective right to determine our own end-of-life choices.

On the second anniversary of Nancy's death in May 2004, many of 'the Nancy Crick twenty-one' – along with Nancy's immediate family – came together on the Gold Coast for a celebratory breakfast. Afterwards, a group of twenty-five took a hire bus up to Brisbane to visit police headquarters, where 94-year-old retired dairy farmer Fred Short and another Exit member, Bron Norman, requested of the police that they be allowed to make a statement to the effect that they were present at Nancy's death. Fred has repeatedly said that for him '10 years [imprisonment] is life . . . Either charge me or let the whole matter drop and let us know we are no longer under suspicion'.[26]

June 2004 was to prove an eventful month. We successfully used the media to lobby to obtain Nancy's autopsy report (something understandably very important to the Crick family). In this report of only a few pages it was noted some forty-three times that Nancy was cancer-free at the time of her death. Talk about the politicisation of an autopsy! Also of importance in the report, however, was the fact that it took 'at least one hour of unpicking . . . dense adhesions' in the loops of the bowel and in the abdomen to allow 'for an assessment of large and small bowel'. In medical terms, such adhesions indicate that this was a seriously unhealthy bowel, a condition that would cause anyone excruciating pain (a point also noted in the report). These 'numerous peritoneal adhesions', it was stated, 'would adequately account for her abdominal pain'.[27] Also, the Queensland police commissioner finally announced that the group of people who sat with Nancy would not be charged. Amazing, isn't it? It took a full twenty-five months to decide that Nancy's family and friends committed no crime – they did not 'assist' with Nancy's suicide – and hence would not be charged.

While I do, of course, accept the autopsy report when it says that she didn't have cancer, it is important for everyone to understand that what Nancy *did* have were extensive adhesions that can occur as a consequence of cancer surgery. And these – as any doctor knows – can lead to a situation that is far worse than having cancer itself. Indeed, not long after the media coverage of the 'no-cancer verdict' I was phoned by a retired surgeon. This octogenarian wanted to know if Nancy had adhesions from the surgery. It seemed he had been involved in many a discussion about Nancy's condition with friends, family and acquaintances, and was being called on for his professional opinion. 'Yes, Nancy did have extensive adhesions,' I told him. 'Aha,' he said, in the most understanding way. 'Just as I suspected, this is one of those occasions where every time you operate to try to correct things, they only get worse.'

When reporting the finding, Brisbane's *Courier-Mail* also made reference to 'extremely densely-bound adhesions of Mrs

Crick's large and small bowel' and I was quoted as saying it was the scar tissue from previous cancer surgery that had caused Nancy's suffering. As Nancy's son Daryle put it: 'Whether she had cancer or didn't have cancer is neither here nor there. Mum was in terrible pain . . . and her life was a misery. She's in a better place now.'[28]

Nancy Crick would never have experienced her peaceful death without technology. Similarly, the hundreds of Exit members who now possess the knowledge of how to make a plastic bag – and soon, how to make a Peaceful Pill – would not have peace of mind without the know-how and the show-how that has come from Exit's technology focus and our research and development program. These are just small examples of how central technology already is to the ageing process. They should also be seen as indicative of the road ahead and how DIY technologies present limitless opportunities, particularly in the gerontechnological field. The age of invention? Indeed.

Chapter 10

Exit Clinics and Workshops

Exit currently operates three programs of advice and assistance for its members wanting information about end-of-life options, all of which are designed to help people get around bad laws. These consist of private home visits (called clinics), introduction workshops (where groups of people come together for an overview of end-of-life issues), and practical workshops (which provide specific, practical information). They are conducted in all states and territories of Australia and in New Zealand. Plans for an international expansion are well under way. Exit's fourth program, the construction workshops known as the Peanut project, is commencing in 2005.

Over the past seven years, the Exit clinic program has consistently had around one hundred seriously ill patients on its books at any one time. Since the introduction workshop program began in late 1997, more than 2000 people have attended. Exit's practical workshops – where members get together to discuss how to make devices such as the CoGenie, Exit Bag or Peaceful Pill – were begun in Queensland in late 2003. Already over 200 people have participated.

Exit's program of private clinics and introduction workshops was established in response to the increasing demand from people wanting information about end-of-life options. The short period during which the ROTI law operated changed Territory culture and it changed Australian culture too. For that brief time it became acceptable to talk openly about death and dying with your doctor. Doctors could answer questions without fearing the consequences of the law. Patients and their families felt these were questions they had the right to ask. All of society benefited. With the loss of the legislation, Australia reverted to a climate where discussion was once again difficult. But by then people had seen what was possible and the sick and elderly and their families have continued to want answers.

To meet this need, I registered myself as a doctor in all states and territories of Australia and began Exit's clinic program in which I visited sick patients in their homes. However, almost as soon as I began these clinic visits, I noticed that many of the people I was called upon to visit were not very ill, and certainly not terminally ill. Most were elderly, and many were in good health. This group of people seeking clinic appointments simply wanted information about their end-of-life choices, should things deteriorate. They wanted to be prepared for the future. The introduction workshops were established to address this group's need to know and the first workshops were conducted in Melbourne in late 1997. Since this time, the format of Exit workshops has been copied by others in Australia and overseas.

Exit clinics

Clinic visits are offered to individual members of Exit and those whom I visit are usually seriously ill, often terminal. These visits are conducted mostly at the homes of these patients, although I sometimes visit hospices, hospitals and nursing homes. Requests for visits come from people from all walks of life. The patient decides the issues that receive most attention during our discussion, but the most common question I receive is 'If things get worse, can I get drugs, or use something else, to ensure I have a peaceful death if and when I want it?'

During the first visit I often find myself having to ask a seriously ill person a blunt question: 'Do you know anyone who would be prepared to risk fourteen years to life in prison to help you die?' If the answer is yes, there is usually more to discuss and the trusted friend is included. If the answer is no, then that patient is on their own, and that can be very sad. Often the person is simply too sick to organise or acquire the means necessary to act themselves. I recently visited a 95-year-old patient in Adelaide whose diagnosis of motor neurone disease had only just been made. She knew it was too late for end-of-life assistance; she also knew there was precious little I could do for her. People's end-of-life options greatly contract when there is no one to help, and yet it is help such people so greatly need.

On many occasions I leave a clinic visit knowing that it wouldn't matter what I said, it really is too late to alter the inevitable. I do not charge for these visits, although a donation to Exit is encouraged. Neither Australia's Medicare nor any private system is called upon for support.

The following request for information is typical of the many letters of enquiry I receive daily:

> Dear Dr Nitschke,
>
> First of all let me congratulate you on the most courageous and human service that you strive to provide to society in the face of enormous difficulties contrived by the political system of this country.
>
> I am a professionally qualified engineer who held very senior positions in the electronics industries in Australia and abroad. Unfortunately I have been suffering from major spinal cord related problems over a long period of time which required surgery and radiation therapy several times in the recent past.
>
> The current situation is that a tumour exists inside my spinal cord spanning some 70 per cent of the spinal cord. The prognosis by eminent neurologists and neurosurgeons who I consulted in Australia and the US is that further surgery is not possible due to the critical state of my spinal cord and my clinical condition will continue to deteriorate.
>
> Over the last few years paralysis of my legs has worsened to a point that currently I am able to walk only a very short distance and that with great pain and difficulty. Due to the progressive nature of my tumour and the degeneration of my spinal cord, my clinical condition continues to deteriorate.
>
> I'd appreciate very much if you could grant me an appointment to meet with you to discuss some critical

aspects of my life in the face of the progressive deterioration of my condition that would transform me to the status of an invalid in the not so distant future.

In the event that you are unable to meet with me in Perth, I will be able to make arrangements to visit you in any other state. I am also in a position to absorb all costs associated with an appointment.

Thanking you in anticipation.

David Smith

Some people who contact Exit for clinic visits make it clear when I talk to them that they are angry there is no easy way to get their questions answered. They tell me that they want to use their experience – their death – to make a difference. Clinic patients like Sandy Williamson in Victoria and Shirley Nolan in South Australia are two such examples. Both women were seriously ill at the time I met with them and they wanted information about their end-of-life options. They both probably would have qualified to use the ROTI law, had it still existed. These women were angry that they had to go to such lengths to get the help to die that they wanted, and they chose to speak out publicly, hoping their statements would prompt change.

Sandy Williamson's story

Sandy Williamson had good reason to remember the attack on the World Trade Center in her birthplace of New York on 11 September 2001, since it was also the day she received her diagnosis of motor neurone disease (MND). It would be nine months later, on 23 July 2002, that Sandy would die from an overdose of the barbiturate Amytal.

At the time of diagnosis, Sandy did not know how much time she had left. And this is usually the case with MND. This relentless neurological disease gradually destroys the body's muscle control, slowly paralysing the patient and trapping their active mind in an immobile body. Premature death is inevitable, but the timing can vary greatly, from a few months to many years (as in the very unusual case of Stephen Hawking). This is a disease for which there is little treatment and certainly no cure. Patients fear the inevitable dependency they will have on others and the knowledge that their options will contract with time. Many sufferers contact Exit seeking advice on how they can retain the option to end their lives if it all gets too bad. The disease is feared, and sufferers of MND evoke considerable sympathy from their carers and loved ones.

Sandy Williamson first contacted me in late 2001. In her early fifties, she had been a high-flying creative talent in the advertising industry. Responsible for many well-known ad campaigns, MND was the last thing on Sandy's mind – at least until her diagnosis came through. An articulate, financially independent, professional woman, it was understandable that Sandy would want to take control of her death just as she had done with her life. Not one to be told 'No', she was infuriated at the lack of options available to her. What Sandy most wanted was to acquire lethal drugs and, with the comfort of knowing they were there, enjoy what was left of her life. She knew, though, that by the time she was ready to take them, her arms could well be paralysed.

Slowly, the implications of Sandy's spreading paralysis dawned on her. She told me how terrified she was of waking up one day, unable to move her arms. If she could not do this, she would have lost her 'window of opportunity' to die in her own time and in her own way. If she waited too long and became trapped, her only choice would be to ask someone to help her prepare the drugs, hold the glass to her lips, and to risk many years in prison. The other choice – enduring what she saw as an unbearable existence of a totally paralysed person – she regarded as no choice. I remember Sandy lying there, staring at me, feeling nothing but a huge wave of frustration and anger, primarily at her disease but also at a society that denied her assistance in her hour of need.

Over the ensuing few months I visited Sandy regularly for clinic consultations at her home in the upper-crust Melbourne suburb of South Yarra. She was by then living with her twin and another sister, both of whom had come out from New York to be with her. She told me she would never ask her sisters to help her die. Privately, her sisters told me that if asked, they would help. Time dragged on and while Sandy knew that nothing would change, she did not want to feel that her death would be in vain. We talked about this and I suggested she go public with her story. She embraced the idea and I contacted *60 Minutes*. On a cold winter's night in July 2002, Sandy and her sisters told Ray Martin about her plight. When the story ran, it was cleverly put together and included footage from Holland of Willem van Beek, another motor neurone disease sufferer (of about the same severity as Sandy) who was also considering his options.

In a powerful piece of television, the two patients talked by phone about their hopes, their fears, and their futures. A large audience across Australia watched as the injustice of Sandy's situation was spelt out. Because Australia now has no VE law, Sandy would have no choice but to take her life prematurely. She could not risk involving her sisters and she could not risk leaving her suicide so long that her ability to administer drugs by herself would be lost. In Holland, on the other hand, if a MND sufferer wakes one day to find they are unable to move their arms, they simply have to ask someone to call their doctor, who can then lawfully provide the drugs to end their life. Here was the evidence. When there is voluntary euthanasia legislation in place, patients live longer. Take away the law, and in many cases you reduce the length of these patients' lives.

The next day, *The Age* newspaper ran a feature article on Sandy. Her voice was finally being heard, and she felt she was making a difference. Sandy even asked the Victorian Premier Steve Bracks to come and visit her. She wanted to explain to him first-hand what his government's inaction on the issue had cost her. Needless to say, Bracksie had an excuse and declined, although the then local Liberal member for Prahran, Leonie Burke, did have the courage to visit. Yet, in the face of no choice, Sandy eventually took matters into her own hands. She had stockpiled the lethal drugs required and took an overdose in late July.

Sandy took the drugs before she wanted to. She took them while she could still move her arms, prepare the drugs, mix them with water and bring the glass to her mouth. However, things did not go to plan – the Amytal acted very slowly and Sandy fell into a deep coma. In the morning her distressed sisters called the local doctor, expecting him to come around and make Sandy comfortable as she died. However, instead of the doctor arriving, an ambulance appeared, closely followed by several police cars. Sandy's plans for a peaceful death were interrupted and four more days were added, not to her life, but to her death. These were days spent in a coma, ventilated, hovering between life and death in the intensive care unit of Melbourne's Alfred Hospital.

After these four fruitless days, the hospital doctors agreed to let Sandy go. She was finally granted her wish and they arranged for her to be moved back to her own home and to have the fluids switched off. In the end, Sandy Williamson died in the way that she most wanted to avoid. After questioning by the police, Sandy's traumatised sisters left for New York. In a letter sent to me in November 2002, Carmen wrote:

> Dear Dr Nitschke,
> Thank you so much for the support you gave Sandy for so long. You gave her tremendous comfort and the courage to go on. I appreciate how often you came to see her and your strength to stand up for your beliefs. I will always think of you with great respect and affection.
> Carmen

I remember Sandy as a courageous woman. Her attitude to dying is a sign of things to come. A quintessential baby boomer, she was furious at her lack of control over the fate that was forced upon her. In retrospect, it seems clear that her decision to make a difference and to speak out before she died directly affected her treatment at death. And this is too often the case. You can speak out by all means, as this is the only way things will ever change, but don't be surprised when, on your death, the police turn up and those closest to you are taken off for questioning. The stories of my patients described in this book who spoke out all prove this point. The public road to challenging the lack of VE laws can be very long and fraught with difficulty.

Diane Pretty and her fight for justice

Diane Pretty is undoubtedly the most famous MND sufferer to draw attention to the VE issue. Diane died in mid-2002 after a protracted legal battle in the courts of the United Kingdom and in Europe. Her condition had worsened to the point that she had become trapped in her body, but refused to cease asking court after court for the right to die, for her husband to legally give her the drugs that would end her suffering. All courts said no, including finally the European Court of Human Rights in Strasbourg, but the conscience of the Western world was pricked as media coverage reached saturation level. Her name is now known in all UK households and we are all a little wiser knowing of her fight to die with dignity. Diane had wanted her death to make a difference and she succeeded.

Shirley Nolan's story

Shirley Nolan is perhaps best known as the co-founder of the Anthony Nolan Trust, which she established in her son's name

in 1974. Through this Trust, Nolan created the world's first
bone marrow register, one which is said to have saved more
than 4000 lives globally. In honour of her work, she was presented to the Queen in 1992 and awarded an OBE in 1999.
Shirley was also one of Australia's most high-profile sufferers
of Parkinson's disease, and eventually took her life at her home
in Adelaide on 15 July 2002. She first made contact with me,
requesting a clinic visit, in 2000.

Shirley migrated to Australia in the early 1990s, and
although she had been diagnosed with Parkinson's while still in
her thirties, most of her life was relatively uncompromised by
the disease. In her late fifties, though, her deterioration gained
pace and her quality of life took a turn for the worse. Like
Sandy Williamson, Shirley Nolan was a headstrong woman and
she too was outspoken about the unfairness of her situation –
not because she had Parkinson's disease, but because she had
no options about how to put an end to her suffering. Her first
attempt to take her life was, as she put it, 'botched'. On that
occasion, the plastic bag method failed her. Shirley chose to
have her views about her situation released publicly only after
her death. This can be an important consideration if one wants
to spend one's final months without the constant intrusion of the
media. It does, however, limit the interactive dialogue between
the sufferer and the public, dialogue that can be so effective, as
in the case of Nancy Crick. In an interview published after her
death in the *Sydney Morning Herald*, Shirley said:

> I have always believed in the right to exit with dignity . . .
> I am not advocating going to nursing homes and disposing

of old people, but I want the right to make that decision myself.

Shirley wanted it known, the article continued, that she sought death because her life 'had suffering but no meaning'. To find mobility each day she would shoot dopamine into her blackened thigh up to a dozen times. She fluctuated between hot sweats and being freezing, and would lie trapped with the airconditioner on high after her temperature dropped, chilled to the bone but unable to move.[1]

In the last few years of Shirley's life, I made several clinic visits to her home in Adelaide. Each time we discussed her options. Each time the difficult questions would arise: 'If I become so disabled by the disease, how am I going to be able to physically end my life? If I have lethal drugs, will I be able to prepare them if the tremour becomes too severe? Would it be even possible, with Parkinson's, to use a plastic Exit Bag? And, if help is needed, who will risk South Australian laws and provide it?' Shirley's questions were typical of someone in her condition. And, by their very nature, they are difficult questions to answer. There are so few answers and even fewer solutions.

In April 2002, Shirley wrote the first of several open letters to the media in an attempt to share her thoughts about her situation:

TO WHOM IT MAY CONCERN
My Life and My Death
I have battled Parkinson's disease for more than 25 years to the stage of losing control of my body. Now, at times,

I cannot even move, speak or breathe. I am further demeaned by staggering, shaking and falling, appearing to be inebriated. It is easy to appreciate the loss of self-esteem in Parkinson patients when they see the look of disgust when observed by the unenlightened.

Parkinson's disease becomes increasingly degenerative. I am beginning to stoop, my muscles too weak to hold my body upright. My feet claw like talons and recently, my hands cramp and become exceedingly painful.

My muscles are almost constantly in spasm, i.e. rigid, heavy and aching. Most of the time in this latter stage of the illness, I find it impossible to relax sufficiently to read a book, view TV or even lie on my bed. I can no longer even control my body temperature. I hover between a state similar to hypothermia and menopause. My face can be hot and perspiring and my feet blue and icy. Passing from one room to another of a different temperature causes me to freeze, i.e. rendered completely immobile and helpless.

Those blocking research for Parkinson's (and other neurological conditions) should experience the indescribable terror of this paralysis. They should experience the slow erosion of self-confidence, self-worth, freedom and independence; the inability to even walk alone; leave one's home unassisted; go to a movie, dine out, visit friends – those few stalwarts who remain.

It is a life without quality. It is a living hell. I place what is left of mine on the altar of compassion in the hope that my death will highlight the plight of others and thus serve some purpose.

I pray for the speedy success of a change of the law to allow people like me to have assistance to die. Meanwhile, I must take my release into my own hands. I have already exercised my legal right to take my own life but, unfortunately, I botched it. Consequently, I have now planned with greater care and I hope fervently that I will succeed the second time.

Shirley Nolan OBE

Determined that her death should not be in vain, Shirley penned another letter on the morning of the day she would die. In it she wrote:

To whom it may concern

I hope today I can end the horror my life has become.

Parkinson's disease has slowly debilitated me for some 25 years, leaving in its path an almost unrecognisable parody of my former self.

No one has assisted me to end my life and the detailed account of my deplorable condition will affirm its necessity and blessed release.

Here today, my last day, I am an advocate of death, yet for over a quarter of a century, as founder of the Anthony Nolan Trust I have worked with fervour and determination to give to children and adults throughout the world, suffering leukemia and related diseases, the greatest gift of all, THE GIFT OF LIFE.

YET, as valuable as that life is, when shown it no longer has quality reduced to intolerably cruel days and nights of pain and suffering, I have always believed in THE RIGHT TO DIE WITH DIGNITY.

From the heart, I should have that right.

Like Nancy Crick, Shirley wanted people to understand *why* she wanted to die. But unlike with those suffering from terminal cancer, questions do arise about the terminal – or non-life-threatening – nature of chronic, neurological debilitating diseases like Parkinson's, which, on their own, might not necessarily shorten life expectancy. Parkinson's is also the condition affecting well-known Melbourne businesswoman Suzan Johnston who, prior to her diagnosis, established one of Australia's first deportment schools in 1959. Today, at sixty-five, Suzan struggles on with her disease, furious at the damage it has wrought on her body and her life, and she is anxious to ensure that she has access to viable end-of-life options, should things 'just get too difficult'. Parkinson's sufferers can endure a poor quality of life for many years. Had the ROTI Act still been in place and had someone like Suzan or Shirley tried to use it, questions would have been asked about the terminal nature of their disease. Quite possibly they would have been unsuccessful in seeking permission to use it. This highlights a particular problem with legislation – if we restrict access to it to only the terminally ill, we fail to address the needs of those suffering interminably with a disease that may not actually kill them. In many ways people with chronic suffering are the forgotten victims in the endless debates on the benefits of the legislative approach to end-of-life choices.

Exit introduction workshops

Exit offers its members the chance to participate in introduction workshops that are run several times a year in all states of Australia and in New Zealand. I also occasionally receive requests from people further overseas to attend our workshops, as in the letter below:

> Dear Dr Nitschke,
> Will you please email me your workshop dates in the next six months. I read in Hemlock's newsletter you will have six a year. I am visiting my son, who is married to an Australian in Melbourne. I would adapt my visit to fit one of your dates for your workshops. I tried to see you last November but you changed the days and city.
> Thank you sincerely,
> Gloria
> California

The majority of people who attend Exit workshops are elderly. Most are in good health (66 per cent),[2] and simply want to learn more about their options, although around a quarter have a terminal or serious chronic illness. Another much smaller group of participants are those who are best classified as being 'tired of life'. These people are not ill but, like Lisette Nigot, they are old and often feel they have lived long enough. Included in this group are people like Bundaberg couple Sydney and Marjorie Croft, who died together in 2002.[3]

Participants have included lawyers, doctors, scientists and engineers. Secretaries, business executives, clergy, builders, teachers and housewives also attend. That we continue to see more than a few retired judges at workshops suggests that even those who administer the law from the highest benches in the land still need information about their end-of-life choices.

The workshops cover a wide range of topics including the law; advance medical directives/living wills; psychiatric illness; palliative care and slow euthanasia. We also discuss issues such as death certificates; inquests; coronial inquiries and autopsies. The workshops conclude with a general discussion of drug options and non-drug methods to end life. Most people (77 per cent) come to gain specific information about their own end-of-life options. The rest come for general information or on behalf of a sick or elderly relation. Participants say that the three most useful topics covered are information about drugs (85 per cent); Exit's own inventions (84 per cent); and the current legal situation (83 per cent). Workshops are usually held in local community centres and sometimes at people's homes. In some states we work with the local voluntary euthanasia societies to organise the day. The workshop program takes about three hours.

Workshop safeguards

To attend a workshop, participants must be members of Exit. Attendance is free. Occasionally some people are excluded. All workshop participants sign a disclaimer that reads:

> I acknowledge that none of the information provided in this workshop will be used in any way to advise, counsel or assist in the act of suicide, either of myself, or any other persons.

I further agree not to photograph or electronically record by any means the discussion and commentary that takes place during the workshop without prior arrangement.

The disclaimer is then countersigned by a witness at the workshop.

Referrals by doctors

Seriously ill patients are occasionally referred to Exit's introduction workshops or clinics by their treating doctors. And the reasons are clear. There is plenty of evidence that some doctors have difficulty in talking about death with their patients.[4] This may be because they are aware of the legal risks in answering questions, but sometimes it is because the doctors don't know the answers to the queries put to them as they are often of a technical nature, for example 'How much of a certain drug will prove lethal?' or 'Will an overdose of a particular drug reliably cause death?' Exit workshops answer these questions.

At a personal level, I have found considerable support for our introduction workshops among many Australian GPs. Our workshops provide a respectable referral point that is often greatly appreciated by doctors.

Workshops – improving quality of life

Voluntary euthanasia opponents often accuse me of promoting suicide and of encouraging well people to die prematurely. They claim that those who attend our workshops will rush home, find lethal drugs and immediately end their lives. Yet our research reveals a totally different story.

Our longitudinal research study of people who attend Exit workshops examines for the first time the effect of providing accurate and concise end-of-life information in a workshop setting. Preliminary findings put an end to many of the concerns of the pro-life lobby. Just as the conservatives jumped up and down when sex education was first provided in schools, arguing that greater knowledge would encourage young people to have sex, so Exit has been accused of encouraging older people to die. However, just as there is no evidence that the provision of sex education increases sexual activity among young people, there is also no evidence that information about end-of-life options increases the suicide rate among the elderly or the seriously ill.[5]

The vast majority of people (84 per cent) who attend Exit's introduction workshops report that their attendance has a *positive* effect on their lives as they leave with more knowledge about their end-of-life options and as a result feel better able to make decisions. Their queries and concerns are put to rest because they are better informed. The remainder say the workshops have no discernible impact.

One of the key tenets of the new public health ethos of the World Health Organization has been the importance of empowering patients through knowledge. Our introduction workshops are therefore consistent with this approach to patient health, with an intrinsic respect for personal autonomy. That 95 per cent of participants leave our workshops feeling that their questions have been well answered is testimony to the effectiveness of the program, and to Exit's positive effect on those who choose to become members of our organisation.

A word of warning

In recent years, Exit workshops have been criticised by a number of groups and organisations, including Right to Life Australia and the Australian Medical Association. The former has claimed that our workshops 'should be closed and police should act to put Nitschke out of business'. They accuse me of 'missing the point'. Margaret Tighe says, 'People might want to say "good-bye, cruel world" because of the circumstances of their lives. They feel that nobody cares whether they live or die. We have to be able to recognise that and reach out to them.'[6]

To date, the police have not acted on the concerns of Right to Life, pointing out that no one attending has ever made a complaint. If such an allegation was to be formally made, I would highlight that giving people access to accurate information neither encourages suicide nor is diminishing of life. Precisely the opposite, in fact. As often as not, the providing of accurate information dissuades a person from dying prematurely, and outlines more appropriate options.

The AMA has also attacked Exit workshops, albeit from a slightly different angle. Describing me as exploiting 'fragile and vulnerable members of our community', Dr Simon Towler (former president of the AMA's West Australian branch) has called our workshops 'a cynical publicity gimmick which only deals with one aspect of what is a very complex and sensitive issue'.[7] Towler's criticism begs the question of how he knows this, since neither he nor anyone else from the AMA has formally ever asked to attend. More importantly, though, almost all participants report that an Exit workshop lowers their anxiety about end-of-life decisions and increases their peace of mind. In their criticism of the workshops, the AMA would do well to note the ethics manual of the Royal Australasian College of Physicians, which states:

> The trust which is essential to effective consultation [should] be based not on the traditional paternalistic model, but on a requirement for honest and effective communication between doctor and patient.[8]

As long as our workshops fulfil this criterion, I remain cautiously optimistic that the introduction workshop program will continue in all states and territories of Australia. As long as the program's contribution to wholistic health continues to be recognised – not only by participants, but by the medical profession, albeit silently – it will remain an integral part of Exit's activities.

Practical workshops

In 2003, Exit International initiated a new and unique program of practical workshops where members come together to discuss how to build the devices that can give them end-of-life choices. These workshops have a quite different focus from that of the introduction ones described above – they are about conferring practical empowerment on those who want it. Participants are encouraged to form networks so they can help each other aquire, manufacture or construct devices such as the Exit Bag or CoGenie. These information-sharing sessions are only available to members of Exit. They operate as follows.

Exit holds practical workshops regularly in all states of

Australia. They are usually held at private homes and involve around twenty-five participants, depending on the size of the host's lounge room or garage. To attend a workshop, Exit has instigated the following safeguards. Participants must have been a member of Exit for more than six months and must have attended an introduction workshop at a prior time. The third criterion for attendance is that participants must agree to contribute through their attendance and to co-author the next edition of the workshop handbook (currently in its fifth edition). This document contains the most explicit information about DIY end-of-life options, but it is not the intellectual property of any one person. Rather, it is a collectively written document of around 200 authors. The handbook contains basic instructions, a full list of materials required and personal tips about construction. To date, the collective contributions to the handbook have led to significant improvements in design and innovations in the materials used. Indeed, the workshops are extremely effective because they draw upon the pool of expertise that exists among the retired engineers, chemists and home inventors – male and female – who are members of Exit.

The focus of these workshops differs, depending upon the interests of those attending. Sometimes there is much interest in how the plastic bag works to cause a peaceful death, while other workshops concentrate on strategies to obtain prescription drugs which, when taken in certain combinations, can provide a dignified, peaceful death. What is most important and useful at these workshops, however, is the networking that occurs between members. This means that those who live locally are put in touch with each other, and it is in collaboration that they can make for themselves devices that provide end-of-life choices.

Construction workshops

Construction workshops provide Exit members with the opportunity to physically come together to make or acquire devices that provide real end-of-life choices. Similar to practical workshops, construction workshops are based around a collective model whereby members assist other members. The first construction workshop was held in Queensland in late 2002, and at this gathering a group of Exit members each built themselves a CoGenie. In 2005 the format was extended to the making of the Peaceful Pill – the so-called Peanut project. Interest in Peaceful Pill weekends seems likely to eclipse that of all other Exit programs.

The aim of members who attend construction workshops is simply to ensure they are prepared for the future. None of these people is rushing home to die. They are just ensuring that they know what to do and how to create real end-of-life choices for themselves in the event they feel they need them, choices that are independent of political process and legislative change.

At a theoretical level, the construction and practical workshops are a form of mass civil disobedience. A challenge is being laid down to the authorities. Will they prosecute the many authors of handbooks that show people how they can die with dignity? Although this is legally possible, the political impact of putting a large number of eighty-year-olds on trial for simply wanting real options that the state does not offer makes this unlikely. That hundreds of elderly people are willing to throw in their lot with this DIY approach, accepting the risks and possible legal consequences, should serve as a wake-up call to the politicians.

The goal of Exit's clinics and workshops is the same: the empowerment of the individual, the provision of genuine choice. All of these programs are independent of the legislative process and highlight how irrelevant the need for a VE law can be when DIY solutions are within reach. None of the Exit devices require the cooperation of our politicians. Real end-of-life options are available *now*. And since the documentary *Mademoiselle and the Doctor* has been shown around the world, demand for all Exit programs has increased markedly. People want to know, and they deserve to know.

Chapter 11

Peace in a Pill

The late Dutch Supreme Court Judge Huib Drion was the first person in the world to call openly for the introduction of a pill that would provide a peaceful, pain-free death at a time of a person's individual choosing, a pill that is taken orally and available to 'most' people.

As discussed in chapter 7, Drion's letter to a Dutch newspaper was the result of his own frustration at being hamstrung and dependent upon the medical profession for assistance should he wish to die. If Drion had been a doctor, he would know how to obtain a peaceful death when he felt the time was right. Yet, despite Huib's distinguished legal career, he was unable to do this. And this was his point. All people, he argued, should have the right to die at a time of their choosing. A pill would confer this power. He wrote:

> Elderly and often ailing people realise that, at some time in the future, they will find themselves in an unacceptable and unbearable situation which only can get worse, never better.

A pill to end life at one's own discretion would solve the problem. Not a pill for now, but for the unforeseeable future so that the end can be humane.[1]

Drion proposed that the 'Drion Pill', as it came to be known, should be taken in two parts, a day or so apart. This would provide a safeguard so that a person would not die as a result of a rash decision. (The science required to formulate a two-part pill makes this problematic and, as such, is not yet on our research agenda.)

Thus the concept of an accessible and reliable pill was born, a concept highly relevant to older people and the terminally ill. And just as the first 'pill' – the contraceptive pill – broke new ground for women's reproductive rights in the 1960s, so I believe the Peaceful Pill will revolutionise the quality of life of other groups within our community. While some feminists still argue that the introduction of the contraceptive pill has granted men unprecedented access to women's bodies, it is widely acknowledged that the primary benefit of the pill – women being able to control their own fertility – far outweighs any negatives. Similarly, possession of the Peaceful Pill would provide not only peace of mind for its owner, but the ability for them to have control over their own life and death.

More than a decade after he wrote his letter, Drion remained surprised by the considerable reaction he received to the concept of his pill. When I visited him at his home in Leyden in late 2003, he talked at length about the idea and wished Exit well in our efforts to realise his vision. Drion was to die a few months after that visit, in April 2004.

The history of the suicide pill

The idea of a Peaceful Pill – that is, a substance or liquid that when taken orally results in a reliable and peaceful death – is not new. Indeed, in Athenian times, the herb hemlock was the drug of choice for suicide and it was taken in liquid form. Closely related to the carrot and parsnip family, hemlock depresses the nervous system in a way similar to nicotine, although the effect of hemlock is far stronger.[2] The most famous suicide involving hemlock was that of Socrates, discussed in chapter 7.

More recently, cyanide has been used to make suicide pills. Cyanide is a chemical that has many forms and occurs naturally in a range of bacteria, fungi and algae. Certain cyanides are also found in car exhaust fumes and in tobacco smoke. So why is the cyanide suicide pill not more commonly used? One reason is that there is conflicting evidence of the type of death that cyanide may provide. While anecdotal reports tell of cyanide taking up to fifteen minutes to work, all the while causing an agonising death – burning of the mouth, nausea, vomiting, etc. – other reports suggest a different effect. For instance, some of the reports of the videotaped suicide of disabled man Ramon Sampedro in Spain in 1998 say that his death – which was brought about by potassium cyanide – was as quick as it was peaceful. Importantly, though, sleep does not precede the death, and it is death while asleep that most people seek.

This conflict in evidence aside, for years cyanide was the most commonly used substance in pill form for suicide. Intelligence agents were issued with potassium cyanide pills as part of their job. It was such a pill that allowed Heinrich Himmler, Hitler's head man in the SS and the Gestapo, to escape interrogation upon arrest by the British. He suicided before he could be questioned. Hermann Goering, head of the Luftwaffe, also avoided execution by taking a pill of potassium cyanide. Cyanide mixed with Kool-Aid was used by most of the members of the People's Temple for their mass suicide at Jonestown in Guyana in 1978. While cyanide might be a subject of curiosity, especially given its infamous past, the substance is of little use to the Peaceful Pill project of today. For this project, peace, ease and, most importantly, manufacturability are all preconditions.

Barbiturates

The barbiturate Nembutal is the drug that comes closest to what Exit seeks to provide in a Peaceful Pill, although its manufacturability and limited availability put it beyond the reach of most elderly or seriously ill Australians. However, Nembutal is an important and historically significant drug. For this reason some detail about its history is warranted.

Nembutal is one of a class of drugs that was derived from an original discovery. Known as barbiturates – or 'peanuts' as they came to be known by street dealers in the 1950s – these drugs were made from the salts of barbituric acid. Barbituric acid was first synthesised on the feast day of Saint Barbara, on 4 December 1863 by Adolph von Bayer, hence its name. Barbiturates were found to be pharmacologically active as sedatives or sleeping tablets.

By the 1950s, production of barbiturates peaked and in Australia there were more than twenty marketed forms of the drug, with almost all available as sleeping tablets. They included

Veronal, Amytal, Seconal, Soneryl and, of course, Nembutal. Back then, Nembutal was recommended to help babies sleep, and it could be bought over the counter in bottles from the chemist. Along with these drugs' popularity as sleeping tablets came the discovery that they were particularly useful if you wanted to end your life. Many a famous person died using barbiturates, including Marilyn Monroe, Judy Garland and Jimi Hendrix. Their emerging use as drugs of abuse and drugs that caused death ensured that by the end of the 1950s they had fallen out of favour with doctors. Also, by that time there were better sleeping tablets available – drugs like Valium. This new class of drug – the benzodiazepines – did not have the serious side effect of overdose causing death.

Over the last thirty years, barbiturate sleeping tablets have been slowly taken off the market in Australia. In 1998 there were only two left, and in that year Nembutal was suddenly withdrawn. The last of these barbiturates, Amytal, disappeared in 2003. The common misconception left from this period is that taking sleeping pills with alcohol is an effective way to suicide. While this was true of the old-style barbiturates, this is no longer the case.

Of all barbiturates, the best for ending life was the moderate to fast-acting Nembutal. It was the drug I used in the Deliverance Machine in Darwin during the life of the ROTI Act. In countries where VE is legal and any drug can be used, Nembutal remains the drug of choice. In Australia, Nembutal is now only available from veterinarians who use it as an anaesthetic agent during surgery, and as a drug to euthanase pets. While it may have *just* been possible to convince your trusting doctor before Nembutal's withdrawal that your insomnia was so bad that only the dangerous Nembutal could help you get a good night's sleep, there is no plausible story you can give to the vet about why you need it. You can't claim an urgent need to operate on the family cat this weekend! Furthermore, the Australian Veterinary Board has recently become aware of people's interest in this drug, partly because of my speaking in the media about it. In 2001, they published the following warning to their members in the *Australian Veterinary Journal*:

> A worrying issue that recently came to the Board's attention was that information being distributed by the (human) pro-euthanasia lobby notes that potent euthanasia solutions are routinely held by most veterinary practitioners. This should serve as a timely warning to all of us to adequately guard our stocks of euthanasia solution.[3]

A case study in Nembutal

When asked about Nembutal at introduction workshops or clinics, I often tell people that it is handy to know a vet. Some time ago, I was making a clinic visit to the bedside of Harry, a dying patient. With his wife at his side, he asked me which drugs would allow him to peacefully end his life. As I normally respond when asked these questions, I started by explaining that the 'best' drug was Nembutal, but that this was only available in Australia from a vet.

I asked, 'How many vets do you know *really* well – well enough for them to risk a jail term in helping you?' Their silence answered my question, and I went on to talk about other more easily available, but less effective, drugs. After the visit, I left the bedroom and accepted an invitation to have a cup of tea with Harry's wife. Tentatively, she said, 'You know when you asked about knowing a vet? Well, I *knew* a vet, very well indeed. In fact, many years back I had an affair with a vet that my husband knows nothing about. That vet owes me some bloody big favours. I'm going to call them in.'

Later, after Harry had died of his disease, I heard that his wife did indeed call in the favour and obtained a 100 mL bottle of liquid Nembutal. Despite this, however, Harry never used it. She told me it sat in his bedroom over the last weeks of his life and that he drew immense comfort from knowing it was there. As he faced every new day, he was reassured by the knowledge that if things became too difficult for him, he could find relief by simply drinking the drug. Indeed, the presence of Nembutal helped to prolong his life.

Of course, the number of people who have a vet on their shortlist of friends who would risk jail for them is very small. There has only been a handful of occasions I know of when help was obtained in this way. Perhaps the question I should put to patients should be 'Have you ever had an affair with a vet?' When I recently told this story in a public meeting, one elderly woman shouted: 'I wish you'd told me that forty years ago!'

Veterinary drugs only rarely appear on the street. I know of cases where dying people have paid up to $5000 for a single 100 mL bottle of Nembutal that would retail to a vet for less than $100. It is not clear how the drug is getting onto the black market. One presumes it is obtained during the theft of other drugs from veterinary practices, perhaps by those targeting more tradable black market items like veterinary steroid users. While the mark-up for Nembutal can be significant, it is easy to see why an organised illegal trade in the drug has never been established. Unlike heroin or steroid users, the purchaser of this drug never wants more than one item.

Many people can and do travel overseas to obtain Nembutal. Good results have been obtained by searching out the product in countries where less rigorous controls apply. Its availability in countries like Mexico and Indonesia has been investigated by Exit, and we have asked our members travelling to these and other countries to visit veterinary supply shops in order to test how easy it is to obtain. It is certainly no crime to ask for the product, and the information when compiled is of great assistance to our members.

I also often get asked about obtaining Nembutal via the Internet. On this front, Exit members have tried repeatedly to make such a purchase, but they have always been unsuccessful. The only person to obtain Nembutal this way was Nancy Crick (see chapter 9), but she was able to use her unique Internet diary to appeal for help to do so.

Those members of Exit who were lucky enough to obtain Nembutal when it was still prescribed continue to report having peace of mind just knowing they have a bottle in the cupboard. When taken as a drink and followed by alcohol, this clear, odourless liquid with a bitter taste provides a fast, peaceful and pain-free death.

Given how difficult it is to obtain reliable, effective drugs like Nembutal and the difficulty of home synthesis of the product, in 2004 Exit committed itself to creating its own Peaceful Pill formula. Exit's aim in developing a Peaceful Pill is clear: to replicate the painless, easeful death provided by a drug like Nembutal.

> As my health is good and I haven't reached seventy it is hard for me to visualise needing a pill but of course I shall, as people near and dear to me in the past were desperate to find such a method to end their suffering. Just knowing that a pill could be available if necessary would be wonderful. Thank you so much for putting so much effort into its research.
>
> – Joy, sixty-eight years, nurse (retired), Henley Beach, South Australia

The Peaceful Pill project mark #1

I first outlined the possible role of a Peaceful Pill in a paper I presented at the World Federation of Right-to-Die Organisations in Zurich in 1998. Seven years on, we have two very different projects under way, although both have the same aim, and that is to create the means by which Exit members can provide for themselves the *option* of a peaceful death, at a time of their choosing.

The first of these projects concerns the creation of a home-made version of the Peaceful Pill from ubiquitous, unrestrictable ingredients using equipment no more complicated than what is found in the average kitchen. In our initial thinking about the manufacture of the pill we thought it important to make use of requirements that are safe from being banned or confiscated by the authorities. Our focus was upon ingredients that have such widespread use in society that they will never be restricted. Nicotine, alcohol and paracetamol are just a few examples. The idea of the state forgoing the revenue it collects from substances like alcohol or nicotine is unimaginable, no matter how they might wish to curtail the Peaceful Pill project. Similarly, the restriction of a drug like paracetamol, so widely used, would be hard to envisage.

To date, this project has led to a pill being developed from nicotine and chlorinated alcohol, but with testing so problematic, laboratory trials are set to continue into the foreseeable future.

The Peanut project

The second project – the Peanut project – is a more ambitious undertaking that is expected to have its first phase completed by mid-2005. It involves a group of Exit members coming together to manufacture their own professional-strength Nembutal-like barbiturate. Again using the political strategy of mass civil disobedience, the members undertaking this project have worked long and hard to make it happen. They are lucky to have a number of retired chemists and engineers in their ranks. The input of these former scientists, laboratory technicians and academics has been vital in determining the logistics and practical issues associated with the project. This takes the issue of a self-manufacturable Peaceful Pill to a new level. No longer is it good enough to offer Exit members the means to make an untested and unvalidated copy of the original. Why not aim for the best? The best is Nembutal. The goal of the Peanut project is to create a pill that is reliable and one that provides a peaceful, dignified death. These are the preconditions demanded by the majority of Exit members of the Peaceful Pill.

In late 2003, Exit carried out an exhaustive survey of our members' views and expectations about the Peaceful Pill. These results have guided our activities and form the basis for the discussion that follows.[4]

This research found an overwhelming preference among our members for the Peaceful Pill over all other forms of 'self-deliverance', with 89 per cent reporting they would prefer to take a pill than use traditional drugs, the CoGenie, or a plastic bag.[5] Also, most Exit members tell us that if a Peaceful Pill was available, they would like to obtain it from Exit, rather than make it themselves. This hesitance about unassisted production I think reflects our members' low level of awareness of the legal implications of what they are asking Exit to do. While suicide is legal, assisting a suicide is illegal. Given that I wish to strongly avoid the latter charge, there is simply no legal means for me or Exit to be the manufacturer and distributor of the Peaceful Pill in the way that our members would like.

This finding may also reflect a collective lack of confidence in members' own ability to make the pill, although this is currently being addressed through the Peanut project, in which all tasks are truly joint activities. This means that everyone present is part of the manufacturing team, and their actual contribution will never be able to be fully established. Responsibility is shared equally, as is the benefit of everyone's labours.

I certainly don't think the Peaceful Pill should be handed out willy-nilly, but should be available to those of us with nothing to look forward to but suffering. This is simply being human. I am a practising Christian and since my God brought me into this world as a human being – and one capable of making choices – I do not believe it is His will to take me out as a vegetable. The choice is mine as always, and I hope to go with spirit and soul intact – not with a spirit that is broken and cringing. Roll on Peaceful Pill.

– Terri, seventy-two years, housewife, Palm Beach, Queensland

Perceived benefits and concerns about the Peaceful Pill

One of the main reasons behind the establishment of the Peanut project was our members' overwhelming concern about the reliability of the Peaceful Pill. Eighty-eight per cent of those surveyed stressed that the pill must be reliable: it must work without fail. Eighty-seven per cent of Exit members reported that ease of use was important in the pill's appeal, unlike the CoGenie, whose various pieces of equipment must be set up. And there should be no 'mess' as a result of the death. Almost 72 per cent of Exit members were concerned that the pill might cause vomiting and fail to work. As Jean explains:

> Both my parents died in their fifties following incapacitating strokes. My concern is that a pill be easy to obtain/use if one can only use . . . one hand or [is] wheelchair bound. My other concern is that the person – say one's children – finding the body not be alarmed by any mess such as blood, vomit, machinery, etc. It should not look like a suicide . . .

– Jean, sixty-three years, nurse (retired),
Booral, Queensland

Finally, death by Peaceful Pill must be dignified. Most Exit members (85 per cent) think that a pill can fulfil this criterion. They believe that a death produced calmly, while asleep, and one that doesn't require several pieces of equipment is desirable. Understandably, the aesthetics of death is a concern raised by many contemplating the use of an Exit Bag or CoGenie. Compared to dying with a plastic bag on your head or with the CoGenie's nasal prongs fastened around your face, a Peaceful Pill has clear advantages. Lisette Nigot's view of the Exit Bag is typical of our members:

> I don't like that [Exit Bag] at all. I don't think it's nice. I think it's as if you were wrapping a piece of ham or something like that, it's not a nice way to die . . . It's not a very attractive idea to stick a plastic bag on your head as if it was a sausage or a piece of ham that you wrap in plastic. However, if all else fails, I have a plastic bag.[6]

While there is strong support for the Peaceful Pill concept, some Exit members also have significant concerns about it. Just over 40 per cent are worried that the pill might fall into the wrong hands (perhaps those of a mentally ill person or a troubled teen). Indeed, there are risks associated with the Peaceful Pill, but does that mean we shouldn't proceed? I think not, as there are so many people who would benefit from having access to the means to peacefully end their life. So in weighing up the benefits and drawbacks, I believe there are a good many more benefits than drawbacks.

This view was supported at a large public meeting of elderly people in Wollongong in late 2003 where I conducted a straw poll on how concerned those present were about safeguards for the pill. When I asked for a show of hands to the question 'Who would want to pick up their own pill at the door on leaving the meeting?' there was unanimous support. Very few elderly people, it would seem, are concerned about their own ability to deal with the power and risk of the Peaceful Pill. The perceived benefit and comfort it offers seems to overrule any other concerns about possible risks.

While many older people realise that society might be anxious about their desire for end-of-life choices, they do not like being patronised by younger people who do not yet understand the suffering one can endure from serious illness and old age. This reminds me of Huib Drion's remarks. Several years ago, Drion was confronted by a number of young people who said that his pill concept proved 'contempt of old age'. Drion's initial response was to say that he was sympathetic to their reasoning. 'But, I remember', he went on, 'a meeting where a young woman of about forty-five pleaded against the pill for the elderly . . . [and] an old woman grabbed the microphone and said: "You made a wonderful plea against the pill but could I please have it?" '[7] At Exit's 2003 conference in Sydney, I watched with interest as hordes of young Christians gathered outside our Wentworth Street venue. As they chanted, hoping to drown out the proceedings inside, one couldn't help noticing the age difference between the two groups. In the street, the average

age of protesters was early twenties, while inside it was mid- to late seventies. On that day I saw the same reaction among the audience members to the protesters as that noted by Drion: the elderly do not appreciate being told by the young what they should believe and do.

I already have an Exit Bag. I have Neur-Amyl. These provide me with what I call my 'insurance' should the necessity arise if my quality of life is not acceptable to *me*. I hope I might be able to attend a practical workshop. The Peaceful Pill would provide further ease of mind. I would then wish for advice on which would be the most peaceful and reliable method on any decision I chose to make regarding the end of my life.

– Violet, seventy-two years, teacher (retired), Hervey Bay, Queensland

---

A Peaceful Pill from the supermarket shelf?

In 2001 I undertook an interview with Kathryn Jean Lopez, associate editor of the right-wing American magazine *The National Review*. In retrospect, this was a mistake. I should have realised that a quote from the interview would be taken out of context and used repeatedly by those seeking to discredit the Peaceful Pill philosophy. I have reproduced Lopez's question and the answer I gave below so that the context in which the 'supermarket shelf' comment was given is clear:

> **Lopez:** Do you see any restrictions that should be placed on euthanasia generally? If I am depressed, do I qualify? If an elderly woman's husband dies and she says she no longer

has anything to live for, would you help her kill herself? What about a troubled teen? Who qualifies? Who decides if a life is worth living?

Nitschke: This difficult question I will answer in two parts. My personal position is that if we believe that there is a right to life, then we must accept that people have a right to dispose of that life whenever they want. (In the same way as the right to freedom of religion has implicit the right to be an atheist, and the right to freedom of speech involves the right to remain silent.) I do not believe that telling people they have a right to life while denying them the means, manner, or information necessary for them to give this life away has any ethical consistency.

So all people qualify, not just those with the training, knowledge or resources to find out how to 'give away' their life. And someone needs to provide this knowledge, training, or recourse necessary to anyone who wants it, including the depressed, the elderly bereaved, [and] the troubled teen.

If we are to remain consistent and we believe that the individual has the right to dispose of their life, we should not erect artificial barriers in the way of sub-groups who don't meet our criteria.

This would mean that the so-called 'Peaceful Pill' should be available in the supermarket so that those old enough to understand death could obtain death peacefully at the time of their choosing. It's hard to imagine how such a development would affect society, but I believe the impact would not be as great as people fear . . .

The final question that needs to be answered though is 'Whom do I want to help?' While acknowledging that all have the 'right' to receive assistance without fear of legal consequence, I do not personally want to involve myself in helping those who can manage the act themselves.

The purpose of the Deliverance Machine . . . was to allow the individual to initiate the process and to take the responsibility for their actions. My guidelines for those whom I am prepared to assist are of course arbitrary. In this country, without protective legislation, I could do what I liked, or rather, what I could get away with.

However, I choose to restrict myself to that group identified in the overturned legislation. I involve myself with terminally ill adults who are articulate, lucid, and not suffering from clinically treatable depression.

The point I wanted to make in that interview was that I can envisage a day when a Peaceful Pill will be freely available. My euphemism for universal access was the concept of the supermarket shelf. Since that time, the supermarket shelf analogy has been used persistently by my critics to denounce my work and paint me as irresponsible and even anarchic. Nevertheless, it remains a metaphor that is useful in any discussion about universal access and for this reason it was included in the Peaceful Pill survey. Less than 1 per cent of survey participants, however, thought that the pill should be available on the supermarket shelf. Some members went beyond the metaphor, however, and took the survey's questions very seriously. Cameron was one such respondent:

If a Peaceful Pill was developed by Exit, all effort will have to be made that the pill and its distribution is controlled by Exit only and given to its members only. Otherwise all the do-gooders, so called Christians and Kevin Andrews of this world will have a field day and enforce a legal injunction. A core group of members committed to Exit will have to supervise the distribution of the pill and its recipe.

I consider that the distribution of the pill to just any-body will be a legal disaster and will close down Exit. I consider it very sensible to challenge the establishment but we should not be stupid and dig our own grave. And yes, I consider it absolutely essential that we develop the Peaceful Pill.

– Cameron, sixty-one years, engineer (retired),
Brownlow, South Australia

While Cameron's comments reflect his concern about the logistics of responsible pill distribution, he was one of a minor-ity who expressed anxiety about the issue. Rather, around 65 per cent of those surveyed thought the pill should be avail-able to 'any rational adult who wants it'. So while Exit has been responsible in restricting access to information about the pill and other devices – especially where the Internet is concerned – it appears our elderly members are much less concerned about whose hands this information may fall into.

After nursing both parents until their deaths and watching their slow, painful passing, I feel strongly that there should be a pill available to those who feel very strongly about being kept alive with no quality of life. I do think that initially, perhaps, for a period of years, it should only be available at a cost to Exit members. This ensures that the person has considered the situation and consequences thoroughly. Thereafter, release of the pill to others could become accepted. With the population exploding throughout the world [and] medical science discovering cures for so many physical causes of death, I am sure it is pointless and senseless keeping people alive, using precious medical facilities, when they feel the time has come to exit . . . because of fatal illness, unbearable pain or the fragility and dependence of old age. When I am no longer independent because of my severe arthritis or some other reason, I feel satisfied that I have a plastic bag from Canada. However, a pill would be so much more suitable.

— Jill, seventy-two years, secretary and RAAF Officer (retired),

Hawthorn, Victoria

Dodging the law

At the heart of the Peanut project is the legality of suicide. While showing someone in a one-on-one situation how to make a pill may leave the instructor open to the allegation of assisting with or inciting a suicide, if hundreds of people do it, there will be safety in numbers. Older Australians – baby boomers included – well remember the efficacy of these types of political actions. The 1960s were characterised by mass civil disobedience on many issues from black equality to gay rights and the women's movement. Exit is finding that strategies of mass civil disobedience are once again proving effective in challenging bad laws.

The following letter is representative of the requests Exit frequently receives:

> Several months ago I wrote to Exit and offered a donation of $2000 if they could provide me with a CO Generator. I explained in detail that I am still healthy and am not intending to use it but I just like to have it in case I need it.
>
> I am Dutch and we have an obsession with 'being prepared' . . . There must be a way to provide me with the CO Generator, even if every part has to be sent separately or at least give me a description of how to make it and the names of the chemicals.
>
> – Gerard, sixty-nine years, security guard (retired),
> Maylands, Western Australia

While Gerard might not see any danger in his request, the current law means that there are significant risks for Exit should we act on it. This is why if people wish to make a Peaceful Pill or build a CoGenie, they must do it by themselves, for themselves. And this is why the 'mass' part of the civil disobedience concept is so important if the program is to continue into the future.

Let us be clear about this. Exit's aim is not to help people suicide. Rather, our focus is on helping create the opportunities by which people can take responsibility for their own beliefs and decisions – decisions so important and so central to one's sense of self that they are the business of no one else.

In two months' time I will be eighty years old. Except for some osteoarthritis I am healthy and can very well look after myself and my house. As long as I stay this way I'll be happy to live and quietly enjoy my life but I realise this could change soon now and I would need help.

This pill is worth to me the top price because it will give me the security to decide for myself when my end will come. Nobody depends on me any more so I won't do anybody any harm by going quietly.

– Tom, seventy-nine years, shop assistant (retired), Carrum, Victoria

A hostile reception – the right-to-die movement's turn away

Until recently, Exit's research and development program has been financed, in part, by the Hemlock Society in the United States. This organisation is America's foremost right-to-die group. In helping to fund Exit's R&D, Hemlock has been explicitly supportive of our direction and activities. Aware that law reform could take many years and cognisant of people's need to have practical end-of-life choices now, Hemlock's significant annual donation was a welcome part of our overall budget. Our report back to Hemlock at the end of each funding year kept them informed about Exit's new ideas and developments.

More recently, however, the society has undergone a makeover and a name change. The new-look Hemlock Society – now known as End of Life Choices – has chosen to focus solely upon legislative reform. This has meant that our funding has been cut. One reason for this change of heart may be the criticism of Hemlock by Right to Life in the US of their support of Exit.

Writing in 2002, the anti-euthanasia crusader Wesley J. Smith in an article titled 'Australia's Dr Death Spreading the Assisted Suicide Gospel' told the world that the Hemlock Society had finally revealed its 'true colours' through 'their moral and financial support of the odious Philip Nitschke'.[8]

But Hemlock's decision to focus upon law reform is not unique and their change of heart may reflect a bigger paradigm shift, one that characterises the movement as a whole. The preference for legislative reform over practical strategies is shared by some VE societies in Australia (especially South Australia and Victoria), as well as the British Voluntary Euthanasia Society, which, incidentally, is the world's oldest and one of the wealthiest VE lobby groups. At the local level, the Victorian VE society continues to distance itself from Exit's activities, particularly the Peaceful Pill project. In their 2003 President's Report, the head of the Victorian VE Society, Dr Rodney Syme, made his opposition to the pill clear.[9] Previously, when discussing the pill on the 7.30 Report in 2001, Syme had said that the Victorian society was a 'responsible organisation and we will not associate ourselves with behaviour or developments which could be seen to be irresponsible and which might be irresponsible'. During that interview, the right-to-die activist found himself in the same corner of the ring as the staunchest of anti-euthanasia doctors, the then vice-president of the AMA, Dr Trevor Mudge. However, even Mudge surprisingly conceded that the Peaceful Pill might be acceptable, saying:

> The ethical argument is that doctors should not be assisting in the euthanasia decision. If patients make their own

decision about deciding to end their life without any form of external coercion or support, then I think it's hard to argue ethically against it.[10]

The South Australian VE Society has also consistently stated that the 'pursuit of law reform and vigorous support for the "peaceful pill" are incompatible'.[11] I see no problem in different VE groups having different priorities. But neither the South Australian nor the Victorian society has ever surveyed their membership. This in itself raises questions about the legitimacy of their legislation focus. In contrast, Exit remains strongly committed to a practical, hands-on approach that provides information and strategies for end-of-life choices. And we remain sceptical about the legislative process or the goals it purports to be able to deliver, particularly in the current political climate.

Peace of mind – in a pill

While the Peaceful Pill project has many aims, at its core it has always sought to create peace of mind by extending people's end-of-life choices. An overwhelming 90 per cent of Exit members tell us that they are in favour of the Peaceful Pill because of the comfort it would give them, knowing it was there. As one Exit member put it:

My quality of life is still good but it would give me great peace of mind to know that I could end it should the situation change and with something that would be peaceful (e.g. Peaceful Pill) and less traumatic for my family and friends than the means now available (plastic bag). I also consider that it is my right to do so without interference from Church or state. Realising this will take time, money and a lot of work, one day we may live in more enlightened times and reason will prevail.

– Betty, seventy-two years, business proprietor (retired), Churchlands, Western Australia

Or as Veronica writes:

The manner of death is very much in the minds of people reaching senior years – inevitable whether sudden, terminal or long drawn-out dementia or living in a nursing home. Peace of mind that you have some choice to be in control.

– Veronica, seventy years, office manager (retired), Donvale, Victoria

For many older people, peace of mind is priceless. This is why 'peace in a pill' is what the Peanut project is all about.

The future of the Peaceful Pill

It seems clear that the Peaceful Pill has a big future, and not only for the seriously ill but for all rational, elderly members of our community. We foresee a future that offers people the option of a peaceful death, at a time and place of their choosing: an option that so many rightly demand.

For many years now, I have argued that the provision of

practical end-of-life choices significantly enhances one's quality of life. When people are allowed options at the end of life, they live longer and are happier as a result. This view is now confirmed statistically by the results of the Peaceful Pill survey *and* our longitudinal study of people attending Exit's introduction workshops. This applies regardless of age, as this letter from a 41-year-old member testifies:

> Thank you for continuing to explore this important pill. There are times when I feel unwell and I panic. I haven't gone to a workshop, I haven't stored drugs to end my life. As I am so well, I don't think about it. But *how relieved* I'd be if you had such a pill . . .
>
> My disease is such that when it gets into my internal organs I will live three months only. For now, it is only on my skin, and tumours have been radiated from my right upper buttock. So it's the 'real thing'. I'm going to try and live to the end, but I won't cop agony or leave such a memory on my sons who are now seventeen and ten. I believe in the right to choose, as my bumper sticker says.
>
> Thank you for being there. Your being there really helps me sleep at night. You are like a lifeline thrown to me on a dark night as I flounder in the endless sea. God bless you. I hope I won't need your help for another ten-plus years, but keep going.
>
> – Daryl, forty-one years, diagnosis: mycosis fungoides,
> Tasmania

And regardless of whether the person is currently sick:

> I have no relatives or younger friends who would be able
> to look after me or carry out my last wishes. I fear becom-
> ing an invalid, unable to care for myself. I would only use
> the Peaceful Pill if and when my life would become unbear-
> able. Having the pill now would give me peace of mind
> and I would actually enjoy life more. As at present – I am
> always worried.
>
> – Duncan, eighty years, librarian (retired),
> Carlton, Victoria

When seniors cards will be edible

With the Peanut project now well under way, it is interesting
and important to ponder the type of world we are creating. Are
we opening the floodgates for mass suicide, or are we setting a
new agenda for ageing? Will there be an avalanche of suicides,
or will there be a wave of comfort that spreads rapidly through
the swelling ranks of the elderly? Will society be better or worse
off? These are important and vital questions to consider as we
embark on this program. I have long pondered the answers and
believe they are clear. Take nursing homes as a case in point.

If a Peaceful Pill was widely available, nursing homes would
only be inhabited by people who were happy about still being
alive because they would know that they could leave if things
got too undignified. No one would live there against their will,
unlike the situation we find at present. Residents could, if they
wished, have their own deaths planned and all the arrangements

made. Only those wanting to extend their life by every possible second would be catered for, rather than our current approach of trying to force everyone into this group, whether they want to continue living or not.

What about older people who still live independently at home? For these people, a Peaceful Pill would lead to fewer people being fearful about asking for help – for anything from the grocery shopping to end-of-life options. They are fearful because they do not want to risk being seen as needing institutionalisation in an aged-care facility in which they might lose their independence and their control. Surely, knowing that one could choose between a peaceful death and nursing-home care, or a combination of both, would change mindsets significantly.

Just imagine.

And what about families, for whom the horrific, unnecessarily slow and often undignified deaths of their loved ones leave in their wake lasting trauma and horrible memories? And then there are the terminally ill. These people could maintain their sense of self and dignity right up to the end if a Peaceful Pill was on hand.

Just imagine.

And, finally, what about the medical profession? This profession could, with the pill in place, finally acknowledge the duplicity of slow euthanasia. Doctors could openly engage with their patients as equals, and patients would have real choice, real options, and such a person's relationship with their doctor would no be longer fearful or dependent. Would not the standards of patient care increase?

Just imagine.

We could live in a world in which those who want to die can die, and those who want to live are given every chance, a world where Drion's 'universal access' model prevails; a better world than the one we've got now.

Conclusion

The Empire Strikes Back

Since the Rights of the Terminally Ill Act was overturned by the Kevin Andrews bill in 1997, Exit has consistently sought to clarify the questions that surround suicide and euthanasia; to put out a challenge to what is legal and what is not; and to help people everywhere establish real end-of-life options, options independent of the vagaries of the political process.

For example, can a husband sit with his wife when she takes her own life due to illness or old age? Can a doctor answer patients' queries in group workshops or in individual clinics about the lethality – or not – of particular drug combinations? Can I tell someone where to buy Nembutal? Can I explain to them the science of a low oxygen death? Can a group of elderly people show another group of elderly people how to make a device that makes carbon monoxide? Can this same group of people come together for a chemistry class to make a Peaceful Pill that none of them will take any time soon? Exit's raison d'être is to establish the answers to questions like these.

In the absence of an Australian VE law, and the unlikelihood of a law being enacted any time soon, Exit remains preoccupied – almost to the exclusion of everything else – with the practical realities of people's everyday lives and deaths. To reach this goal we have needed to push the boundaries of the law, and we have annoyed many a politician along the way. Now – it seems – we are paying the price. Just when we thought that technology and the Internet would be the answer to our metaphorical prayers, making information available for Exit members everywhere, federal legislation has been drafted that makes a mockery of free speech and the tenets upon which the Internet was founded.

Changing the law – making Internet use a crime

Over the past two years, Exit's online activities have come under increasing scrutiny from the authorities. Ever since Nancy Crick used the Net to obtain the Nembutal that gave her a peaceful death – and published a web diary that told her story straight – the Federal Government has been investigating ways to prohibit the use of the Internet in providing information about end-of-life choices to our members – that is, information to the elderly and the seriously ill.

In early 2003, Federal Justice Minister Chris Ellison quietly announced a new offensive in a press release that was boxed to the parliamentary press gallery late one Friday afternoon.[1] His release stated that using the Internet for right-to-die information would soon be illegal in Australia. Ellison sought to justify his move by citing two 'expert studies'. One of these was no study at all. Rather, it was a letter to the editor from the *American Journal of Psychiatry* that had no status and next-to-no relevance to the use of the Internet by Exit and its members (Ellison's cited letter concerned mentally ill teenagers on the other side of the world, in an obscure suicide chat room, talking about the gory details of violent deaths).[2]

As one of many politicians in the Howard Government who is driven more by God than by the wishes of his electorate, Ellison's fiddling of the evidence is not surprising. After all, this is a government that is said to have its social policies 'determined by Rome' and for whom a courting of the Catholic vote is a major preoccupation.[3] (However, the ALP is hardly able to throw stones, with the recent appointment of one of the Catholic ringleaders in the 'Euthanasia No' campaign – Tony Burke – to the ALP's front bench, not to mention fundamentalist Christian Peter Garrett to the back.) Ellison's basic message is that changes will be made to laws controlling the Internet and little justification is needed.

It was only the announcement of the 2004 federal election that prevented what has become known as the Criminal Code Amendment (Suicide Related Materials Offences) Bill 2004 from finishing its legislative journey. Just as I was about to travel to Canberra to appear before the Senate Constitutional and Legal Committee which was reviewing the proposed legislation, John Howard called his October 2004 election, and the hearing was cancelled. My submission to the committee focused upon two issues: Exit's recent research that found that keeping the elderly well-informed about their end-of-life options makes for healthier, happier people; and, second, that the proposed legislation would exceed parliament's authority, and that this was untenable, based upon part V of our Constitution.[4]

The submission of Anthony and Beryl Saclier from Victoria outlined a different but equally important point and made a laughing stock of anti-euthanasia Liberal MP Peter Slipper's scaremongering about the dangers of the Internet and the need for families to be protected. In response, the Sacliers wrote: 'We looked up [on the Internet] "suicide – means of", but didn't have the patience to wade through all the sites that argued against suicide, had plans to prevent suicide, theologically abominated suicide, etc. We could find not a solitary site that urged suicide or revealed a tinge of "destructive intent". "Easily accessible?" Not to us.'[5]

As with any legislation that is in progress when an election is called, the Criminal Code Amendment was shelved and now needs to be reintroduced into parliament. I am told by Labor insiders that if Mark Latham had led an ALP victory in the 2004 election, it would have been extremely unlikely that this draconian legislation would ever have seen the light of day. However, with the Coalition now firmly in control of both houses of parliament, I am resigned that it is only a matter of time until this legislation is passed; and this time the Greens or other concerned politicians will have no way to send the legislation to a review committee. Straight through it will go, and the elderly of this country will know precious little about it: that is, until it is too late. So what is it that I am so concerned about?

The Criminal Code Amendment (Suicide Related Materials Offences) Bill 2004 seeks to ensure that it will soon be a crime for a person to use the Internet to view, copy, download or transmit 'suicide promotion material'. And this means *all* manner of right-to-die/end-of-life choice information. Upon analysis, it would seem that this legislation has been drafted with one person and one organisation in mind. *Philip Nitschke and Exit International.*

The objective of the proposed legislation – to curtail my work – was noted in a submission to the government by the Internet rights/free speech group Electronic Frontiers Australia. The EFA was one of a small number of groups who made its submission to the government during the very short period when the bill was open to public comment. It stated:

> The proposed offence appears to have the primary purpose of silencing the speech of one particular high profile Australian resident, but only in relation to use of the Internet.[6]

Given that our opponents often say that one shouldn't legislate on the basis of a few difficult cases – 'hard cases make bad law' – it would seem the government is doing just that. In their unbridled enthusiasm to silence Exit, these Liberal Party thought police are using a sledgehammer that will crush a great deal more than the chosen walnut Philip Nitschke. As Sydney QC Bruce Donald has commented:

> On any view of it, this bill if enacted will seriously expose proponents of a debate on euthanasia to risk of criminal conduct by use of web-based information and communications.[7]

If enacted, which it no doubt will be, as John Howard takes control of the Senate from July 2005, Exit may risk breaking the law as part of its everyday operations. Remember, this bill makes it illegal to even *possess* information about suicide (or 'end-of-life choices' as I see it), regardless of whether or not this material is ever loaded on the Internet, and regardless of whether such information is ever used. Overnight, my computer and hundreds, if not thousands, of computers owned by other Exit members will become legally dangerous items.

While the overseas hosting and editing of our web site will go some way to circumventing these draconian conditions, Internet service providers (ISPs) could be forced to offer filtering software that would lead to our site being unable to be accessed by *anyone* in Australia. In countries like China, which are well known for their human rights abuses, this type of censorship is perhaps to be expected. For free, democratic countries like Australia, such moves are entirely inappropriate and disturbing. Thus the time may soon come when I am so harassed by the Howard Government that I will have little choice but to relocate overseas. This, however, would be a last-resort, and not a decision I would take lightly. Older Australians and those seriously ill would have their right to obtain the most basic of information about end-of-life choices restricted to an even greater degree. One might ask, where will the tyranny against the old and the seriously ill end?

The Andrews bill may have passed, but this debate is not over.

– Letter to the Editor, *Sydney Morning Herald*, 25 March 1997[8]

A pre-Socratic Australia – preventing the import and export of ideas

Australian author and businesswoman Dr Jill Kerr Conway once accused Australia of being 'pre-Socratic', in that we are incapable of thinking critically.[9] That the Australian Government is now seeking to regulate the type of information and ideas that can be brought in and out of Australia and shared around among registered members of Exit seems to prove her right.

In both the offline world and the online world, Exit has long occupied too much of the Howard Government's attention. It should have been enough for God-botherer politicians to have removed the Northern Territory's groundbreaking legislation on voluntary euthanasia, replete with its strict qualifying conditions and proper safeguards. And it should have been enough for them to totally restrict the access of dying people to a drug like Nembutal, or to prohibit the import of the Exit Bag.

All these measures *should have been enough*. But this is not the case. Now it is debate and information that our Federal Government sees fit to stifle; and with this our most fundamental of freedoms – our right to determine when and how we die. Suicide, after all, is legal.

Everywhere one looks, there is a smell. It is the stench of books burning, of ideas being suppressed, and of people's rights and hopes being crushed. But one thing the government can't stop – no matter how hard they try – is the groundswell of support among the Australian people themselves for end-of-life choices. Try as they might, the elderly and the seriously ill cannot be stopped from organising, from forming DIY groups and *teaching themselves* all they need to know: how to create their own end-of-life choices and how to collaborate with others so the instructions – the solutions – are handed around and around and around. This ensures that how to die – and how to live life to its fullest – becomes a real option for us all.

Notes

Chapter 1 – Will the Real Philip Nitschke Please Stand Up?

1   Frank Hardy, *The Unlucky Australians*, Nelson, Melbourne, 1968.

Chapter 2 – Lessons from Darwin

1   Marshall Perron, email, 29 September 2004.
2   'Australian medical, church groups challenge euthanasia law', Reuters, 18 June 1996. Retrieved at http://www.aegis.com/news/re/1996/RE960673.html.
3   A. Toulson, 'AMA Pledge to end Right to Die', *Northern Territory News*, 31 May 1995.
4   Northern Territory, Seventh Assembly, *Rights Of The Terminally Ill Bill (Serial 67)*, Parliamentary Record no. 11, 1995.
5   See A. Bentley, *Interim Report Summary of Findings Poll of Public Opinion Northern Territory*, Market Research Services, North Adelaide, 1995.
6   Australian Bureau of Statistics, *Australian Social Trends 1994*, cat. no. 4102.0, Canberra, 1995.
7   M. Gordon, 'Holy Alliance: The inside story of euthanasia's demise', *The Weekend Australian*, 29 March 1997.
8   D. Nason, 'Death Bill nearly costs leadership: Stone', The Australian, 29 May 1995.
9   Media reports erroneously stated that Max was forced to return to Broken Hill because the ROTI law was overturned at that time. Rather, it was because no doctors would break ranks with the AMA.
10 Contrary to Reg Cribb's depiction of Max in his play *Last Cab to Darwin*, Max was no victim. Rather, he was a strong-willed man who knew what he was doing. Max invited the media to document his dying experience so that those who opposed the ROTI legislation could see what they were putting him through. In addition to presenting Max's character so inaccurately, the same play is ruthless in its depiction of me as an arrogant, media-hungry doctor. Anyone who knows me also knows the extreme creative licence that Cribb has taken with the portrayal of my character. While I cannot deny I am hurt by the play, the right-to-die issue is bigger and more important than Cribb and his play will ever be. If this is the price of ensuring the injustice done to Max in this play is never visited again, I'll wear it.
11 After the *Four Corners* program was aired, Channel Seven's *Witness* pursued the story. At the helm of this second production was film-maker Janine Hosking (who has gone on to make the documentary film *Mademoiselle and the Doctor*). Janine and her crew arrived in Broken Hill just as Max

was admitted to the palliative care unit at the hospital. The second round of filming captured the days that immediately preceded his death.

12 As early as May 1995, at the invitation of *The Australian*'s national affairs editor Mike Steketee, Jim Dominguez would appear in the paper under the guise of opinion writer and in the letters to the editor. All the while his biography would fail to acknowledge his early commitment to the 'Euthanasia No' campaign. Instead, he appeared variously as 'Jim the Banker', and 'Jim from Hunters Hill'. *The Australian*'s duplicity was complete.

13 Gordon. A full analysis of the 'Euthanasia No' campaign can be found in Gordon's article: 'Holy Alliance: The inside story of euthanasia's demise', *The Weekend Australian*, 29 March 1997.

14 Australia, House of Representatives, *Speech, Second Reading Euthanasia Laws Bill 1996*, 1996, p. 5920.

15 K. Beazley, media release: transcript of doorstop [Wik decision], Canberra University, 22 January 1997.

16 Australia, House of Representatives, *Speech, Second Reading Euthanasia Laws Bill 1996*, 1996, p. 7325.

17 Commonwealth of Australia, Senate: Official Hansard, Canberra, 26 March 1997.

18 ibid.

19 ibid.

20 'Democrats seek to Overturn Euthanasia Law', ABC News Online, 3 March 2004. Retrieved at http://www.abc.net.au/news/newsitems/s1058035.htm. Indeed, Martin, a Catholic, has never supported the bill. *The Australian* reported at the time of her election on 10 August 1995 that she expressed concern about the 'excessive haste' of the law.

21 M. Perron, *Private Member's Bill*, media release, 24 March 2004.

Chapter 3 – The State of Voluntary Euthanasia Laws around the Globe

1 Oregon Department of Human Services, *Sixth Annual Report on DWD*, 10 March 2004. Retrieved at http://www.dwd.org/law/ohd.asp.

2 Despite being editorialised in the *British Medical Journal* as the fifth 'medical hero' in the history of medicine, a description I strongly support, it greatly saddens me that Kevorkian is currently in a Michigan jail serving a 10–25 year sentence for second-degree murder of motor neurone sufferer Thomas Youk.

3 R. Jonquière, *Van der Wal/Van der Maas report*, Right to Die Netherlands, 23 May 2003. Retrieved at http://www.nvve.nl/english/info/remmelinkreport23-05-03.htm.

4 See B.D. Onwuteaka-Philipsen, A. van der Heide, D. Koper, I. Keij-Deerenberg, J.A.C. Rietjens, M.L. Rurup, A.M. Vrakking, J.J. Georges,

M. T. Muller, G. van der Wal, & P. J. van der Maas, (2003) 'Euthanasia and other end-of-life decisions in the Netherlands in 1990, 1995, and 2001', *The Lancet*, vol. 362, no. 9381, 2003, p. 395.

5   'Belgium second country to legalize euthanasia', Agence France-Presse, 23 September 2002.

6   'Medical body relaxes rules on euthanasia', SwissInfo, 6 February 2004. Retrieved at http://www.swissinfo.org/sen/Swissinfo.html?siteSect=511&sid=4696720.

7   'Switzerland's Suicide Tourists', *60 Minutes*, CBS, United States, 3 July 2003. Transcript retrieved at http://www.cbsnews.com/stories/2003/02/12/60II/main540332.shtml.

8   S. A. Hurst & A. Mauron, 'Assisted suicide and euthanasia in Switzerland: allowing a role for non-physicians', *British Medical Journal*, vol. 326, 2003, pp. 271–273. Retrieved at http://bmj.com/cgi/content/full/326/7383/271.

9   ibid.

10 One recent case concerned the 'suspicious' death of Victoria Vincent, wife of Ralph Vincent.

11 L. Martin, *To Die Like a Dog: the Personal Face of the Euthanasia Debate*, M-Press Ltd, Wanganui, 2002.

12 'Euthanasia campaigner convicted', 1 April 2004, *The Guardian*. Retrieved at http://www.guardian.co.uk/medicine/story/0,11381,1183301,00.html.

13 Martin.

14 'Jailed euthanasia campaigner turned down for home detention', *The New Zealand Herald*, 1 March 2004. Retrieved at http://www.nzherald.co.nz/index.cfm?ObjectID=3575683.

15 A good summary of this issue can be found at the Death With Dignity National Center web site at http://www.dwd.org.

Chapter 4 – An Unholy Trinity – Medicine, Law and the Church

1   J. Harris, 'Euthanasia and the Value of Life', in J. Keown (ed.) *Euthanasia examined: ethical, clinical and legal perspectives*, Cambridge University Press, Cambridge, 1995.

2   M. Foucault, *The Birth of the Clinic: An Archaeology of Medical Perception*, trans. A. M. Sheridan Smith, Tavistock, London, 1973.

3   A. Kellehear, 'Health and the dying person', in A. Petersen and C. Waddell (eds) *Health Matters sociology of illness and prevention and care*, Allen & Unwin, St Leonards, 1998.

4   B. S. Turner, *Medical Power and Social Knowledge*, Sage, London, 1987.

5   ibid.

6   B. McNamara, 'A good enough death', in A. Petersen and C. Waddell (eds), *Health Matters sociology of illness and prevention and care*, Allen & Unwin, St Leonards, 1998.

7 Australia, House of Representatives, *Speech, Adjournment: Euthanasia*, 26 June 1996, p. 2904.

8 J. Muller & B. Koenig, 'On the boundary of life and death: the definition of dying by medical residents', in M. Lock & D. Gordon (eds), *Biomedicine Examined*, Kluwer, Netherlands, 1988.

9 L. Spinney, 'Playing God: Interview with Dr Philip Nitschke', *New Scientist*, 4 October 2003.

10 A. Petersen & D. Lupton, *The New Public Health: health and self in the age of risk*. Allen & Unwin, St Leonards, 1996.

11 McNamara.

12 J. Davies, 'Patients in Limbo', *The Bulletin*, 3 February 2004, pp. 28–33.

13 If people are well-informed, in line with the new public health ethos, then a greater feeling of wellbeing results and better choices can be made. See chapter 10 for more discussion on this.

14 W.L. Macdonald, 'Situational Factors and Attitudes towards Voluntary Euthanasia', *Social Science and Medicine*, vol. 46, no. 1, 1998, pp. 73–81. While the legislation makes no mention of whether a doctor can or should be present at a death, it does require the physician to 'counsel the patient about the importance of having another person present when the patient takes the medication'. Source: Oregon Death with Dignity Revised Statues General Provisions, 127.815s.3.01. Attending physician responsibilities are listed at http://www.dhs.state.or.us/publichealth/chs/pas/ors.cfm.

15 The NuTech group is a loose assembly of individuals who are interested in the practical means of self-deliverance. Since the group was established in 1998, it has met four times. The group's members are from Australia, the United States, Canada, France, Netherlands, Germany and Belgium.

16 McNamara.

17 H. Markel, 'Becoming a physician: "I swear by Apollo" – on taking the Hippocratic oath', *New England Journal of Medicine*, vol 350, no. 20, 2004.

18 R.D. Orr, N. Pang, E.D. Pellegrino & M. Siegler, 'Use of the Hippocratic Oath: a review of twentieth-century practice and a content analysis of oaths administered in medical schools in the U.S. and Canada in 1993', *Journal of Clinical Ethics*, vol. 8, 1997, pp. 377–88.

19 D. Humphry & A. Wickett, *The Right to Die: Understanding Euthanasia*. Collins, Sydney, 1986.

20 McNamara.

22 B. Kitchener & A. Jorm, 'Conditions required for a law on active Voluntary Euthanasia: a survey of nurses' opinions in the Australian Capital Territory, *Journal of Medical Ethics*, vol. 25, 1999, pp. 25–30.

21 D. Humphry & A. Wickett, *The Right to Die: Understanding Euthanasia*. Collins, Sydney, 1986.

22 I. Margalith, C. Musgrave & L. Goldschmidt, (2003) 'Physician-assisted dying: Are education and religious beliefs related to nursing students' attitudes?' *Journal of Nursing Education*, vol. 42, no. 2, 2003, pp. 91–97.

23 J. Moody, 'Euthanasia: a need for reform', *Nursing Standard*, vol. 17, no. 25, 2003, pp. 40–44.

24 L. Doyal & L. Doyal, 'Why active Voluntary Euthanasia and physician assisted suicide should be legalized', *British Medical Journal*, vol. 323, 2001, pp. 1079–80.

25 J.C. Batlle, 'Legal status of physician-assisted suicide', *JAMA*, vol. 289, no. 17, 2003, pp. 2279–81.

26 A.R. Idol & J.D. Kaye, 'The discursive positioning of people who are terminally ill in terms of power: a parliamentary debate on Voluntary Euthanasia', *Australian Psychologist*, vol. 34, no. 3, 1999, pp. 188–97.

27 It is a major regret that my name appears as co-author for this article. I do not agree, nor ever did, with the arguments Kissane presents.

28 D.W. Kissane, A. Street & P. Nitschke, 'Seven deaths in Darwin: case studies under the Rights of the Terminally Ill Act, Northern Territory, Australia', *The Lancet*, vol. 352, 1998, pp. 1097–1102.

29 Bill did not want his full name to be made public.

30 Australia, House of Representatives, *Speech, Euthanasia Laws Bill Second Reading*, 1996, p. 6742.

31 SAVES Fact Sheet No. 15 retrieved at http://www.saves.asn.au/resources/facts/fs15.htm.

32 Rodney Syme, email, 8 October 2004.

33 'Euthanasia Bill Rejected', *The Adelaide Advertiser*, 4 June 2004.

34 Australia, House of Representatives, *Speech, Second Reading Euthanasia Laws Bill 1996*, 1996, p. 7934.

35 Australian Institute of Health and Welfare, *Australia's Health 2002: the seventh biennial health report of the Australian Institute of Health and Welfare*, AIHW, Canberra, 2003.

36 In one letter, Horrocks reminded me that a 2001 *Herald Sun* poll had reported 80 per cent public support for his execution.

37 Jonathan Horrocks, letter, 2003 and 2004.

38 *Mademoiselle and the Doctor*, documentary film, iKandy Films, Sydney, NSW, 2004. Directed by Janine Hosking.

39 Life Week, 'The Life Debate: Professor Anthony Fisher's argument', Sydney, 12 August 2003. Transcript retrieved at http://www.lifeweek.org/Anthony_Fishers_argument.php.

40 R. Syme, 'The Father, Son and Euthanasia', *The Age*, 13 April 1998. Retrieved at http://www.vesv.org.au/docs/symereligion97.htm.

41 J.S. Spong, 'A Supportive Voice from the Pulpit', Death with Dignity Vermont, January 2003. Retrieved at http://www.deathwithdignityvermont.org/spong_interview.htm.

42 W.L. MacDonald, 'Situational Factors and Attitudes Toward Voluntary Euthanasia', *Social Science and Medicine*, vol. 46, no. 1, 1998, pp. 73–81.

43 K. Puntillo, P. Benner, T. Drought, B. Drew, N. Stotts, D. Stannard, C. Rushton, C. Scanlon & C. White, 'End of life issues in Intensive Care Units: A national random survey of nurses' knowledge and beliefs', *American Journal of Critical Care*, vol. 10, no. 4, 2001, pp. 216–29.

44 I. Margalith, C. Musgrave & L. Goldschmidt, 'Physician Assisted Dying: Are education and Religious Beliefs related to Nursing Students' Attitudes?' *Journal of Nursing Education*, vol. 42, no. 2, 2003, pp. 91–97.

45 K. McGlade, L. Slaney, B. Bunting & A. Gallagher, 'Voluntary euthanasia in Northern Island: general practitioners' beliefs, experiences and actions', *British Journal of General Practice*, vol. 50, 2000, pp. 794–97.

46 Vatican Information Service, 'Ideal Politicians Live Moral Integrity, Fight Injustice', *EWTN News*, 30 April 2003. Retrieved at http://www.ewtn.com/vnews/getstory.asp?number=35621.

47 Australia, House of Representatives, *Speech, Second Reading Euthanasia Laws Bill 1996*, 1996, p. 7914.

48 M. Mellish, 'Garrett: Christian in Radical Clothing', *Australian Financial Review*, 25 September 2004.

49 ibid.

50 M. McKenna & M. Cole, 'Family First Backs Liberals into Corner', *The Courier Mail*, 6 October 2004.

51 T. Hassan, 'Interview with Family First Federal Chairman Peter Harris and Founder Andrew Evans', audio recording, *The Religion Report*, Radio National, 29 September 2004. Retrieved at http://www.abc.net.au/rn/talks/8.30/relrpt/stories/s1209308.htm.

52 A. Bolt, 'Power of the pulpit', *Herald Sun*, 22 September 2004. Retrieved at http://www.heraldsun.news.com.au/common/story_page/0,5478,10838521%255E25717,00.html.

53 J. Harris, 'Consent and end of life decisions', *Journal of Medical Ethics*, vol. 20, p. 13, 2003.

54 Commonwealth of Australia, Senate: Official Hansard, Canberra, 26 March 1997.

Chapter 5 – Palliative Care – Between the Truth and Lies

1 World Health Organization, *Cancer pain relief and palliative care*, Technical Report Series 804.11, Geneva, 1990.

2 C. Seale, *Constructing Death: The Sociology of Dying and Bereavement*. Cambridge University Press, Cambridge, 1998.

3 Australian Institute of Health and Welfare, *Australian Hospital Statistics 2001–2002*, AIHW, Canberra, 2003.

4   R. Hunt, 'Palliative Care – the Rhetoric-Reality Gap', in H. Khuse (ed.), *Willing to Listen: Wanting to Die*, Penguin, Ringwood, 1994.
5   Lieberman.
6   McNamara.
7   M. Davis, 'Euthanasia debate sweeps world', *BBC News Online*, 26 September 2003. Retrieved at http://news.bbc.co.uk/2/hi/europe/3143112.stm.
8   R. Ogden, 'Palliative Care and Euthanasia: a Continuum of Care?' *Journal of Palliative Care*, vol. 10, no. 2, 1994, pp. 82–85.
9   R. Daly, 'Pioneers in palliative care remaining cool to euthanasia', *The Toronto Star*, 27 September 2000.
10 Seale.
11 J.C. Battle, 'Legal Status of Physician-Assisted Suicide', *Journal of the American Medical Association*, vol. 289, no. 17, 2003, pp. 2279–81.
12 Palliative care staff maintained there was a lucid moment when I was away from the hospital during which Max had asked for a priest to be brought to his bedside. However, in all previous lucid moments, he had insisted that he did not want this.
13 Pope John Paul II, 'Declaration on Euthanasia. The Sacred Congregation for the Doctrine of the Faith', Vatican, 5 May 1980. Retrieved at http://www.vatican.va/roman_curia/congregations/cfaith/documents/rc_con_cfaith_doc_19800505_euthanasia_en.html.
14 Daly.
15 For a transcript of the Life Week debate, see http://www.lifeweek.org/Life_Debate_Questions_Hour.pdf.
16 Australia, House of Representatives, *Speech, Second Reading Euthanasia Laws Bill*, 1996, p. 7347.
17 K. Cornette, 'For Whenever I am Weak, I am Strong', *International Care of Palliative Care Nursing,* vol. 3, no. 1, 1997.
18 B. Rumbold, 'Pastoral Care of the Dying and Bereaved', in A. Kellehear (ed.), *Death and Dying in Australia*, Oxford University Press, South Melbourne, 2000.
19 Commonwealth of Australia, Senate: Official Hansard, Canberra, 24 March 1997, p. 2293.
20 Australia, House of Representatives, *Speech, Second Reading Euthanasia Laws Bill*, 1996, p. 5904.
21 John Goss, email, 13 April 2004.
22 V. Menec, L. Lix, C. Steinbach, E. Okechukwu, M. Sirski, M. Dahl & R. Soodeen, *Patterns of Health Care Use and Cost at the End of Life*, Manitoba Centre for Health Policy, Manitoba, 2004. Retrieved at http://www.umanitoba.ca/centres/mchp/reports/pdfs/end_of_life.pdf.
23 Australian Institute for Health and Welfare, *Australia's Health 2002*, AIHW, Canberra, 2003.
24 Productivity Commission, *Economic Implications of an Ageing*

Australia, Draft Research Report, Productivity Commission, Canberra, 2004.

25 Audience member submission, Australia, Legal and Constitutional Legislation Committee Euthanasia Laws Bill 1996: Discussion, 1996, p. 144.

26 L. Ganzini, E. R. Goy, L. Miller, et al. 'Nurses' experiences with hospice patients who refuse food and fluids to hasten death', *New England Journal of Medicine*, vol. 349, p. 359–365, 2003.

27 B. Ferrell, R. Virani, M. Grant, P. Coyne & G. Uman, 'Beyond the Supreme Court decision: Nursing perspectives on end-of-life care', *Oncology Nursing Forum*, vol. 27, 2000, p. 445–55.

28 J. Gardiner, 'Martin trial told patients often asked for death', *New Zealand Herald*, 27 March 2004.

29 H. T. Engelhardt, 'Death by free choice: modern variations on an antique theme' in B. Brody (ed.), *Suicide and Euthanasia: Historical and Contemporary Themes*, Kluwer Academic Publications, Boston, 1989.

30 H. Kuhse, P. Singer, P. Baume, M. Clark & M. Rickard, 'End-of-life decisions in Australian medical practice', *Medical Journal of Australia*, vol. 166, 1997. Retrieved at http://www.mja.com.au/public/issues/feb17/kuhse/kuhse.html.

31 M. Angell, 'Euthanasia in the Netherlands – Good News or Bad?' *New England Journal of Medicine*, vol. 335, 1996, pp. 1676–1678.

32 'Call to spend more on palliative care', *The Press*, 1 August 2003.

33 Australian Medical Association, *Media Conference: Dr Kerryn Phelps, Dr Trevor Mudge, Professor Margaret Somerville, Dr Philip Nitschke, Professor David Currow*, Media Conference, Sydney, 26 May 2002. Retrieved at http://www.ama.com.au/web.nsf/doc/WEEN-5GB4C6.

34 K. Bryant, *Singer: A Dangerous Mind*, Serendipity Productions, 2004.

35 B. Smoker, 'On advocating infant euthanasia', *Free Inquiry*, 1 December 2003.

36 E. Day, (2004) 'Infanticide is justifiable in some cases, says ethics professor', *The Sunday Telegraph*, 25 January 2004. Retrieved at http://www.telegraph.co.uk/news/main.jhtml?xml=/news/2004/01/25/nbaby25.xml&sSheet=/news/2004/01/25/ixhome.html.

37 H. Kuhse & P. Singer, *Should the Baby Live? The Problem of Handicapped Infants*, Oxford University Press, Oxford, 1988.

38 P. Singer, 'Moral Maze, *The Mail on Sunday*, 2 November 2001.

39 Daly.

40 Hunt.

41 Ogden.

42 The World Federation of Right to Die Societies, 'The Zurich Declaration on Assisted Dying', Zurich, 12–15 October 1998. Retrieved at http://www.worldrtd.net/about/page/?id=560.

43 Commonwealth of Australia, Senate: Official Hansard, Canberra, 26 March 1997.

44 Daly.

Chapter 6 – What's Wrong with Slow Euthanasia?

1   Kuhse, Singer, Baume, Clark & Rickard.
2   C. Douglas, L. Kerridge, K. Rainbird, J. McPhee, L. Hancock & A. Spigelman, 'The intention to hasten death: a survey of attitudes and practices of surgeons in Australia', *Medical Journal of Australia*, vol. 175, 2001, pp. 511–515; H. Kuhse & P. Singer, 'Doctors' Practices and Attitudes Regarding Voluntary Euthanasia', *Medical Journal of Australia*, no. 148, 1988, pp. 623–627.
3   W. May, 'Double Effect', in W. Reich (ed.), *Encyclopedia of Bioethics*, The Free Press, NY, 1978.
4   C. Norton, 'An end soon to hypocrisy of treating the dying?' *The Independent*, 12 May 1999.
5   J. Laurence, 'Death on prescription?' *The Independent*, 13 May 1999.
6   Triple Helix, 'Euthanasia: Where are we now?', Christian Medical Fellowship, 1999. Retrieved at http://www.cmf.org.uk/index.htm?helix/sum99/euth.htm.
7   E. Hannan, 'Kennett's Rhetoric Far from Reality', *Sydney Morning Herald*, 7 January 1997.
8   Jeff Kennett, email, 22 March, 2004.
9   D. J. Schumacher, 'There's light at the end of the tunnel for America's end-of-life care', *Knight Ridder/Tribune News Service*, 3 August 2001.
10 Commonwealth of Australia, Senate: Official Hansard, Canberra, 26 March 1997.
11 C. Barnard, '*Good Life / Good Death: A Doctor's Case for Euthanasia and Suicide*', Prentice Hall, Englewood Cliffs, New Jersey, 1980.
12 S. Fraser & J. Walter, (2000) 'Death – whose decision? Euthanasia and the terminally ill', *Journal of Medical Ethics*, vol. 26, 2000, pp. 121–25.
13 Moody.
14 Australian Medical Association, media transcript, 19 November 2001. Retrieved at http://www.ama.com.au/web.nsf/doc/SHED-5EXHND.
15 T. Cohen, 'Proposal for Dying Patients Expected', *Associated Press Online*, 16 September 2002.

Chapter 7 – Tired of Life

1   H. Drion, 'The Intentional Ending of Life of Old People', *NRC/Handelsblad*, 19 October 1991.
2   *Mademoiselle and the Doctor*.
3   I. Dikkers, 'Special "Drion Pill"', *Magazine of the Dutch Voluntary Euthanasia Society (NVVE)*, vol. 28, no. 1, January 2002. Retrieved at http://www.nvve.nl/english/info/summaries/summ02-1.htm.
4   G. Evans & N. Farberow, *The Encyclopedia of Suicide*, 2nd edn, Facts on File Inc, New York, 2003.
5   Roberts & Gorman.
6   Humphry & Wickett.

7   L. I. Dublin, *Suicide: a sociological and statistical study*, Ronald Press, NY, 1963.

8   L. Lieberman, *Leaving You: the Cultural Meaning of Suicide*. Ivan R. Dee, Chicago, 2003.

9   The eighteenth-century philosopher David Hume was later to take issue with the inclusion of murdering oneself in the interpretation of the sixth commandment. In his famous essay 'Of Suicide', Hume argued that the sixth commandment applied only to murder.

10 Lieberman.

11 Engelhardt.

12 Lieberman.

13 S. E. Thorne, rev. & trans. *Bracton on the Laws and Customs of England*, The Selden Society and The Belknap Press, Cambridge, 1968.

14 Humphry & Wicket.

15 Lieberman.

16 ibid.

17 Evans & Farberow.

18 ibid.

19 C. J. Ryan, 'Depression, Decisions and the Desire to Die', *Medical Journal of Australia*, vol. 165, 1996, p. 411.

20 Australian Institute of Health and Welfare, *Mental Health Services in Australia 2000–01*, AIHW, Canberra, 2002.

21 See http://www.beyondblue.org.au.

22 Australian Bureau of Statistics, *Suicides: Recent Trends, Australia*, cat. no. 3309.0.55.001, AGPS, Canberra, 2003.

23 D. Humphry, 'Cutting-edge debate on elder suicide in the Netherlands', AuthorsDen.com, 21 December 2001. Retrieved at http://authorsden.com/visit/viewarticle.asp?AuthorID=312&id=3438.

24 According to the Australian Bureau of Statistics, there were on average nine deaths per year of 10–14 year olds from suicide over the period 1992–2002. Having suicide recorded as the cause of death for under ten year olds is extremely rare and there have only been a handful of such deaths since statistics were first collected (1907). Source: Australian Bureau of Statistics, *Causes of Death, Australia*, cat. no. 3303.0, ABS, Canberra. Unpublished data available on request.

25 ibid.

26 Australian Bureau of Statistics, *Suicides, Australia, 1921–1998*, cat. no. 3309.0, ABS, Canberra, 2000.

27 P. Berger & T. Luckmann, *The Social Construction of Reality: a Treatise in the Sociology of Knowledge*, Penguin, 1967.

28 Harris.

29 D. Clark, Autonomy, rationality and the wish to die, *Journal of Medical Ethics*, vol. 25, 1999, pp. 457–62.

30   ibid.

31   Lieberman.

32   A. Giddens, *Modernity and Self Identity Self and Society in the Late Modern Age*, Polity Press, Cambridge, 1991.

33   It is important to note that individual worlds vary greatly depending upon our gender, ethnicity, sexuality, educational background and occupational status; these structure the choices we have and the decisions we make.

34   Giddens.

35   E. Goffman, *Stigma: Notes on the Management of Spoiled Identity*, Prentice Hall, New Jersey, 1963.

36   B.S. Turner, *The Body and Society*, Sage, London, 1987.

37   D. Menadue, *Positive*, Allen & Unwin, Crows Nest, 2004.

38   P. Mellor, (1993) 'Death in High Modernity: the Contemporary Presence and Absence of Death', in D. Clark (ed.), *The Sociology of Death*, Blackwell, Oxford.

39   Lieberman.

40   J. Lavery, J. Boyle, B. Dickens, H. Maclean & P. Singer, 'Why do people desire euthanasia or assisted suicide?' *The Lancet*, vol. 358, no. 9270, 4 August 2001.

41   John Howard quoted in G. Roberts, M. Metherell & R. Pollard, 'Inside Dr Nitschke's Traveling Death Show' *Sydney Morning Herald*, 27 November 2002. Retrieved at http://www.smh.com.au/articles/2002/11/26/103827430-4499.html.

42   *Mademoiselle and the Doctor.*

43   ibid.

44   Life Week Debate, Sydney, August 2003. Transcript retrieved at http://www.lifeweek.org/Life_Debate_Questions_Hour.pdf.

45   We are more likely to understand the suicide of those who are seriously ill. For these people, the future can look bleak indeed. By its very definition, with terminal illness there is usually no turning back. Miracle cures are few and far between.

46   *Mademoiselle and the Doctor.*

47   CNN, 'Dutch minister favours suicide pill', CNN.com, 14 April 2001. Retrieved at http://www.cnn.com/2001/WORLD/europe/04/14/netherlands.suicide/.

48   R. Kalbag, 'In search of a good death', *British Medical Journal*, vol. 327, 26 July 2003. Retrieved at http://bmj.bmjjournals.com/cgi/content/full/327/7408/226.

Chapter 8 – Legal Constraints and Legal Opportunities

1   D.W. Kissane, A. Street & P. Nitschke, 'Seven deaths in Darwin: case studies under the Rights of the Terminally Ill Act, Northern Territory, Australia', *The Lancet*, vol. 352, 1998, pp. 1097–1102.

2   R. Koenig, 'More Among Living Interested in How to Die', *St Louis Post*, 19 June 1994.

3   ibid.

4   M.J. Teno, S. Licks, J. Lynn, N. Wenger, A.F. Connors, R.S. Phillips, M.A. O'Connor, D.P. Murphy, W.J. Fulkerson, N. Desbiens, W.A. Knaus, 'Do Advance Directives Provide Instructions That Direct Care?' *Journal of the American Geriatrics Society*, vol. 45, no. 4, April 1997, pp. 508–512.

5   J. Williams, 'Analysis: Alternatives for patients faced with making end-of-life decisions', *NPR: Talk of the Nation*, 21 August 2001.

6   McNamara.

7   Francis Polak quoted in 'Odd Spot', *The Age*, 6 March 2003.

8   E. Lindblom, 'Where there's a living will . . . (use of living wills to cut Medicare costs)', *Washington Monthly*, 1 November 1995.

9   T. Thompson., R. Barbour & L. Schwartz, 'Adherence to Advance Directives in Critical Care decision making: vignette study', *British Medical Journal*, no. 327, 2003, pp.1011–4.

10 We should add, however, that as this was not a decision made by the court, assisting with a suicide in Queensland is still illegal.

11 G. Lower, 'Mum's mercy kill son wins freedom', *The Mercury*, 27 May 2004.

12 'Court Decision Reignites Euthanasia Debate', television program, *7.30 Report*, Sydney, 27 May 2004. Reporter: J. Nettleford. Transcript retrieved at http://www.abc.net.au/7.30/content/2004/s1117601.htm.

13 J.A. Davies, 'Is it Time to Let Them Go?' *The Bulletin*, 3 February 2004.

14 A. O'Connor, 'Deaths Go Unexamined and the Living Pay the Price', *New York Times*, 2 March 2004.

Chapter 9 – The Joys of Technology

1   M. Myrick, 'Has Technology Stolen the Focus? (behavioural medicine)' *Behavioral Healthcare Tomorrow*; 1 June 2003.

2   This is despite the fact that a provisional patent application was logged with Intellectual Property Australia in early 2003, before the CoGenie was demonstrated publicly for the first time. The patent application is less about protecting intellectual property and more about testing the IP system overall. It also stems from my belief that, one day, the CoGenie may be seen as another great Aussie invention. Clearly, that day is still some time off.

3   See http://www.gerontechnology.info/Default.htm.

4   Myrick.

5   J. Coughlin, 'Technology Needs of Aging Boomers', *Issues in Science and Technology*, 22 September 1999.

6   Denton.

7   J. Durant, email, 21 October 1999.

8   S. Forbes, 'The Need to Revise Assumptions about the End of Life: Implications for Social Work', *Health and Social Work*, 1 February 2001.

9   A. Niewijk, *Tough Priorities*, The Hastings Center, 1 November 1999.

10 H. Morreim, *Profoundly Diminished Life: the Casualties of Coercion*, The Hastings Center, 1 January 1994.

11 ibid.

12 Commonwealth of Australia, Senate: Official Hansard, Canberra, 26 March 1997.

13 For Jack Kevorkian, the Mercitron allowed him distance from the suicide that was to take place. He could then argue that because it was a machine and not a person who administered the lethal dose, he was not actually involved in the dying process. This made it all the harder for the law to prosecute him. Thanks to the ROTI legislation, at the time I used the Deliverance Machine I did not share Jack's legal concerns about prosecution.

14 Last Rights, *The Art and Science of Suicide. Self Deliverance and Plastic Bags: Introducing the Customized EXIT BAG*, A Last Rights Publication, Version 1.2, March 1997, Ottawa.

15 ibid.

16 D. Shanahan, 'Mail order suicide kit', *The Australian*, 20 August 2001.

17 D. Meissner, 'Crown opens case against B.C. woman charged with aiding in two suicides', *Canadian Press*, 12 October 2004. Retrieved at http://www.medbroadcast.com/health_news_details.asp?news_id=4990.

18 For legal reasons, in this book we do not name the required chemicals nor provide constructional instructions for building a CoGenie. This information is only available through Exit practical workshops.

19 When this web site was first created, 'Frog' was enthusiastic about the method of generation and the use of carbon monoxide. Now, his site is highly critical of the method. I have never engaged with Frog, and have never bothered to refute his current list of objections. However, all of them can be readily addressed.

20 B. Gates, *Business @ the Speed of Thought*, Warner Books, NY, 1999.

21 M. Franklin, G. Stolz & C. Griffith, 'Crick died cancer free', *The Courier Mail*, 25 May 2002.

22 L. Scott, 'A life in pain is a life in prison', *The Weekend Australian*, 30 March 2002.

23 G. McManus, T. Rindfleisch & I. Haberfield, 'As Crick debate rages, a Melbourne woman says: I'm going to end my life', *Sunday Herald Sun*, 26 May 2002.

24 D. Nason & N. Strahan, 'Nitschke has explaining to do: Premier', *The Australian*, 28 May 2002.

25 'Beattie Raises the Spectre of Murder Plots', *The Courier Mail*, 28 May 2002.

26 'Frustrated Crick witness to confess', *The Age*, 20 May 2004.

27 Autopsy Report of Nancy Crick, 2004.

28 G. Stolz, 'Supporters defend suicide help', *The Courier Mail*, 9 June 2004.

Chapter 10 – Exit Clinics and Workshops

1   P. Debelle, 'Shirley's Dying Plea a Mission for the Living', *Sydney Morning Herald*, 16 July 2002. Retrieved at http://www.smh.com.au/articles/2002/07/15/1026185160587.html.

2   In 2002, Exit International commenced a new, longitudinal research program aimed at capturing information about participants at introduction workshops. To date, over 309 workshop participants have completed a ten question, anonymous survey. The survey sample consists of 59 per cent female participants and 41 per cent male. The vast majority (72 per cent) are aged sixty years or over and they come from all states of Australia. More detailed results of this research are currently being published in a range of journals.

3   See chapter 7 for more information about this couple.

4   McNamara.

5   A. Grunseit, *Impact of HIV and sexual health education on the sexual behaviour of young people; a Review Update*, Joint UN Program on HIV/AIDS, Geneva, 1997.

6   Margaret Tighe quoted in G. Roberts, 'Dicing with Death', *Sydney Morning Herald*, 20 December 2002. Retrieved at http://www.smh.com.au/articles/2002/12/19/1040174343273.html.

7   Australian Medical Association of Western Australia, 'AMA Says Death Clinics are Not Needed in WA', media release, 30 March 2001.

8   The Royal Australasian College of Physicians, *Ethics: A manual for Consultant physicians*, The Royal Australasian College of Physicians, Sydney, 1999, p. 15.

Chapter 11 – Peace in a Pill

1   Dikkers.

2   See http://www.chm.bris.ac.uk/webprojects2001/gerrard/coniine.html.

3   *Australian Veterinary Journal*, vol. 79, no. 3, March 2001.

4   To ensure that our research and development program is in line with member expectations, in late 2003 Exit undertook its first survey on the subject of the Peaceful Pill. A four-page paper survey was mailed to over 2600 Exit members and a response rate of 45 per cent was achieved. Of the 1163 members who participated, 47 per cent were male and 53 per cent female. The median age of participants was seventy-two years and most were retired (77 per cent). Around half of all respondents had been a member of Exit or another VE organisation for five or more years. Participants were from all states and territories of Australia. Four per cent were from overseas. Fifty-five per cent of participants reported their health as 'very good', with a third saying their health was 'fair'. Eleven per cent said their health was 'poor', with 3 per cent reporting a terminal illness.

5   Four per cent of participants preferred the CoGenie, 3 per cent preferred tra-

ditional drugs, less than 1 per cent preferred the Exit bag, and 0.3 per cent preferred slow euthanasia (3 per cent of responses answered the question incorrectly and are not reported).

6 *Mademoiselle and the Doctor.*

7 Dikkers.

8 W.J. Smith, 'Australia's Dr Death Spreading the Assisted Suicide Gospel', *National Review*, 26 November 2002. Retrieved at http://www.national review.com/comment/comment-smith112602.asp.

9 R. Syme, 'President's Message', *VESV Report*, no. 124, November 2003.

10 Dr T. Mudge, television interview, *7.30 Report*, Australian Broadcasting Corporation, Sydney, 31 July 2001. Transcript retrieved at http://www.abc. net.au/7.30/content/2001/s338233.htm.

11 South Australian Voluntary Euthanasia Society (SAVES), *The VE Bulletin*, South Australian Voluntary Euthanasia Society, vol. 19, no. 3, 2002. Retrieved at http://www.saves.asn.au/resources/newsletter/nov2002/six.htm.

Conclusion – The Empire Strikes Back

1 C. Ellison, (Minister for Justice & Customs), *New offences to clamp down on Internet Child Pornography*, media release, Parliament House, Canberra, 4 April 2003. It is apparently common practice for government ministers to release information that they do not want to attract media scrutiny late on a Friday. However, it was precisely because it *was* put out on a Friday that one suspicious press gallery journalist read it and noticed the paragraph that related to assisted suicide and the Internet.

2 A.O. Adekola, J. Yolles & W. Armenta, Cybersuicide: the Internet and Suicide, *American Journal of Psychiatry*, vol. 156, 1999, pp. 1836–1837.

3 Mark Latham cited in L. Tingle, 'PM Proves Liberals can Have Very Catholic Tastes', *Australian Financial Review*, 8–12 April 2004, p. 78.

4 Part V of our Constitution states that the parliament's authority and scope only applies to Australia. Yet the proposed legislation has clear implications for people who live in other parts of the world – for example, Exit members from overseas who email me with their questions. While I have to abide by the laws of Australia, our international members who request answers to their questions are not under the same jurisdiction. What happens then?

5 Private Submission: A. & B. Saclier, Legal and Constitutional Committee, Australian Senate, Criminal Code Amendment (Suicide Related Material Offences) Bill 2004.

6 See http://www.efa.org.au/Publish/efasubm-agd-teleco.html#47416.

7 Legal advice to Philip Nitschke from Bruce Donald QC, 16 April 2004.

8 Commonwealth of Australia, Senate: Official Hansard, Canberra, 26 March 1997.

9 H. MacKay, 'Let's enjoy our national identity', *The Age*, 26 January 2000.

Photograph Credits

Index

exit

Donate / Join Exit International

Exit membership provides:

- Workshops
- Private clinic visits
- Exit's research and development (the Peanut project and the Peaceful Pill)
- A monthly newsletter – *Deliverance*
- Nancy's Friends network
- Exit lapel badges and membership card

Title . . . . . First name . . . . Last name . . . .

Address . . . .

. . . . Postcode . . . .

Email . . . .

Date of birth . . . . Phone . . . .

Occupation (if retired, pleases state previous) . . . .

Where did you hear about Exit? . . . .

I am donating $ . . . . (amount) on . . . . (today's date)

I am paying by:

☐ Visa   ☐ MasterCard   ☐ Bankcard   ☐ Cheque

Credit card no . . . . Name on card . . . .

Signature . . . . Expiry Date . . . .

Exit International

PO Box 37781

Darwin NT 0821

Australia

Membership averages $150/year

Or join online at:

www.exitinternational.net

Phone: 0500 83 1929

Fax: 61 8 8983 2949

info@exitinternational.com